OUTED

AMERICA
UNSETTLED

Edited by Geraldo L. Cadava, Brent Cebul,
N. D. B. Connolly, and Lily Geismer

OUTED

LBJ'S CONFIDANT AND THE ARREST THAT TRANSFORMED A PRESIDENCY

Timothy Stewart-Winter

THE UNIVERSITY OF CHICAGO PRESS
Chicago and London

The University of Chicago Press, Chicago 60637
The University of Chicago Press, Ltd., London

Published 2026
Printed in the United States of America

35 34 33 32 31 30 29 28 27 26 1 2 3 4 5

ISBN-13: 978-0-226-84102-1 (cloth)
ISBN-13: 978-0-226-84103-8 (ebook)
DOI: https://doi.org/10.7208/chicago/9780226841038.001.0001

Library of Congress Cataloging-in-Publication Data

Names: Stewart-Winter, Timothy, 1979- author
Title: Outed : LBJ's confidant and the arrest that transformed a presidency / Timothy Stewart-Winter.
Other titles: LBJ's confidant and the arrest that transformed a presidency | America unsettled
Description: Chicago ; London : The University of Chicago Press, 2026. | Series: America unsettled | Includes bibliographical references and index.
Identifiers: LCCN 2026008597 | ISBN 9780226841021 cloth | ISBN 9780226841038 ebook
Subjects: LCSH: Jenkins, Walter (Walter Wilson), 1918–1985 | Johnson, Lyndon B. (Lyndon Baines), 1908–1973—Friends and associates | Sex scandals—United States | Outing (Sexual orientation)—United States—History—20th century | Homosexuality—United States—History—20th century | United States—Politics and government—1963–1969 | United States—History—1961–1969
Classification: LCC E847.2.S75 2026 | DDC 973.923092—dc23/eng/20260220
LC record available at https://lccn.loc.gov/2026008597

♾ This paper meets the requirements of ANSI/NISO Z39.48-1992 (Permanence of Paper).

Authorized Representative for EU General Product Safety Regulation (GPSR) queries: **Easy Access System Europe**—Mustamäe tee 50, 10621 Tallinn, Estonia, gpsr.requests@easproject.com
Any other queries: https://press.uchicago.edu/press/contact.html

In memory of Beth
And for Greg

Those who would carry on the great public schemes must be proof against the most fatiguing delays, the most mortifying disappointments, the most shocking insults, and worst of all the presumptuous judgment of the ignorant upon their designs.

ATTRIBUTED TO EDMUND BURKE AND FRAMED ON THE WALL OF WALTER JENKINS'S WHITE HOUSE OFFICE

CONTENTS

INTRODUCTION

Walter Jenkins was eating lunch at the Hotel Congressional when he heard the president had been shot. He rushed back to the Executive Office Building. Soon it became clear he was needed across the street at the White House.

"Do you know whether or not this is some sort of plot?" asked Lyndon B. Johnson, his boss, when he telephoned from aboard Air Force One at Dallas's Love Field. Johnson had become commander in chief at the instant of John F. Kennedy's death, that much was certain. But other questions abounded. "Are they out to get a lot of us?" he asked Jenkins.[1] Jenkins didn't know. And there were decisions to make: Should Johnson take the oath of office? Where? When? Who should administer it?

In an East Wing office, Kennedy aides at his side and a phone pressed to his ear, Jenkins suddenly had the burden of authority. He later recalled the strangeness of that moment, when the dead president's aides—who normally directed him—instead deferred to his judgment. "They knew I was in contact with Mr. Johnson," he explained. With Johnson still aloft, Jenkins found himself weighing who should make the dozen-mile trip to Andrews Air Force Base and whether they should go in government cars or by helicopter. For Kennedy's men, the logistics of presidential travel had been routine;

for Jenkins, they were unfamiliar, and yet he was the one making the decisions now.[2]

Jenkins arranged for high-ranking government officials to be assembled on the Andrews tarmac when the plane touched down at 5:58 p.m. Television lights blazed and network cameras rolled as Kennedy's coffin was lowered from the plane and into a waiting ambulance. Johnson, pale and hoarse, spoke into the microphones, his words nearly lost beneath the thrum of helicopter rotors preparing to lift him back to the city. After speaking for less than a minute, he moved among congressional leaders and exchanged a word with Jenkins before ascending the steps of Marine One. Jenkins followed him aboard for the short flight to the White House.[3]

For twenty-four years—as congressman from Texas's Tenth District, as US senator, and as vice president—Johnson had relied on Jenkins's judgment above all others' save that of his own wife. Jenkins was forty-six, Johnson fifty-six. With hazel eyes, wavy brown hair, and a high forehead over thick eyebrows, the five-foot-ten Jenkins cut a modest but alert figure beside his much more imposing boss. He soon proved as essential to the triumphs of Johnson's accidental presidency as he had been to his rise in Congress. Weeks after the assassination, when the new president needed a bloc of wavering House Democrats to move the Civil Rights Act out of committee—a crucial step toward his landmark achievement—it was Jenkins who secured their support.[4]

• • •

Eleven months later, at 3:56 p.m. on October 14, 1964, another urgent call reached Johnson—now campaigning to win the presidency in his own right, with less than three weeks left before Election Day. Abe Fortas, Washington lawyer and longtime adviser to Johnson, informed him that Jenkins had been arrested by plainclothes officers who had spied on him during a sexual encounter with another man in the basement men's room of the G Street YMCA, two blocks from the White House. Fortas added that this was Jenkins's second arrest in that same men's room in six years. Johnson spent the rest of the afternoon and evening huddled with allies and on the phone, debating what he should say or do.

The first phone call had instantly made Jenkins one of the most powerful men in America. The second, a year later, nearly destroyed him. Five hours after Fortas's call, Jenkins resigned, leaving Johnson without his most trusted and effective partner for communication and governance. Suddenly the president had to negotiate with foreign leaders and members of Congress—to make decisions about war and peace, life and death—without Jenkins's steady voice at his side. Theirs had been a professional marriage, and its abrupt dissolution stunned colleagues and unsettled White House operations. Jenkins, who had helped reassure Americans that their government was functioning on November 22, 1963, did not even attend Johnson's inauguration in 1965, instead watching it on television.[5]

Before he was at the center of a scandal, Jenkins was a key operator in the machinery of mid-century Washington. His relationship with Lyndon Johnson—intimate, durable, strategically indispensable—explains the speed and scope of the response. He not only resigned but was hospitalized, purportedly for "nervous exhaustion," where he remained secluded for nearly a month after resigning. Johnson also ordered J. Edgar Hoover to launch an "immediate and comprehensive inquiry." FBI agents questioned Jenkins in his hospital room, one of at least 435 people they interviewed in just eight days, nearly as many as the Warren Commission questioned in its ten-month probe of the Kennedy assassination. On October 22, 1964, the bureau released only an eight-page summary, which stressed that nothing suggested Jenkins had compromised national security; the full ninety-four-page report, with ten attached exhibits, remained secret for decades.[6]

The Jenkins scandal had special meaning and consequences for Americans who violated heterosexual norms. It came at the crest of a broader effort to exclude homosexuals from all government jobs as threats to national security, a rule that lasted from 1953 to 1975, and more broadly to purge queer people from American life. These policies have come to be called the Lavender Scare. In the furor surrounding Jenkins, it reached into the White House and briefly threatened LBJ's reelection campaign. Men who engaged in same-sex acts witnessed their worst nightmare—what might happen to any one of them at the hands of the police—come to life in screaming headlines.

For these Americans, Jenkins's downfall illustrated the real costs of exposure: arrest, job loss, family rejection, expulsion from schools, or loss of child custody. "My prayers for you," a father of four wrote him anonymously from Cleveland, "are joined with those of the many thousands of other good, church-going family men who have lived your torture but who have had the good fortune to escape public notice." For every Jenkins, there were countless quiet resignations and close calls. "I, too, have been through the shadow of the same horror as yours," one woman wrote Marjorie Jenkins, Walter's wife, from Connecticut. "Three times I have been through the hell of public exposure," she added. "I never knew another woman with the same problem, never confided the trouble to anyone. . . . There are probably many of us."[7]

Such letters underscore how antigay policing did not target only men with gay identities or exclusively same-sex erotic lives; it reshaped the lives of wives, children, friends, colleagues—and, in Jenkins's case, even the president of the United States. Johnson was forced to avoid contact with his most trusted aide for the rest of his presidency. Their tie was a different form of male intimacy that Cold War America pressed into a closet. "One homosexual can pollute a government office," a Senate subcommittee warned in 1950, fueling purges that Dwight Eisenhower codified three years later by executive order. Between five and ten thousand suspected homosexuals were expelled from the federal government, while police conducted as many as a million arrests between 1945 and 1970 for consensual acts such as kissing, dancing, or holding hands.[8] By 1964, a morals charge was the ultimate political weapon; never before had such a grenade exploded so high. Earlier presidents had endured sex scandals—Grover Cleveland's illegitimate child, Warren Harding's adultery—but none carried the uniquely discrediting force of a Cold War–era charge of homosexuality.

This was no ordinary scandal, in part because Jenkins was no ordinary employee. In 1964, he had been working for Mr. Johnson, as he called his boss, for twenty-five years—longer than he had known Marjorie, the woman he married in 1945. In the 1950s, Johnson became the preeminent legislator in a capital where loyalty endured unless and until a man was "guilty of a morals conviction or a murder rap or membership in the Communist Party," in the words of a character in *Advise and Consent*, Allen Drury's bestselling 1959 novel of Washington.[9] At the height of the Cold War, Drury suggested, only three things had the power to leave a man stranded without any allies—being a communist, being a murderer, or being caught by police in a same-sex act.

The Jenkins case looked as if it might seriously damage Johnson, but the White House contrived to reduce it to a detail. Lady Bird Johnson cast it as the tale of a loyal aide worn down by years of service, someone who had reached the "end point of exhaustion." The FBI and two trusted columnists—William S. White and Betty Beale—assisted the administration's effort to label the affair as an instance of illness rather than deviance. Beale's scoop that J. Edgar Hoover had sent flowers to Jenkins in the hospital provoked an uproar among Barry Goldwater supporters, but it also captivated the public and became a news event in its own right. Lady Bird gave the episode a language of compassion; Beale gave her interpretation the sanction of Hoover's authority.

Jenkins returned to Texas after an uncomfortable renegotiation of his relationship with the president. Still in the hospital, he was furious that the FBI's public statement exonerating him nonetheless implied he had confessed to the acts in question—so furious that he demanded a press conference to rebut it, refusing to yield until, Fortas recorded, "the nurse on instructions from the psychiatrist gave Jenkins some sort of 'knock out' drug." Weeks later, when a reporter quoted Marjorie Jenkins saying her husband was home and "coming along just fine," Johnson exploded. He phoned Fortas and instructed him to deliver this blunt message to Jenkins: "If y'all can't listen . . . and can't stay out of the papers, I can't help you."[10]

The Johnsons *did* help, but only behind the scenes. Walter Jenkins, once omnipresent in Lyndon Johnson's House and Senate offices and during the first 327 days of his presidency, all but vanished from high-level correspondence after the scandal. "Now Jenkins' name is never mentioned in the White House, except when a staffer inadvertently says, 'When Walter was here . . . ,'" one journalist observed in 1965. Banished from government, he was forced to reinvent himself with help from the Johnsons, who drew on Washington contacts and even enlisted New York philanthropist Mary Lasker to send a substantial Christmas check to help him start over. Jenkins left politics forever and built a management consulting business, careful to avoid any firm's permanent payroll. Even at the 1966 weddings of their daughters Luci Baines Johnson and Beth Jenkins—where the two women served as each other's bridesmaids—only the bride's father attended. The prospect of the two men appearing in the same room was deemed too fraught. They did not appear together at a public event until the 1971 opening of the LBJ Library.[11] In fifteen oral history interviews Jenkins gave in the 1970s and early 1980s, neither he nor his interviewers from the Library made a single reference to the resignation or the affair.

The White House did not want this history told, nor did Jenkins, whose loyalty and dread of harming Johnson kept him silent. With his cooperation, Johnson removed him abruptly, sealed off further inquiry, and reframed it as a private drama about a fallen individual. After speaking to police and the FBI, and submitting a short written statement to the bureau, Jenkins never again spoke or wrote on the record about a defining event of his life.

Jenkins's own correspondence and the other sources generated by the investigation, however, offer a glimpse of the age of antigay policing and purges as ordinary Americans lived it, rather than through the retrospective filter of the gay rights revolution. The FBI cataloged every potential thread of gayness in the tapestry of his life. Yet the people who mattered most to him were his wife, children, and the Johnson family. Until his life took an unusually sharp turn, he was a characteristic father of the baby boom—"a Roman Catholic steady Eddie," in Luci Baines Johnson's words, the kind of man who "dotted all the i's, crossed all the t's."[12] He belonged to a generation in which many men who had sex with men did not adopt a gay identity. The Jenkins "case" thus provides a vantage point on men who never came out or identified as gay, and on the many others who remained silent, closeted, or fearful—helping correct the selection bias in litigation, oral histories, and LGBTQ organizational records, sources that emphasize the voices of those who embraced a gay identity. It shows both the reach of state power and the private realities of those who lived under its shadow.

This book tells the story of a single arrest—a few brief minutes in a YMCA bathroom that became shockingly public, with a blast radius that touched the Jenkinses, the Johnsons, gay and nongay Americans alike, and even the Johnson presidency. "LBJ's greatest loss," one journalist called it. It provides the definitive account of an episode that brought queer life into the national spotlight more dramatically than any before it, and of the concerted efforts that soon followed to redirect and dim that light. What began as a routine arrest in a "tearoom," as gay men referred to public toilets where they cruised for sex, was reported on the front page of every major US newspaper, dissected and reanalyzed by an FBI investigation, and became known to Americans. In a nationwide poll that October, 88 percent of respondents had heard of "the Jenkins case."[13]

• • •

My interest in the Jenkins affair grew naturally out of my research on the history of antigay policing. In 2016, as I began to pursue it in earnest, I received a Moody Research Grant from the LBJ Foundation to travel to Austin and examine the available records. There, a bit nervously, I cold-called his eldest daughter, Beth Jenkins Bromberg, who had been a seventeen-year-old freshman at Marquette University in 1964, to ask about her father. She agreed to meet at her lake house in the Hill Country outside Austin, where her younger brother Walter Jr.—sixteen at the time of the upheaval—also joined us. While her husband barbecued brisket, Beth and Walt spoke candidly. Beth confirmed that Jenkins had never come out or identified as gay and had remained married to their mother until his death in 1985. "Walt and I have never discussed this with my father, as a matter of respect," Beth said early in our conversation. I soon learned they had barely spoken of it with each other. "I just compartmentalized it," Walt told me. "I didn't really talk about it with anybody much and was very successful at that."[14] Yet, like many Americans, they understood homosexuality differently in 2016 than they had when their father died. Beth had a gay stepson, and she recognized why her father's experience might matter to gay people.

The sources for this book include the previously unexamined personal papers of Walter Jenkins, which were transferred to the LBJ Library in Austin after his death in 1985. The collection—306 acid-free boxes—was still closed until, with Beth's support and assistance, I persuaded the Johnson Library in 2017 to open the collection to me. In 2022, Beth's youngest sibling, Anne Jenkins Mauel, shared additional materials in her possession, which I reviewed alongside Anne and Beth during a memorable weekend at Beth's lake house. I then drove the materials to Austin in a rental car, pulled up to the LBJ Library's rear loading dock, and delivered them to be added to the Jenkins papers. I have also used a range of other sources: White House records, the Johnson tapes, FBI files I obtained, the papers of journalists, politicians, and gay activists, and oral history interviews with members of the Jenkins and Johnson families and others who saw it up close, including Bill Moyers, who, Johnson announced on October 14, 1964, would take over Jenkins's duties.

Although the episode is deeply entangled with the history of gay politics in America, it drew little response from the nation's small band of organized gay activists at the time. To Frank Kameny, dismissed from the Army Map Service in 1957 for being gay and the first to challenge such a firing in court, the incident offered little immediate political value. It didn't fit the kind of story he wanted to tell about "the homosexual American citizen." Kameny warned fellow activist Barbara Gittings that homophile groups should stay quiet. The "circumstances of [the] arrest do not warrant [a] test case," he said. What is more, he said, "Intercession by homophile groups will do more harm than good if we want to see Johnson elected."[15]

The Jenkins affair was politically inconvenient, not only for Lyndon Johnson but also for the gay movement then beginning to articulate a coherent vision of gay rights. To figures like Kameny and Gittings, the case confirmed the need to resist the state's persecution of homosexuals. Yet it also complicated that cause. Jenkins did not identify as gay, never joined the movement, and was deeply invested in the institutions it critiqued. His arrest drew national attention, but his life did not easily fit the narrative homophile leaders were constructing and trying to publicize. Precisely for that reason, it expands our understanding of the Lavender Scare era. The federal purges of the 1950s and early 1960s were in part a deliberate attack on homosexuality, one that provoked an organized response from gay people.[16] But the effects of that repression were far broader and messier than its architects had imagined.

Queer history has often been centered on self-consciously gay protagonists pursuing liberation. Jenkins doesn't fit that mold—nor did a great number of the men who had sex in tearooms during the postwar years. Kameny's legal battle and other homophile activism shaped American sexual politics. But there were many more Jenkinses than Kamenys: men whose same-sex encounters remained secret, whose identities remained ambiguous, and whose place in queer history has often gone unacknowledged.

This book makes three central arguments about what the Jenkins case reveals. First, it shows that in the very years when heterosexual marriage was at its apex legally and culturally, it coexisted with—and at times even facilitated—the expression of same-sex desire.[17] Same-sex encounters were a feature of countless married men's lives in the postwar era, including men whose lives were rooted in worlds presumed to exclude them. In a study of participants in tearoom sex in St. Louis between 1965 and 1968, 54 percent were married and living with their wives.[18] As Lauren Gutterman has likewise shown for women, same-sex intimacy wasn't outside the postwar family ideal; rather, the queerness of straight marriage was hidden in plain sight.

Second, the Jenkins affair marked a watershed in straight Americans' knowledge of gay life. For many gay people, the facts were perhaps shocking but unsurprising: sex in public restrooms, vice-squad surveillance, and the range of possible consequences of arrest were well known. But for many straight Americans, Jenkins's arrest revealed an invisible world all around them, where men were having sex in bathrooms, including seemingly straight Catholic fathers, and where vice officers watched behind peepholes and transoms. This turn of events raised uncomfortable questions about the queerness of "normal" men, including family men, and about the intrusiveness of the state. It laid bare not just gay sex but also the surveillance state.

Public reactions registered the change. News of J. Edgar Hoover's sending flowers to Jenkins's hospital room and Lady Bird Johnson's public expression of sympathy signaled to Americans that knowledge of homosexuality did not necessarily lead to condemnation—a notable departure in 1964. Jenkins's proximity to power and ability to function at the highest levels of government cast doubt on the rationale behind the Lavender Scare. His firing triggered not outrage, but compassion. In the aftermath, the *Washington Post* ran a five-part front-page series on gay life in the capital, observing, "The public response to the Jenkins arrest has been encouraging of a more enlightened public attitude." For Frank Kameny's legal battle against the government's employment ban, the series marked its most significant media breakthrough to date.[19]

Post-Jenkins, queer activists were emboldened to assert that they should be part of the Great Society. "Fair Employment Applies to Homosexuals, Too," declared one of the signs at a gay protest in front of the Civil Service Commission in the summer of 1965. Even though the architects of Johnson's domestic program did not incorporate their ideas, the Jenkins episode perceptibly changed the climate they found in Washington. The DC Circuit Court began narrowing the government's ability to fire employees for same-sex acts unless job performance was demonstrably affected. Two key rulings—issued in 1965 and 1969—involved plaintiffs arrested on morals charges in downtown Washington. In retrospect, 1964 was an interregnum between the purges of the Lavender Scare and the politics of liberation to come. The Jenkins affair helped make straight Americans more aware of the damage wrought by antigay policies—and in doing so, helped create the preconditions for change.[20] It was during the Johnson presidency that gay Americans held their first public protests and forced the government's lawyers to defend antigay policies in court. The organizing that followed Jenkins's outing treated the Great Society as a framework that ought to include gay Americans, years before presidents Carter, Clinton, and Obama gradually made that inclusion part of policy and ritual.[21]

Third, the episode illustrates how state power operated not only through punishment, but through discretion, in both senses of the word. Vice officers didn't always act to punish; sometimes, they intervened to protect family men. That protectiveness—evident, for instance, in the quiet handling of Jenkins's first arrest—invites closer attention to how whiteness, marriage, and political connectedness could shield men.[22] Single men without wives or children rarely received such protection. Still, the range of possible outcomes—from police brutality to low-key cover-up—suggests that part of the state's power lay in its arbitrariness. Fear stemmed not only from the threat of punishment but from the unpredictability of what would happen next.

Beyond the affair itself is the figure of Walter Jenkins. Though this book is not a biography, it fundamentally recasts how Jenkins has been portrayed by Johnson's biographers, accounts often shaped by hindsight and antigay assumptions or that work backward from his downfall. Drawing on stereotypes, they have painted Jenkins as weak, neurotic, or broken. One early Johnson biographer described Jenkins as "a mystery man" who avoided cameras from his 1959 arrest onward. Robert Caro, in 1982, introduced Jenkins as a psychological dependent and "a true successor" to a lesser Johnson aide who resigned after having a nervous breakdown. As evidence, Caro quoted "a friend of Jenkins" named Edward Puls who told Caro that, when he visited Jenkins in Washington in 1941 "for a few nights," he found that "Johnson was working him like a n***** slave." Caro later repeated this quotation—twice—in his book on Johnson's Senate years.[23] But such an account, shaped by knowledge of Jenkins's later disgrace, could well be distorted by hindsight.

Jenkins was unquestionably hardworking, as he had to be—"Working for Lyndon Johnson was not eating bonbons," Johnson's daughter Luci observed—but he was also ambitious. In 1951, he left Johnson's staff to run for Congress, placing second in a crowded special election. He continued rising in government even after his 1959 arrest, assuming the risks that entailed. "I don't deserve what is being written," he wrote after being praised following the Kennedy assassination, "but being human—I like to hear it."[24] Even after he was forced out of public life, he was enterprising. Walter Jenkins & Associates prospered, and he expanded into new projects, including a cable-television company and a travel agency for bridge tournaments, a business centered on a lifelong hobby.

Those who worked with him knew his value. Jenkins was not simply obedient; he was discerning, especially in his interactions with Johnson. Far from having a breakdown, Jenkins worked for Johnson with steady competence year after year in the Senate and the White House. "Walter 'read' him better than anyone else," Bill Moyers recalled.[25] His skill lay in knowing when to push back—and in doing so effectively. He was among the few with the authority and tact to moderate Johnson's worst impulses without provoking his wrath.

Some of the Johnson presidency's most fraught decisions came in Jenkins's absence. In 1966, Johnson took heat for heeding Marvin Watson's ill-advised recommendation to monitor all White House telephone traffic; Jenkins suggested he would have blocked that idea.[26] Jenkins did not speculate further. But we might. In the spring of 1965, might he have offered discreet counsel as Lady Bird Johnson struggled with depression? Could he have softened the "rude dismissal" of press secretary George Reedy that summer? Late in 1965, might he have made plainer to Johnson the likely political consequences of understating the Vietnam War's costs and forgoing a tax increase, a short-term expedient that later corroded congressional trust? In 1966, as J. William Fulbright's televised Senate hearings challenged Johnson's framing of the war, might he have pushed back against two conspiratorial explanations the president entertained—John Connally's claim that Robert Kennedy was orchestrating the proceedings and Johnson's own suggestion to a skeptical senator that the Soviets were behind them—and steered him back toward repairing relations with Congress? If Jenkins had still been in charge of the president's "night reading" during the Tet Offensive in early 1968, might he have flagged crucial passages in reports from the CIA station chief and the US commander in Vietnam that Johnson overlooked?[27] Jenkins might not have advised Johnson to get out of the Vietnam War, but he surely would have influenced how he conducted it.

Absence, too, has a politics. To understand Jenkins's role in the rise of Lyndon Johnson—and what it meant for Johnson to lose him—we must begin earlier, in the long years of service that bound the two men together.

CHAPTER 1

TWO WASHINGTONS

Walter Jenkins moved between two Washingtons. One was the official city: the marble corridors of the Capitol and the anterooms of power, and the low-ceilinged back rooms stacked with filing cabinets and memo baskets where the work of governing ground forward. The other was an often invisible world of coded glances and unspoken rules, where men who desired other men moved cautiously through downtown parks, restrooms, and a small number of bars, watching who might be watching them. These two Washingtons had long overlapped, but during the Cold War the federal government's all-out campaign against nonconformity sharply raised the stakes of exposure.

Jenkins first arrived in the capital in the late 1930s, a young Texan with shorthand skills, quiet ambition, and a willingness to serve, and quickly became one of Representative Lyndon Johnson's most trusted aides. He took dictation, ran the office, managed the flow of information, and worked long hours uncomplainingly, earning a reputation for competence and loyalty. As a young congressman on the rise, Johnson relied heavily on Jenkins to keep his operation running smoothly, including during long stretches when Congress was out of session and the two returned to Texas.

As Washington's professional ranks swelled after World War II, Jenkins became a top congressional staffer. The Legislative Reorganization Act of 1946, which gave both individual members and congressional committees "decently paid, expert staff aides," reflected the United States' postwar global ambitions and the expanding workload of its national legislature.[1] Jenkins rose alongside Johnson from the House to the Senate and then to that body's leadership. By the late 1950s, the Jenkinses lived in a leafy northwest Washington neighborhood where the family belonged to Blessed Sacrament Parish. From modest beginnings during the lean years of the Depression, Jenkins came to serve the ambitious government of a new superpower.

Professional success, however, coincided with escalating danger for men with secrets. The Cold War strengthened federal institutions and lent new urgency to the task of rooting out "security risks." What would later be called the Lavender Scare gathered force. We do not know when Jenkins began to cruise—we know only that he was first arrested in 1959—but he understood something of the risk involved much earlier. In 1949, one of his closest colleagues was arrested after an encounter with a plainclothes officer in Lafayette Park; Jenkins answered his call. The arrest would remain a secret for years, even as its implications shaped the choices Jenkins made in the two Washingtons he inhabited.

"A City of Temporaries"

Walter Jenkins was born on March 23, 1918, in the tiny rural north Texas community of Jolly, in western Clay County, the sixth and youngest child of John B. Jenkins and Enna Morgan (see figure 1.1). He was raised in a fairly strict Southern Baptist home.[2] When the family homestead burned in 1925, they resettled in nearby Wichita Falls, a quintessential oil boomtown that grew rapidly after a major oil discovery in 1918. In the early 1920s, with a population of over 40,000, Wichita Falls became a regional hub for drilling, refining, and refinery-equipment manufacturing. The Ku Klux Klan gained power in city government in the 1920s, as in other north Texas cities.[3] A 1927 city directory listed John as the manager of a Continental

FIGURE 1.1 Walter Jenkins (*right*) with his brothers John and Charlie and sister Lela Belle, ca. 1942–45. Courtesy of Beth Jenkins Bromberg.

Oil station.[4] At the 1930 census, John was listed as "bankrupt," though the family still owned their home, which they shared with a white female boarder and a fifty-year-old Black woman servant.

Jenkins graduated from high school at age fifteen, then lived at home while attending Wichita Falls Junior College and working to support his struggling family. He was editor-in-chief of the campus newspaper, whose gossip column at one point included a rumor that he had "gone the way of all handsome men, the lovers lane," and on the yearbook staff, which made Franklin Roosevelt's New Deal alphabet agencies the theme of the 1934 volume in honor of "the President's force and optimism." He also contributed to the *Wichita Times*, profiling a blind classmate who used a typewriter and followed football games by ear. From 1935 to 1937 he worked as a bookkeeper for the state highway department in Wichita Falls. Then he moved to Austin to attend the University of Texas, graduating in 1939 with a degree in business administration.[5]

A skill he learned in junior college—shorthand—would prove central to his future. Jenkins worked in the office of the college dean, who later suggested his name when Lyndon Johnson, then in his first full term in the House of Representatives, asked for help filling an administrative assistant position in late 1939. Johnson was especially impressed by Jenkins's facility with Gregg shorthand. "I think that more than any other one thing," Jenkins later recalled, "because he never had had a man that took shorthand," Johnson was "intrigued by the fact that I took dictation." The shorthand Jenkins had picked up in summer school gave him the ability to store and retrieve information quickly—an ability Johnson would come to rely on.[6]

Jenkins's gender, just as much as his skill set, shaped how he was perceived and what authority he could exercise as a congressional staffer. Though trained in a practice most often taught to young women, Jenkins had no signs of effeminacy, then or later. His "only unusual mannerism," a reporter would note in 1964, is that "Jenkins has a habit of locking his hands together, thumbs up, when talking to persons in his office."[7] Johnson could have hired a woman with this same skill at less expense, but a male employee stood a greater chance of being assumed by other government employees to have the authority to speak for his boss.

Jenkins was one of many ambitious young Americans drawn to Washington in the 1930s, as the New Deal expanded the federal workforce amid the Great Depression (see figure 1.2). Washington "is a city of temporaries, a city of just-arriveds and only-visitings," in the words of the novelist Allen Drury, "built on the shifting sands of politics, filled with people passing through."[8] When Jenkins first arrived, he and John Connally, a friend from the University of Texas who also went to work for Johnson, roomed together at the Dodge Hotel, a no-frills establishment near Union Station known for housing young, unmarried, newly hired government workers.[9] At some point that year, Jenkins moved into a boardinghouse one block east of the House office buildings on Capitol Hill. The 1940 census recorded that he earned $990 as a Capitol policeman, and he was one

FIGURE 1.2 Rep. Lyndon B. Johnson (*left*) with staff members John Connally, Dorothy Nichols, Herbert Henderson, and Walter Jenkins, ca. 1939–40. LBJ Library/Photo by NYA of Texas.

of twenty white lodgers in the boardinghouse—most of them young, unmarried men from the South, and virtually all working for the rapidly expanding federal government.

The foundation of Jenkins's relationship with Johnson was time: long hours, in both Washington and Texas, in the company of a boss who rarely let his staff out of arm's reach. When Congress was out of session, Jenkins's duties included bringing Johnson his mail at breakfast. In 1940, they grew closer when Jenkins drove Johnson on a speaking tour around the district. "That's where I first really felt like I got to know him," Jenkins recalled. On one long drive in 1940, Johnson tried to shock his aide by casually endorsing extramarital sex. Jenkins, taken aback, asked whether that wouldn't trouble him in his own family. "Well, not really," Johnson replied. Jenkins later insisted that Johnson *would* have been bothered and that such behavior "never happened" in Johnson's case (a claim contradicted by John Connally, who said Johnson was already by this time in a yearslong affair with Alice Glass). To Jenkins, the episode showed Johnson's joy in teasing "an innocent young kid"; it also hints that the future president held relatively permissive private views. It was the only time Jenkins ever mentioned sex or sexuality in an interview.[10]

By the time Jenkins went off to war in 1942, one of his earliest allies on Capitol Hill was Norman Powell Heine, a Texan from the Hill Country northwest of Austin who graduated with a business degree from the University of Texas in 1940. Like Jenkins, Heine held a patronage position as a Capitol policeman and soon joined Johnson's small House office. Such patronage posts were a routine device mid-century congressmen used to expand their staffs, with a Capitol Police slot in particular ensuring close access to the office. In March 1942 a wire-service report named both men among Johnson staffers entering the military; within weeks Jenkins was selected for Officer Candidate School in the Quartermaster Corps and sent to Camp Lee, Virginia, for training. Johnson himself, meanwhile, after pressing Roosevelt to send him to a combat zone, left for the Pacific in early May and flew a single combat mission on June 9. At the end of June, Heine wrote Jenkins an update on Dodge Hotel letterhead: "The Boss is still 'somewhere in the South or Southwest Pacific.'" Heine added that he was still in Washington, though unsure for how long.[11]

As a quartermaster officer, Jenkins's service reflected both the logistical sprawl of the US war effort and the racial hierarchy of the Jim Crow Army, which relegated Black troops to segregated support units under white officers like him (see figure 1.3). He was placed in command of a segregated Black quartermaster truck regiment. "I have about 30 colored boys under my command," he wrote a friend in 1942. "I am learning all the mechanical parts of a truck and how to repair them." His mother worried, not unreasonably, that, "them being colored they would be put in the most dangerous place." In early 1943, Jenkins shipped out with a massive supply convoy requested by General Eisenhower to support Allied operations in North Africa and the planned invasion of Sicily. He spent over two years overseas, returning from Italy in March 1945.[12]

FIGURE 1.3 Walter Jenkins in his World War II Army officer's uniform. Courtesy of Beth Jenkins Bromberg.

During the war, Jenkins stayed closely connected to the Johnsons through letters, visits, and brief reunions that reinforced his loyalty and worth. While in training, Jenkins corresponded with fellow congressional staffers and a young woman named Nora who pined for him.[13] Lady Bird Johnson, who managed her husband's Washington office while Lyndon was in uniform, invited Jenkins to visit one weekend from Camp Lee, urging him to bring his friends.[14] Later, during a layover in Wyoming, Johnson dropped by Fort Warren, where Jenkins recalled his commander "bowing and scraping."[15]

Jenkins's correspondence from this period also captured how quickly those around him began imagining a path to the presidency for Johnson. In November 1942, a friend wrote from preflight training in Texas to Jenkins at Fort Ord, California, to say he'd heard columnist Drew Pearson on the radio suggesting Johnson might become the next secretary of the Navy. "You told me that your Boss's career parallels F.D.R. in a lot of ways," the friend recalled. Johnson, he added, might be "going one better, as F.D.R. was only assistant secretary," and could even make it to the White House.[16]

In 1943, serving in the quartermaster corps, Jenkins took part in the Tunisia, Sicily, and Rome-Arno campaigns (see figure 1.4). As a platoon leader, he oversaw convoys that carried food, fuel, and equipment from seaports hundreds of miles inland. By the time the Allies invaded Sicily, Jenkins advanced to battalion adjutant, serving as the commander's chief administrative officer and managing the records and communications that kept the trucks moving. As Allied forces fought their way from the Anzio beachhead to the liberation of Rome, Jenkins continued in the adjutant role, now supporting a unit moving supplies closer to the front lines.[17]

FIGURE 1.4 Walter Jenkins in Army uniform beside a truck chassis stripped for parts, likely Italy, 1943–45. Courtesy of Beth Jenkins Bromberg.

FIGURE 1.5 Marjorie and Walter Jenkins. Courtesy of Beth Jenkins Bromberg.

After the war, Jenkins married Marjorie Whitehill and returned both to Washington and to Johnson's House office (see figure 1.5). The couple met at a mutual friend's home over a bridge hand, a lifelong passion for both, and moved quickly from courtship to an October 1945 wedding by a Catholic chaplain at a military base north of Wichita Falls. Their New Orleans honeymoon ended early when Johnson called Jenkins back to work, a preview of the demands that would structure their marriage.[18] They rented an apartment in a 1930 building along the Connecticut Avenue streetcar line in Northwest Washington. A devout Catholic, Marjorie soon saw Walter join her church: after their first child, Beth, was born in 1947, he took instruction from a priest and converted.[19] The following year, Johnson won a US Senate seat. The move to the upper chamber required Jenkins to expand the staff quickly—and in the process set up an unexpected and painful moment when he encountered, at close range, the two Washingtons.

"What a Person and a Friend You Were"

During the transition and first weeks of Johnson's Senate term, Jenkins handled a steady flow of personnel and logistical problems. As Johnson's 1948 Senate victory appeared likely, Norman Powell Heine, who had left government for the private sector in New York after the war, wrote to Jenkins about the possibility of returning. Jenkins replied warmly, adding, "I'll transmit your regards to all of our official family here." After the election, Heine followed up to say he wanted to "get back to Mr. J.," and Jenkins arranged a job for him in the Senate office.[20]

Heine's return to government work was short-lived, however: an arrest derailed his prospects and forced Jenkins to intervene. Two months after Johnson was sworn in as senator, Louis A. Fochett, a twenty-six-year-old plainclothes vice officer and three-year veteran of the Metropolitan Police Department's Morals Division, shadowed the newly rehired Heine, who was then working under Jenkins, in Lafayette Park. In his arrest report, the officer described a decoy operation that unfolded in stages: initial observation inside the men's room; a deliberate walk to the nearby corner to test whether Heine would follow; a return to the restroom, where they stood side by side for roughly five minutes; and, finally, a move to a park bench, where, according to the report, Heine began masturbating and Fochett placed him under arrest.[21] At the police station, Heine called the one person he thought could help: Walter Jenkins.

Jenkins posted bail, kept the matter quiet, and shielded them both from immediate consequences. By supplying the twenty-five-dollar collateral, Jenkins enabled Heine to avoid prosecution and quietly drove him back to the Dodge Hotel, where Heine was renting a room. Heine resigned from the Senate staff and returned to New York, escaping further scrutiny.[22] In a letter to Jenkins, he expressed gratitude for his help and relief at leaving Washington behind. Heine wrote that "finding out what a person and a friend you were was the nicest thing that could have happened," an elliptical but unmistakable nod to Jenkins having posted his bail.[23] Jenkins replied months later, but warmly.

There is no further mention of the episode in their correspondence, and the reason for Heine's abrupt resignation appears to have remained a secret until 1964. In an FBI interview during the investigation into Jenkins, Heine said he had called Jenkins because, having just relocated from New York, he had no one else to turn to. Some might infer that Jenkins helped out of solidarity or kinship with a man arrested for cruising, but there is no evidence he disclosed to Heine any involvement of his own in such activity. More likely, Jenkins acted out of ordinary kindness and loyalty. In 1949 the Cold War antigay consensus was not yet entrenched, and he may have viewed the arrest as a private embarrassment that he could handle quietly rather than something he needed to report to Johnson. Either way, his actions protected them both.

Heine's arrest had occurred amid a growing crackdown on homosexual activity in the capital. Responding to the *Washington Evening Star*'s demands, the Park Service in 1947 launched a "Pervert Elimination Campaign" to arrest men cruising Washington's downtown parks and monuments. Congress soon followed with a 1948 law permitting the indefinite commitment of so-called sexual psychopaths. Vice arrests like Heine's multiplied. According to Louis Fochett, the detective who arrested Heine, publicity changed the profile of those apprehended by 1950: the "habituals" became more circumspect, using the parks chiefly as meeting places, and arrests increasingly involved first-time or out-of-town men.[24]

In 1950, as the Korean War began and Washington's antigay witch hunt intensified, Heine wrote Jenkins about his reserve status, leaving unspoken the fact that being called up would force him either to disclose or to lie about his arrest. Jenkins discreetly checked with the Navy—reporting that a call-up affecting him was unlikely "but everything is dependent upon what Joe Stalin does"—and the next year again looked into Heine's status "without using your name."[25] Read alongside the FBI report, the surviving correspondence between Heine and Jenkins offers a valuable record of contact between men navigating the postwar nadir of American queer life *without* either one referring to himself or the other as a member of a sexual minority. Antigay policing in postwar America was not simply a purge of those who understood themselves as homosexuals but also the mass enrollment of men in a drama of concealment, avoidance, and rehabilitation. Some of these men understood themselves as homosexuals, but many—perhaps most—did not.[26]

The Hidden City

By the 1940s, a second map of the capital had taken shape in the shadow of the monuments, legible both to men who sought other men and to the vice officers who hunted them. It spanned the city but centered on a small set of places: Lafayette Park and its comfort stations; restrooms along the Mall and in the Federal Triangle; and a small circuit of downtown bars. All were closely watched by the Morals Division. In a segregated city, the hub of white gay life was Lafayette Park, just north of the White House—a seven-acre enclave of footpaths, benches, and trees that "is many things to many people," as the *WPA Guide to Washington* put it. A newcomer in 1945 wrote that "most sex life here seems to center around public toilets and the notorious Lafayette Park" and that police left even obvious homosexuals alone.[27]

Across from the White House, the queer nightlife around Lafayette Park mirrored the city's racial and gender hierarchies and was closely policed. Washington's best-known gay bar, the Chicken Hut, stood just west of the park's north edge. Its campy upstairs piano bar drew men who identified with the gay subculture, but Black patrons were excluded—segregated public accommodations remained legal in Washington until 1953—and many instead went to the Cozy Corner near Howard University. White lesbians gathered at the Showboat one block east of the park until it closed in the mid-1940s, then shifted to a successor bar, known by various names, on L Street three blocks to the north. Some men moved between public spaces and queer bars: "I went to the YMCA because I knew it was 'cruisy,'" one man recalled, "and I got picked up there by a guy . . . who took me out for some drinks."[28] As a married congressional employee, however, Jenkins likely avoided gay bars, where simply being recognized could carry social or professional risk; as visible licensed premises, they were conspicuous and sometimes raided.

Outside queer bars, men often sought sex in parks and restrooms through ambiguous gestures—a glance, a pause at a urinal—recognizable to those in the know but also to plainclothes officers who impersonated cruisers. Meeting men in Lafayette Park was "almost a ritual dance," one man said, with "little signals, toe-tapping and the whole bit" or verbal cues like "'Do you have the time?' or 'Do you have a light?'"[29] Tearooms were commonly sites for anonymous encounters across class lines and were prime targets of vice-squad surveillance and decoy stings. They were located in urban America's parks, libraries, department stores, bus terminals, and YMCAs. Sidelong glances, foot placement, and motions under stall dividers formed a visual language of cautious invitation. For white-collar professionals like Walter Jenkins, cruising required discretion. Parks and comfort stations offered fleeting privacy and, just as important, plausible deniability, since police surveilled many of the same spaces.

In 1950, the US Senate became the cradle of full-scale inquiries into both communists and homosexuals in government. A new subcommittee led by Senator Clyde Hoey began to study "perversion" but soon faced pressure to find homosexuals quickly. The *Washington Post*'s federal-government columnist wrote, "Very few sex pervert cases have been uncovered by the staff despite charges there are thousands in the Government service here." Under its staff director, former FBI agent Francis D. Flanagan, the committee turned to local law enforcement, obtaining 600 arrest records from the DC vice squad that June. In a memo a few weeks later, Flanagan listed nine Capitol Hill employees who had been arrested, including Heine, and noted next to his name, "Johnson's office—?"[30] The question suggests the matter could have been pursued but was not. Heine's quiet resignation had likely shielded him.

The Lavender Scare intensified, fueled by Cold War fears of subversion, partisan hostility toward the New Deal, and anxiety that city life and office work were softening American manhood. These currents converged most powerfully in Washington, where federal employment had long drawn gay men and lesbians. Civil service exams gave women a foothold, and office culture was relatively permissive, making room for men whose style or manner marked them as different. Washington's openness made it a target when the nation took a conformist turn after the war. Alfred Kinsey's blockbuster *Sexual Behavior in the Human Male* (1948) reported that male same-sex experience was more common than assumed, intensifying worries that wartime experiences had led some astray. A Soviet atomic test in August 1949 and the Communist victory in the Chinese Civil War soon afterward shocked and disturbed many Americans. With Senator Joseph McCarthy's rise and the Alger Hiss spy case, fears of subversion and blackmail soon fueled parallel government-wide purges of both leftists and suspected homosexuals.[31]

As the seat of federal power, Washington embodied the very conditions that made conservatives anxious: bureaucracy, urban anonymity, and blurred gender roles. Anticommunists promoted a rigid vision of domestic life while casting homosexuals as security risks—a label that became a euphemism for *pervert*. A State Department report warned that federal jobs enabled queer people to escape "home" and relocate to "a large metropolitan community," framing government service as a gateway to deviance. Legislators pressed executive agencies to identify and dismiss suspected gay employees. The Senate Armed Services Committee, for example, acting unanimously and with Johnson's support, advanced a bill to ease the removal of gay employees in eleven "sensitive" agencies and departments.[32] In December, the Hoey committee's report called for "detecting and removing perverts" across federal agencies. It also criticized DC police for allowing arrestees to forfeit twenty-five dollars and avoid court, a practice it claimed was unique among major US cities.[33] This leniency, Flanagan argued, allowed homosexuals to slip through the net, endangering national security.

Even those men who escaped the harshest consequences of a vice arrest lived with the enduring fear of exposure. As Margot Canaday observed of GI Bill benefits snatched away from gay veterans, those able "to claim benefits because they were undetected" were included only on inferior terms—a second-class form of citizenship.[34] State power reached into daily life in subtle ways that most Americans never saw, through background security checks, police surveillance, eligibility requirements, and formal and informal investigations.

In the first half of the 1950s, the purges spread across the government. President Dwight Eisenhower escalated the effort with his 1953 executive order excluding homosexuals from all federal employment. The military, immigration authorities, and defense contractors took up the call. State regulators drafted rules to close queer establishments.[35] In the ensuing decade and a half, as investigations fell most heavily on federal workers, what Canaday has called "the legal regime of heterosexuality" peaked.[36]

In tandem with these federal purges, local police across urban America escalated their harassment of gay and bisexual men. In the decades after World War II, every major US city undertook antigay surveillance. Many police departments created specialized units to arrest men cruising in public places. In city after city—Atlanta in 1953, Miami in 1954, Boise and Sioux City in 1955, Greensboro in 1957—entrepreneurial police leaders launched roundups of cruisers that dominated headlines for weeks and sent some men to prison.[37] Such arrests were usually made under disorderly conduct or other catchall charges, not sodomy laws, though the latter remained on the books, including in the District of Columbia until 1993, and lent legitimacy to antigay policing. Within departments, specialized "morals squads" were tasked with controlling vice. Facing pressure to justify their existence through rising arrest numbers, officers, as Anna Lvovsky has put it, "frequently found that their simplest option was targeting homosexual men."[38]

Antigay state policies could devastate even a man of high position—and, in some ways, were especially likely to. In 1954, a liberal senator from Wyoming, Lester C. Hunt, was blackmailed not by foreign agents but by two conservative Republican senators, Styles Bridges and Herman Welker, who threatened to expose his son's arrest for cruising a vice cop in Lafayette Park unless Hunt agreed not to run for reelection. With Senate control potentially at stake, they demanded and secured the son's prosecution and conviction on a morals charge. Even after announcing he would withdraw from the race, and after attending his son's trial, Hunt was reportedly tormented about what to do. On a Saturday morning in June 1954, he carried a rifle into his Senate office and killed himself. The political blackmail that shaped his death brought together the era's excesses of anticommunism and of antihomosexualism. Bridges and Welker also moved quickly to stifle coverage: when columnist Drew Pearson reported on their role in exploiting the arrest and worsening Hunt's despair, they pressured newspapers to drop the story and extracted an apology from Pearson's radio sponsor.[39]

Hunt's suicide showed how mere proximity to a morals charge, even through a family member, could end a political career. The press suppressed the episode's queer dimensions, even as the context was widely known in Washington. His staff helped obscure the cause of death; his top aide falsely cited medical problems.[40] At a memorial, Lyndon Johnson called Hunt "one of God's kindly men" and said his death cast a "pall of gloom over the Senate." Yet routine resumed: Jenkins fielded calls from Democratic colleagues advising Johnson on replacements for Hunt on Senate committees.[41]

The tragedy quickly became fodder for political fiction. Former Senate correspondent Allen Drury's bestselling novel *Advise and Consent*, published in August 1959, thinly veiled the Hunt case while portraying a Cold War capital where "a solid married life" was "obligatory upon most ambitious men" and where a senator's opponents had learned "the one thing he hoped no one in the world, particularly the world of Washington, would ever know."[42] In Drury's imagining of the case, the senator's opponents had paid cash for a

World War II–era letter from a former male lover—damaging evidence of a clandestine Pacific-theater liaison. A political conservative as well as a closeted gay man, Drury inverted the politics of the Hunt affair by casting the villainous senator as a wild-eyed liberal. The novel's reach widened with a film adaptation starring Henry Fonda.

The Lavender Scare unfolded in a postwar culture deeply ambivalent about secrecy. Advice columns urged women not to ask whether their husbands had been faithful during the war, and experts counseled concealment in stigmatized circumstances like divorce, adoption, and teenage pregnancy.[43] Yet as the Lavender Scare gathered force, the forms of secrecy cultivated by gay men, lesbians, and men who cruised came under harsher scrutiny and drew greater stigma. By contrast, the Cold War often shielded the transgressions of straight men. In 1959, a West Coast photographer caught astronaut Alan Shepard in Tijuana with a woman who was not his wife. Fellow astronaut John Glenn personally called the reporter, the photographer, and then the publisher to kill the story. Glenn pleaded that the United States was falling behind "godless Communists" and urged the press to let us "get back in the race."[44] The incident never ran, the photo disappeared, and Shepard became the first American in space. For straight white men, even public figures, the press often looked the other way. The major White House scandals of the Truman and Eisenhower years, such as those involving presidential aides Harry Vaughan and Sherman Adams, centered on financial misconduct, not sex.

Even after the Lavender Scare was codified as federal policy, it remained possible—though increasingly rare—for an arrested federal employee to avoid public disgrace. The columnist Max Lerner observed in 1950 that in the hunt for "perverts," unlike the communist purges, "only the accusers and the hunters—Senate probers, security officers, police officials—get their names in the papers."[45] Those protections had eroded by decade's end: more and more, the names of the arrested appeared in print.

A Growing Family

While Jenkins navigated a city shaped by surveillance and suspicion, his life was anchored by conventional milestones of marriage and children. Born on a remote Texas farm, he came of age amid the expanding opportunities of white-collar work and the swelling ranks of the federal government. He was one of "the ones of our middle class who have left home, spiritually as well as physically, to take the vows of organization life," as William H. Whyte wrote of America's new bureaucratic strivers.[46] For ambitious and talented men like him, organizational life promised not just stability but upward mobility.

As the Jenkins family grew, their housing tracked the broader postwar migration of white veterans-turned-civil-servants from city centers to the suburbs. In 1948, with one child in tow, they moved from northwest Washington to Del Ray, a modest Alexandria, Virginia, neighborhood. Two years later, with Johnson's help, they moved to Fairlington, a former wartime housing complex in Arlington that had become a haven for baby-boom families in the rapidly expanding capital.[47] From their redbrick garden apartment, Jenkins's daily commute took him past the Pentagon, over the Fourteenth Street Bridge, and by the Jefferson Memorial on the way to the Senate Office Building. His trajectory from boardinghouses to commuter suburbia mirrored the changing built environment of metropolitan Washington.

The rhythms of Jenkins's family life were shaped by the congressional calendar and the demands of political service (see figure 1.6). "Some years I would come to Texas and some years I would stay in Washington," he recalled. This was common for political families. Political reality, a Senate wife wrote in her memoir, "often means that a husband must be in his home district more often than his wife—or that he must be back in Washington when she is at home." For the wives of staffers, doubly removed from power, the strains could be greater still. At times, the Jenkinses lived in Johnson's

FIGURE 1.6 Lady Bird Johnson and Marjorie Jenkins. Courtesy of Beth Jenkins Bromberg.

home, a sign of their close relationship with the senator. In the fall of 1949, after Congress adjourned, the Jenkinses moved in with Johnson in Washington, while Lady Bird took Lynda Bird and Luci Johnson to Texas. Many years, the Jenkins children attended school in Washington in the fall and in Austin in the spring.[48]

Jenkins found a sense of belonging in government work—and also in the more personalized hierarchies of Lyndon Johnson's political machine and the family broadcasting empire Johnson shared with Lady Bird. From the early 1940s, Jenkins shuttled between Washington and Austin, working in the Johnsons' political and business enterprises. After Lady Bird Johnson purchased an Austin radio station in 1943, he handled station matters alongside congressional business. In a 1947 letter to Johnson, then back in Texas, he noted, "Mr. Marks says that the FM application will probably be granted this week or not later than next week," before adding, "The mail was somewhat heavier today than it has been for several days." Such overlap between public service and private enterprise was generally permissible at the time; Congress did not adopt a modern ethics code until 1968, and meaningful limits and disclosure requirements arrived only in the late 1970s.[49]

Jenkins also returned to Texas to assist with Johnson's 1948 Senate primary campaign, a contest he described as "mean" (see figure 1.7). Marjorie, too, was employed by the Johnsons. In 1946, when a House staffer left mid-month and congressional disbursement rules allowed the remaining salary to be paid only to a new hire, another Johnson aide, Glynn Stegall, suggested putting Marjorie Jenkins's name on the payroll temporarily. A few years later, Marjorie was added to the payroll of the station, KTBC.[50] Stegall's own wife, Mildred, went on to become Walter's devoted secretary. The Johnsons' company later launched television station KTBC-TV.

The same pressures that fused work and household life also kept the family apart. By the late 1940s, even as their family grew, the couple spent long stretches in different cities. Marjorie returned to

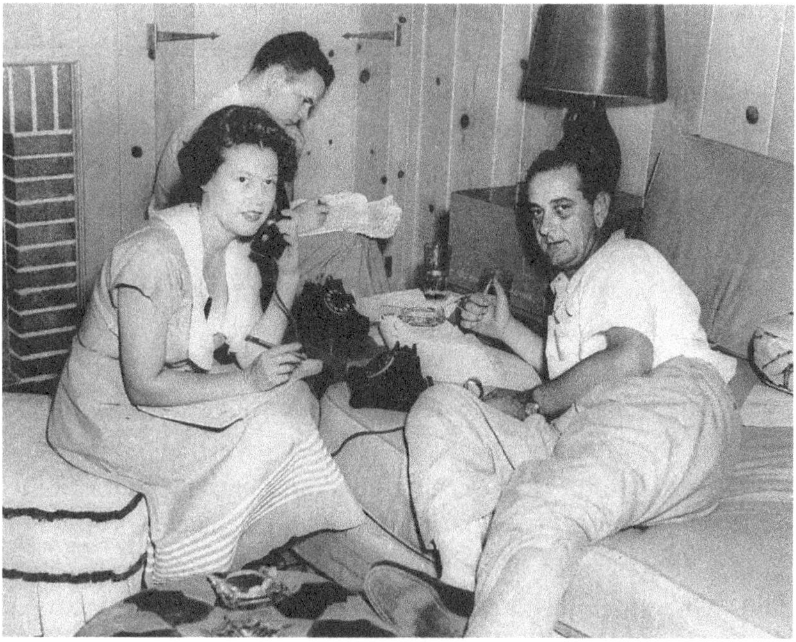

FIGURE 1.7 Lyndon Johnson reclines at his Austin, Texas, home with longtime secretary Mary Rather and Walter Jenkins, August 30, 1948, as he receives election returns in the Democratic runoff primary for the US Senate. AP Photo.

Wichita Falls—often without Walter—for the births of their six children: Beth in 1947, Walter Jr. in 1948, twins John and Joe in 1950, Lyndon in 1955, and Anne in 1961. "I love you, miss you, and am hoping to get slim for you," she wrote to Walter in November 1950 after giving birth to the twins. That Thanksgiving, she signed off on behalf of herself and the children: "We love you, love you and hope you're having a wonderful Thanksgiving today and we're looking forward to a big Christmas with you."[51] These absences often became filled by the Johnson family.

From an early age, the Jenkins children were folded into the Johnsons' "official family," sharing meals, holidays, and the rhythms of political life (see figure 1.8). The relationship offered both emotional closeness and material support while underscoring the Jenkinses' dependence on Johnson's favors. Like political machines that traded services for loyalty, Johnson's personal network operated through patronage. His efforts to electrify rural Texas in the 1940s had created allegiance through material gain; his relationship with the Jenkinses had certain parallels. With housing scarce in postwar Washington, the newly elected Senator Johnson asked the Dallas developer who had purchased the Fairlington housing complex from the government to rent Jenkins the first available three-bedroom duplex. The request reflected both the senator's influence and Jenkins's growing needs as a father of two.[52]

The 1950s, when Lyndon Johnson became the most powerful man on Capitol Hill, was a grueling era for the wives of driven political men. Historian Jessica Weiss has observed that during the baby boom, young middle-class parents inhabited not just emotional but physical separate spheres: fathers' lives had "two loci, home and work," while mothers' lives centered almost entirely on the home. Early childbearing, Weiss notes, meant couples quickly fell into "dissimilar daily existences," and the shared goal of a large family often shifted their focus away from one another. "At night, wives waited for their husbands," recalled the daughter of a congressman. "There were plenty of depressed women, and a lot of wives and mothers who drank heavily"—as Marjorie increasingly did. The wife of an

FIGURE 1.8 Walter and Marjorie Jenkins with their children by the pool at the LBJ Ranch outside Johnson City, Texas, ca. 1958. Courtesy of Beth Jenkins Bromberg.

Indiana senator remembered, "We worried about our husbands' health holding out, at the frantic pace they were keeping. We worried about raising our children alone."[53]

The demands of Jenkins's job began to strain both his health and his marriage. He received regular cortisone injections to treat tightening of the shoulder girdle muscles from constant telephone use, a physical marker of the strain that came with always being on call for Johnson. The emotional toll of political life fell especially hard on Marjorie Jenkins, who became increasingly depressed. The uncertainty, constant interruptions, and long absences were isolating. A senator's wife recalled, "Two homes to worry about, dinner hours that are never definite, social engagements which, even in your own home, have to be made on a tentative basis because late sessions often interfere—all make planning impossible, whether for a vacation or a birthday party." As Luci Baines Johnson later said of Marjorie, "She had six children and a husband that worked all the time."[54]

In January 1955, Marjorie gave birth in Wichita Falls to her fifth child, whom the couple named Lyndon, after the man who one week earlier had become the youngest majority leader in Senate history. That spring, the Jenkinses moved into a six-bedroom white clapboard house with green shutters in northwest Washington, near the Maryland line. Writing to a former high school teacher, Jenkins noted the "seven very beautiful trees in the front yard, including a particularly lovely dogwood now in bloom," along with "a two-car garage and a fairly small backyard where Marjorie is growing flowers and tomatoes."[55]

"Senator, Junior Grade"

Jenkins bridged the political cultures of Texas and Washington, maintaining relationships with constituents and coordinating the work of Johnson's growing circle, which included not only staff but other fellow Texans like journalists Liz and Les Carpenter. In the office, Jenkins maintained social and political ties, the management of a complex office, and the safeguarding of Johnson's secrets. He served as secretary of the Washington Texas-Exes Club, the official University of Texas alumni group in the capital. He helped Johnson navigate the widening divide between Texas Democrats and the national party—a gap Johnson finessed to his advantage. "I'm damned tired of being called a Dixiecrat in Washington and a Communist in Texas," the senator quipped, positioning himself as a moderate, centrist, and unifier. Even Jenkins's sister Lela Belle, now living in Oklahoma, had drifted away from the Democrats in backing Eisenhower in 1952.[56]

In 1951, shortly after Johnson became Senate majority whip, Jenkins briefly stepped away to test his own prospects back home. He resigned from the Senate staff to run for an open House seat in Texas's Thirteenth District, which included his hometown of Wichita Falls. The retirement of Congressman Ed Gossett triggered a special election and thus an unusual political opportunity. His position would be hard to fill, but Johnson could "readily understand that a man of ability" would "seek to advance himself" by elected office. Jenkins opened his campaign headquarters in the former Majestic Theater on Scott Street. His years with Johnson lent him credibility but also made him vulnerable to charges that his ties to the district had frayed. While Johnson did not officially endorse him—he made it a rule never to endorse in primaries—he called "nearly every day," and Johnson's donors, including the construction magnates Herman and George Brown, backed the campaign financially.[57]

Jenkins's platform reflected Cold War conservatism and frustration with the Truman administration. He attacked corruption, taxes, and price controls, while defending farm supports and calling for rural infrastructure and increased military spending. In 1947 he took a somewhat moderate stance on communism, clashing with the hawkish views of the Catholic priest who had taught him the tenets of the faith, but by 1951, like Johnson and much of the public, he was more strident. "We have let [communists] creep into our government," he warned. Yet he also defended New Deal programs, reminding voters of "the hard times of the late thirties" and "the pitifully low price you were getting then for your cotton and your cattle," and praising public power over "the power trust."[58]

His message faltered. In the Baptist-dominated district, anti-Catholic sentiment hurt him. One constituent told Johnson his wife had the "same attitude" about Jenkins as she had had about

Al Smith, the 1928 Democratic presidential nominee whose defeat in Texas was widely attributed to his Catholicism. Opponents portrayed Jenkins as a carpetbagger, publicizing that he had recently voted in Austin rather than in the district. After Jenkins's defeat, a Wichita Falls oilman blamed "the same crowd which belonged in the regulars [a faction of Texas Democrats who opposed Franklin Roosevelt and Harry Truman] and Dixiecrats."[59] Jenkins briefly considered leaving politics altogether, yet he later told his daughter Beth that losing was the best thing that ever happened to him, since it paved the way for his later White House service. Though he returned to Johnson's Senate office, he took another leave in 1952 to sell advertising for KTBC television in New York, a sign that he was open to a life beyond Washington, even as he chose not to pursue it.[60]

Johnson's leap to Senate minority leader gave Jenkins even more responsibility. After Majority Leader Ernest McFarland lost reelection, Johnson was chosen to lead his caucus despite being only a freshman senator. As minority leader, he dispensed rewards in exchange for votes, expanded Senate committees, and reduced the power of seniority—moves that gave him increased influence over both personnel and policy. Jenkins became staff director of the Policy Committee and had administrative oversight over key aides like George Reedy and Gerald Siegel.[61]

Jenkins became Johnson's trusted surrogate. Senate principal office aides, *Newsweek* noted, were "senators, junior grade," and Jenkins was no exception.[62] He fielded requests and managed the flow of favors and obligations, often standing in for Johnson himself. When Senator Stuart Symington needed help securing an appointment for an ally, he called Jenkins. When a Mexican official protested the refusal of service to two consulate employees at a Lubbock hair salon, the complaint went to Jenkins. Even Johnson's lawyer—offering advice on how to handle columnist Drew Pearson's attacks on Johnson's broadcast dealings—went through Jenkins.[63] In short, he was essential to Johnson's ascent.

Jenkins embodied Johnson's strengths and offset his weaknesses. Johnson, for example, could rapidly absorb complex information,

Jenkins recalled. "He was not the greatest organized fellow in the world," however. "Sometimes he wouldn't remember who he told to do what." Jenkins was, with Lady Bird, the key figure who provided calm and order, according to George Reedy. He kept track of promises and smoothed tensions. When Johnson told a UPI reporter to lie to his editors and say he had been unreachable, Jenkins followed up: "I thought you ought to know that he was a little bit unhappy with his conversation with you."[64]

He managed legislative and administrative detail with unusual breadth, from communications to policy to money. Amid Strom Thurmond's record-setting filibuster against the Civil Rights Act of 1957, he watched the Texas mail and pressed for a newsletter emphasizing that the measure addressed voting rights, not "all of the other matters some of them mentioned such as schools, swimming pools, etc." He advised Johnson to introduce a Social Security disability extension but suggested indexing it to the cost of living. When it came to office budgeting, he "never told Mr. Johnson no" and "always tried to find some way to do it," he recalled.[65] He played a key role in securing material benefits for Texas. He was instrumental in negotiating the acquisition from the military of a former magnesium plant in northwest Austin, which the University of Texas converted into a major defense and industrial research facility that attracted Cold War–era industry to the region and thus paved the way for the city's later growth.[66]

In addition to policy and politics, Jenkins managed personal matters. When Johnson had a massive heart attack in 1955, Jenkins was already at Bethesda Naval Hospital when he arrived. Throughout Johnson's recovery, Jenkins brought mail two or three times daily and briefed him on Senate business. Later he submitted Johnson's hospital reimbursement claim to Blue Cross and processed the $612 repayment. He sent monthly support checks to Johnson's mother and alerted him when his brother Sam Houston Johnson was drinking again.[67]

Jenkins not only anticipated Johnson's priorities but advanced them while preserving critical relationships. When CIA director

Allen Dulles asked to reschedule a Saturday security briefing Johnson had canceled, Jenkins told Johnson with studied tact—"I hate to keep bothering you with this, but they keep bothering me"—and offered a face-saving way to decline without slighting a powerful official. Of everyone around him, only Lady Bird Johnson commanded more of Johnson's confidence. He often acted with delegated authority and little need for instruction. "Walter became the other Johnson, in terms of knowing and executing what had to be done confidentially," Bill Moyers later recalled.[68] Then, at a moment of political triumph, his position was suddenly and shockingly placed at risk.

Slipping Through the Net

Jenkins's first arrest occurred on Thursday, January 15, 1959, at 10:20 p.m., in the basement men's room of the G Street YMCA. It was otherwise a triumphant moment for Democrats, who had swept the midterm election and picked up thirteen Senate seats, the largest gain in the chamber's history. On Monday, Johnson had defused a bitter fight over filibuster rules with a characteristic compromise. On Wednesday, the chamber voted to expand major committees, giving more of the newly elected Democrats access to meaningful power, and adjourned until Saturday.[69]

Jenkins was forty years old, a father of five, and the key aide to the Senate's most powerful figure. Unlike Norman Powell Heine a decade earlier, he could not simply resign or relocate without involving his wife or explaining the change. The memory of helping a friend escape detection after being arrested may have suggested he could survive the fallout. And indeed, he did so. Despite being arrested by vice officers in a public tearoom, Jenkins remained at Johnson's side without apparent consequence. Had he avoided returning to the YMCA, the arrest might well never have come to light. That possibility reveals the limits, and the uneven application, of Cold War surveillance even at the height of the Lavender Scare.

Jenkins avoided severe repercussions. As a close daily reader of the newspapers, he would have known how differently such cases could end. In 1960 a World War II veteran and father of five, arrested in the same restroom, lost his military pension; in April 1961 local papers printed the names of seven men arrested there.[70]

In 1959, Jenkins learned—perhaps overlearned—that it was possible to be arrested and continue working in government. Like Heine before him, he received a quiet exception. Washington's overlapping institutions—police, press, FBI, congressional staff—did not always speak with one voice. Even as the Lavender Scare became systematic, enforcement of antigay policies was still shaped by discretion, chance, and human judgment. The state's most powerful accomplices, including the press and the police, sometimes stretched the mesh of surveillance just enough to let someone slip through, especially if he was a family man. Because morals charges "are so damaging to the reputation of a man," one editor explained, Washington newspapers "ordinarily do not report the mere allegation of an offense, where an ordinary citizen is involved."[71] Compassionate exceptions could not usually be expected, but they occurred often enough to inspire hope.

Jenkins was not the only man whose name entered the Morals Division ledger that night. As a colleague followed Jenkins into the YMCA's basement men's room, Officer Louis Fochett—who had arrested Norman Heine in 1949—was on duty nearby in Lafayette Park, where he arrested an eighteen-year-old for an indecent act. At 11:00 p.m., when Fochett returned to the station, Jenkins was already being processed in the Morals Division office. Like Jenkins, Fochett was a practicing Catholic and a World War II veteran who had served in North Africa. Both men had advanced in their careers since the war, and when their paths crossed again a few years later, each held even greater authority.[72]

CHAPTER 2

THE BEST MAN I'VE GOT

As Lyndon Johnson moved from Senate leadership through the bruising 1960 presidential campaign and into the vice presidency, Jenkins was by his side. By 1964, Jenkins's proximity to Johnson placed him at the heart of both historic legislative triumphs and the darker side of Johnson's presidency, including its covert political operations. He served as Johnson's enforcer and vote counter, with a particular ability to wrangle Southern Democrats who balked at liberal legislation. He was also Johnson's point man with J. Edgar Hoover's FBI. Jenkins earned Johnson's profound trust—"he's the best man I've got," he told reporters in the White House one evening—because he combined unmatched administrative skill with an intuitive grasp of Johnson's real aims. More than an administrator, Jenkins understood Johnson. Bill Moyers recalled that if you were unsure what Johnson truly meant, "you went to Walter for clarification." Jenkins himself put it plainly: "He told me one time . . . that the great value he had in me was that I knew when to ignore what he said and *not* do it."[1] Confident in his read of Johnson's intentions, Jenkins knew when a command was for effect and when to let his boss blow off steam.

Looking back on the late 1950s, Jenkins said of his boss, "I felt that we had a possible presidential candidate very early. I did not know whether it was possible for a man from this part of the country to actually ever become president." Though Johnson insisted pub-

FIGURE 2.1 Sen. Lyndon B. Johnson (*center*) with Walter Jenkins and Tennessee Gov. Buford Ellington at the airport in Nashville during a campaign trip, May 9, 1960. LBJ Library/Photo by Frank Muto.

licly he wasn't a candidate in 1960, Jenkins had long worked to help his boss monitor the men who might run or might endorse him (see figure 2.1). "You ought to really be nice to Humphrey," he advised Johnson in a memo in late 1959, noting that the Minnesota senator—and Democratic hopeful—was likely down the road to be looking for someone else to back. After hours, Jenkins often slipped over to John Connally's unofficial Johnson-for-president headquarters on K Street to help. Johnson was outmaneuvered by Senator John F. Kennedy's charisma and family wealth, however. As the Democratic

FIGURE 2.2 Sen. Lyndon B. Johnson with Walter Jenkins (*right*) during the Democratic National Convention in Los Angeles, July 1960. Thomas D. McAvoy/The LIFE Picture Collection/Shutterstock.

convention opened, Jenkins recalled, his mind was not on the vice presidency: "I did not think that he would be asked."[2]

He was with Johnson during the Democratic convention in Los Angeles when Kennedy, fresh off his first-ballot victory, came to his room in the Biltmore Hotel to offer Johnson the vice-presidential nomination (see figure 2.2). Many of the Johnson staff had already left Los Angeles. Johnson and Kennedy talked privately. "I thought he should do it," Jenkins remembered. Declining, he reasoned, might cost Johnson his authority as Senate majority leader, or even the post itself. Though he had not expected the offer, he quickly concluded that Johnson had "no choice, really, once he was asked." When a conservative Texas congressman phoned to protest Johnson joining a ticket led by the less experienced and more liberal Kennedy, Jenkins stood by the choice. "This is what we've been waiting for all this time," he said—words the congressman soon relayed to journalists.[3]

During the fall campaign, Jenkins remained in Washington, where he coordinated Johnson's campaign schedule with the Kennedy operation. From Wichita Falls, his mother-in-law reported local sentiment: "A good many I work with are Democrats but anti-Catholic. I have even heard several say they just won't vote in November." The older courthouse crowd, she said, was especially vocal, while "the younger ones (like us) are not so narrow minded." She enclosed an article from *Petroleum Week* that noted continued grumbling about Kennedy's oil policies. On election night, Jenkins manned the phones in Johnson's Washington office, staying up through the night and into the next day, catching only a few hours of sleep on the office couch.[4]

The Vice Presidency

The transition to the vice presidency narrowed Johnson's formal portfolio and forced a tightening of staff, an adjustment that Jenkins managed. He oversaw the reshuffle required by the office's smaller budget compared to the Senate majority leader's, convened meetings to inform staff, and worked to place those who could not stay on. He recalled proudly that everyone had a new job by the time of the inauguration. Looking back, Jenkins said that under Kennedy, Johnson had his finger in fewer "pies" than he had as a senator—only those the president wanted him to touch—and consequently had "more time on his hands." After 1960, Jenkins himself kept a desk at the Capitol, where Johnson maintained an office, but spent most of his time at the Executive Office Building.[5] He was close enough to know what was happening in the White House but far enough to feel the distance from the center of power.

As vice president, Johnson often felt sidelined. Jenkins maintained a tenuous link to the White House, especially through regular contact with Kennedy aide Ken O'Donnell, and he attended the weekly Tuesday afternoon staff meetings as the lone Johnson representative. Asked later if Johnson awaited his reports, Jenkins demurred: "I wouldn't want to say that he was impatient, sitting waiting for my return. That wouldn't be in his nature to do that. But I kept him informed."[6] Johnson's exclusion was clearest when major decisions were made; neither he nor Jenkins was present at a crucial meeting at the height of the Cuban Missile Crisis—on October 27, 1962—when Kennedy decided to make a secret trade with the Soviets by removing American Jupiter missiles from Turkey in exchange for the removal of the Soviet ones from Cuba.[7]

Even as access to the White House was limited, Jenkins drew on his Senate experience to keep lines to Capitol Hill open. Indeed, he became a conduit for the Kennedy administration, especially to the fractious Texas delegation, handling outreach and smoothing frictions. "We did, in a good many cases, better than we expected," he recalled of the legislative outcomes in this period. But Kennedy's restrained approach to pressure, Jenkins observed, reflected a philosophy that "the president proposed and the Congress disposed," a stance that in Jenkins's diplomatically worded view explained an only haphazard effort to muscle programs through.[8]

Travel and public diplomacy offered Johnson a compensating arena for visibility and influence (see figure 2.3). On a high-profile goodwill and fact-finding tour across South and Southeast Asia, including a principal mission of assessing the situation in Vietnam, Jenkins was present when Johnson halted his motorcade to greet a Pakistani camel-cart driver, Bashir Ahmad. The moment became front-page news after Johnson blurted out an invitation to visit Washington and Ahmad accepted. "Like a few other things, it was

FIGURE 2.3 Vice President Lyndon Johnson and Walter Jenkins at the US Embassy in New Delhi during Johnson's trip to Asia, May 1961. Courtesy of Beth Jenkins Bromberg.

the intellectual establishment that made a lot of fun of it," Jenkins later said, "but I believe that it was appealing to not only a good many people in this country but certainly to a good many ones in other countries around the world." Bearing out Jenkins's view, the historian Mitchell Lerner has argued that despite the sneers of Washington insiders, this and other instances of Johnson's mingling with ordinary people during his vice-presidential trips were in fact highly effective diplomacy and were regarded as such by American diplomats.[9]

All the while, the Kennedy White House's carefully curated image shaped the environment in which Johnson and Jenkins operated. The photogenic First Family cultivated a wholesome presence on television and in magazines, even as reporters tacitly ignored the president's compulsive womanizing. From the outset, journalists helped protect that image—suppressing even a story about a White House party when the president was supposedly observing Lent—and among both officials and reporters, Kennedy's affairs were an open secret. "Kennedy is doing for sex what Eisenhower did for golf," a British aristocrat quipped in 1961. That same year, when a married presidential aide impregnated a secretary who worked for him, Kennedy reassigned him to the State Department; the affair continued, she resigned to have the baby, and the episode stayed out of print—a telling contrast with the scrutiny aimed at those whose transgressions violated the heterosexual norm.[10]

After Dallas

Kennedy's assassination catapulted Johnson—and Jenkins—into the center of an unprecedented crisis. "We had very little help, if any, from the Kennedy people outside of Pierre Salinger," Jenkins recalled. As President Johnson's liaison to the FBI, Jenkins fielded the call from J. Edgar Hoover reporting the shocking murder of Lee Harvey Oswald in Dallas police custody. Among other details, Hoover noted that Jack Ruby, who had shot Oswald, "has the reputation of being a homosexual." It was one of the first times Hoover entrusted Jenkins with highly sensitive information before anyone else, and from this point Jenkins had access to the executive branch's most closely guarded secrets. Johnson asked the FBI to sweep not only White House telephone lines but also Jenkins's home and office lines to ensure they had not been tampered with. Agents duly visited the Jenkins home at 3704 Huntington Street NW, inspecting points where outside access to the lines might have been possible.[11]

In the weeks after the assassination, Jenkins tightly managed access to Johnson, prioritizing meetings that would advance the new administration's priorities. Lobbyists and advocates pressed their claims, often invoking the slain president's wishes, but Jenkins made sure the leaders Johnson valued most were able to spend time with him, including Mary Lasker, who had persuaded Johnson in 1959 to push through a major increase in the federal budget for health research.[12] When Lasker flew in from New York on November 24, 1963, he arranged for her to come immediately to Johnson's home, where she discussed her interest in a major appropriation for clinical research on heart disease, cancer, and stroke. Ten days later, on December 4, Jenkins slipped Johnson a note that Lasker hoped "if it were at all possible" to stop by since "I knew you always wanted to see her if at all possible."[13] Through such interventions, he helped set the agenda for the coming legislative session and the contours of the Great Society.

In this moment of national trauma and institutional chaos, Jenkins served as a steadying force (see figure 2.4). Kennedy aide Lee C. White, seated beside him in the helicopter returning from Andrews Air Force Base and struck by "his great shock and grief," soon regarded Jenkins as the central figure managing the transition: "I just wanted Walter, as the obvious chief of staff for Johnson, to know which particular balls I had bouncing in the air." Ralph Dungan likewise called him "the Rock of Gibraltar" during the transition, "a terrific guy with good judgment."[14]

As Johnson cultivated a reassuring and stable presidential image, Jenkins assembled and ran the apparatus that sustained it. "Americans needed a visible presidency and they got it," George Reedy recalled. Behind the scenes, Jenkins helped oversee daily operations and served as a conduit of sensitive information. Oral histories of the period emphasize the delicate task of uniting Kennedy and Johnson loyalists. It took "a little bit of walking on eggs sometimes," Jenkins said: there was "almost [a] dual staff—a Kennedy man and a Johnson man in nearly every position of some importance and trying to work together."[15] He remembered encountering a bleary-eyed, unshaven Kenneth O'Donnell—Kennedy's longtime aide and appointments secretary—who admitted he was still "weighing it in his conscience" whether he could work for Johnson.[16]

As Jenkins stabilized the White House, his own public visibility rose. On December 7, the day the Johnsons moved in, Lyndon, Lady Bird, and their daughter Lucy Baines Johnson had dinner at the Jenkinses' home, joined by Mildred Stegall and Congressman Homer Thornberry. Reporters waited on the sidewalk. That night, Lucy—soon to change the spelling of her name to "Luci"—brought Beth Jenkins back to the White House for a sleepover. The two girls

FIGURE 2.4 Walter Jenkins on the telephone, White House, December 1, 1963. LBJ Library/Photo by Yoichi Okamoto.

lit a fire in the fireplace in Lucy's new bedroom and then struggled to put it out. Two weeks later, the Johnsons returned for Lady Bird's birthday party, hosted by the Jenkinses and attended by about thirty guests, mostly staff. FBI investigators noted in 1964 that officers of the Eighth Precinct already knew Jenkins's address as a result of these highly visible presidential visits.[17]

As the press turned its attention to mapping Johnson's inner circle, eager to define the personalities replacing Kennedy's Ivy

League team, Jenkins stood out (see figures 2.5 and 2.6). A Washington correspondent called him "the one man who truly runs the Johnson office." Another described him as "doing the legwork that leads to the larger strides of decision." Tom Wicker of the *New York Times* cataloged his many roles—managing staff, settling jurisdictional disputes, chronicling meetings—and noted that other aides all agreed: Jenkins had "total rapport" with the president.[18] In a December column, William S. White, a Texan and former *New York Times* Senate correspondent sometimes derided as too cozy with Johnson, called Jenkins "one of the ablest, most devoted, most truly moral but totally unself-righteous public men this country has known for a long time." Such praise would eventually come with a price. Jenkins was now known as the aide "closest" to Johnson, and Barry Goldwater would later weaponize that word on the campaign trail after Jenkins's resignation.[19]

Jenkins's influence was reflected not only in newspaper profiles but in his physical placement. He occupied the first office in the West

FIGURE 2.5 Jack Valenti, Walter Jenkins, and Bill Moyers in the White House, December 4, 1963. Valenti later led the Motion Picture Association of America; Moyers became a prominent journalist and public-television host. LBJ Library/Photo by Yoichi Okamoto.

FIGURE 2.6 Walter Jenkins and President Johnson in the Oval Office, January 13, 1964. LBJ Library/Photo by Yoichi Okamoto.

Wing, while O'Donnell, still appointments secretary, kept his post just outside the Oval Office. "Mr. Jenkins, most of the time in shirt sleeves, is hard at work," one reporter wrote, adding that "the family is finding it sees less of Mr. Jenkins than it ever did."[20]

Their closeness to the Johnsons also made the Jenkinses a focus of social reporting. In January 1964, columnist Betty Beale described a wedding shower they hosted for a Texas lobbyist's daughter, devoting four paragraphs to the event and singling out each Jenkins child, including two-year-old Anne, "whipping around between floors like a beguiling minx in a saucy red jumper that continually showed her all over ruffled panties." For many Texans hoping to curry favor with the president, Jenkins became a key gatekeeper. In July 1964, Congressman Jake Pickle, newly elected to Johnson's former House seat, hosted a party in honor of Jenkins attended by more than 300 guests. A journalist noted that the president and First Lady not only attended but stayed for half an hour.[21]

Creating the Great Society

With his deep knowledge of Congress and an easy rapport with lawmakers, Jenkins was Johnson's trusted proxy in political negotiations. Jack Valenti said that "Walter alone among the staff members could talk to senators and congressmen on the most important subjects without having them feel that they should talk to the President" because they knew they *were* speaking to Johnson. He handled vote whipping, delivered difficult messages, and maintained crucial lines of communication. "I dealt with the Texas delegation and most of the friendly senators," the ones Johnson could "count on for the important things he really wanted done," Jenkins recalled. Johnson, by contrast, would personally engage only "those that were marginal or unfriendly."[22]

Jenkins handled nearly all personnel matters under Johnson's purview. The Executive Office of the President alone comprised some 1,500 employees. He recalled spending long nights reading FBI background checks: "Hoover recommended we do a check on everybody." As Johnson's liaison to the bureau, Jenkins noted simply, "I did have a lot of FBI contacts." Jenkins, like other top presidential aides, had a chauffeured black Mercury sedan to take him to and from work, equipped with a two-way radio so Johnson could reach him at all times.[23]

In addition to managing a demanding boss, Jenkins was inundated by people seeking access to Johnson. "I saw him earlier and later than anybody else did," he recalled, and, he added with characteristic modesty, "mine happened to be the name that people knew." After a long day, he might share a drink with the president, then return to his desk to find a towering stack of message slips for long-distance calls. He worked through them by time zone: East Coast, then Midwest, then West. A returned call from Jenkins signaled that a caller had the president's respect. As society columnist Betty Beale reported, Marjorie Jenkins grew used to evening interruptions from "people who call Walter at night on business and say they didn't want to bother him at the office. This is something I have learned to live with," she said, "but it is so ridiculous."[24]

Jenkins could be tough. He served as Johnson's hard-edged emissary, delivering firm messages in the guise of friendly counsel. As one Johnson biographer noted, Johnson wanted his employees "totally subservient to him, yet brutally aggressive with outsiders in promoting his interests," and Jenkins was arguably more effective because of his lack of bombast. In January 1964, he urged NASA administrator James Webb to withdraw from a space program event in Jackson, Mississippi, after the Student Nonviolent Coordinating Committee announced plans to picket. Jenkins cited what he believed was administration policy: no senior official should address a segregated audience. Webb, reluctant to offend Senator John C. Stennis, a key NASA ally, resisted. Jenkins checked with Johnson, who told him to warn Webb that "it'd be a serious thing from his standpoint," adding that he was sure Webb had "more judgment than to go to a segregated meeting. The space program's too important to have it segregated." Jenkins took care of it, and Webb backed out. A few days later, it fell to Jenkins to call Texas Congressman Joe Kilgore and all but command him not to run against Senator Ralph Yarborough in the Democratic primary, warning that a contested race might hand the seat to the Republicans.[25]

During his time in the White House, Jenkins played a role in some of the greatest triumphs of postwar liberalism. An especially vivid illustration of Jenkins's talents came on the morning of Saturday, August 8, 1964. Speaking from his Texas ranch—where he had just addressed reporters about both the Gulf of Tonkin incident and the FBI's investigation into the murder of three civil rights workers—

President Johnson phoned Jenkins for a rundown of the House vote on his signature War on Poverty bill. Unlike civil rights legislation, which Kennedy had championed before his death, this bill was Johnson's alone, drafted from scratch in just six months, the fastest passage of any major domestic initiative since the 1930s. With congressional liaison Larry O'Brien predicting the bill would pass "if we can just keep the boys that should be sober, sober, and the ones that should be drinking, drinking," Johnson now turned to Jenkins for the numbers.[26]

In twelve minutes, Jenkins walked Johnson through the votes of forty-three members—twenty-two Southern Democrats and fifteen Republicans among them, blocs known for opposing social spending. Using clipped surnames, Jenkins explained who had flipped, who held, who was fuming, who was absent, and whom he'd persuaded to stay by promising an Air Force flight home. Some lawmakers had begged to leave instead of going on record with a vote, citing the bill's likely passage. "I figured if we ever said yes to one," Jenkins told Johnson, "we'd have a hard time saying no to anybody else." Other members struck tactical bargains: voting yes on bringing the bill to the floor but no on final passage, or vice versa. "He says he's going to vote with us on final passage," Jenkins said of one, "but he said he wanted to have one both ways."

Texans were especially bitter about being stuck in Washington during campaign season. "They were all mad. I called all of them," Jenkins reported. Jim Wright was supposed to host a fundraising breakfast in Fort Worth that morning. "It was just hell to get him to stay," Jenkins said, "but he did." While Johnson remained at the ranch, Jenkins acted as his eyes, ears, and pressure gauge—tracking in real time the fragile coalition that would enact the bill into law.[27]

The Trouble with Bobby Baker

In September 1963, a scandal broke that Lyndon Johnson and Walter Jenkins both instantly recognized as dangerous. It centered on Bobby Baker, the former secretary to the Senate majority leader, who had been a top assistant to Johnson during his years in that position. While Vice President Johnson was in Copenhagen during a goodwill trip to Scandinavia, Jenkins called to alert him to a *Washington Post* story that hinted that Baker was taking advantage of his government position to enrich himself.[28]

The first public sign of Baker's troubles came when a man named Ralph Hill filed a lawsuit against him, alleging that Baker had demanded a fee to secure the contract to operate vending machines at Melpar, a missile component manufacturer. Hill said he paid Baker but still lost the contract. When the story broke, Johnson immediately sent Jenkins to meet with Baker and urge him to settle the matter quietly. Baker refused—and quickly came to regret it. Jenkins also tried unsuccessfully to dissuade Texas reporter Sarah McClendon from writing about the case.[29] As the charges snowballed, Baker resigned his post on October 7.

Reporters covering the story were egged on by Delaware Republican Senator John Williams, known for his fixation on official corruption, including his role in the 1958 downfall of Eisenhower aide Sherman Adams. Baker's closeness to Johnson only heightened the stakes. As the former cloakroom operator and master vote counter, Baker had been essential to Johnson's power in the Senate, and now he threatened to tarnish that legacy.[30]

Baker had capitalized on insider knowledge of Cold War defense contracting. Many of his activities were legal, but they raised persistent concerns about conflicts of interest. Johnson faced similar scrutiny. In 1956, as liberals criticized Johnson's push for natural-gas deregulation, columnist Drew Pearson ran a three-part exposé detailing Johnson's ties to Brown & Root, a pipeline builder, and for the first time disclosed an IRS inquiry into the company's donations to Johnson's 1941 Senate campaign. A longtime Johnson ally, Navy secretary Fred Korth, resigned shortly after Baker amid controversy over the TFX fighter-aircraft contract awarded to Texas-based General Dynamics, a firm with which he had prior ties. Senate critics, the *Times* reported, joked that the TFX plane "should have been called L.B.J."[31]

By the fall of 1963, a Senate Rules Committee investigation was underway, and *Life* magazine was digging deep. On November 8, just two weeks before the Kennedy assassination, *Life* ran a cover story titled "The Bobby Baker Bombshell," featuring a photo of Baker wearing a party mask. "He was known as 'Lyndon's Boy,'" the magazine reported. Johnson, it continued two weeks later, had "sponsored Bobby Baker's election as majority secretary and fashioned him into his legman, mouthpiece and satrap of power."[32] When Baker resigned, reporters redoubled their scrutiny of Johnson's fundraising apparatus—and of the confidants who had handled its most sensitive tasks. Jenkins's visibility and close identification with Johnson made him a natural target. Like Baker, Jenkins had quietly helped channel political money for Johnson, literally ferrying cash supplied by the senator's Texas backers between Austin and Washington to cover campaign expenses during Johnson's Senate years. The practice itself was lawful, but exposure would have been acutely embarrassing.[33]

By January 1964, the Baker story and Jenkins's name had become publicly linked. Don Reynolds, a former insurance salesman, had testified on the morning of Kennedy's assassination that he had been pressured by none other than Jenkins to buy $1,208 in advertising on KTBC, the Johnson family's Austin TV station, as part of a deal to write a life insurance policy on Johnson. In a January 8 *Des Moines Register* article, investigative reporter Clark Mollenhoff described Jenkins as "the second most powerful man in the White House." He also noted that Jenkins "occupies the office that housed Sherman Adams in the Eisenhower administration," an ominous reference since Adams was forced to resign over accepting bribes.[34] Mollenhoff had built his reputation exposing corruption in the Teamsters union, working closely with Robert Kennedy—connections that surely fed Johnson's paranoia.

Jenkins denied Reynolds's claims, but Republicans pressed for him to testify. The story threatened to implicate Jenkins directly in a kickback scheme. According to Reynolds, Jenkins had personally suggested the KTBC ad buy as a condition for landing the life insurance contract on Johnson, whose heart attack had made him difficult to insure. Jenkins, in a statement to investigators, denied "any knowledge of the arrangement by which Reynolds purchased advertising time on the TV station." But Senate investigators obtained letters from a third party that appeared to show Jenkins's familiarity with the transaction.[35]

As Rules Committee members pushed to subpoena Jenkins, Johnson worked feverishly to prevent it. "They're trying to make a big play that Walter Jenkins has committed perjury," Johnson told Senator Richard Russell, "and he's the most honest man I know." Abe Fortas asked Hubert Humphrey to lobby committee Democrats to limit the inquiry. At the same time, Johnson's press team tried to manage the fallout. Following Reedy and Pierre Salinger's advice, Jenkins ducked interview requests from *Newsweek*'s Jay Iselin and columnist Marquis Childs.[36] But the administration also began pressuring news outlets directly. Fortas called editors at the *Washington Evening Star* asking them not to publish a new allegation: that, at Baker's request, Reynolds had given Johnson an expensive hi-fi stereo. The story ran anyway, and so did reports about the heavy-handed pressure tactics of Fortas and others. It was one of the earliest breaches in the Johnson White House's credibility with reporters. When columnists Drew Pearson and Jack Anderson later published damaging information about Reynolds's Air Force record, many suspected Johnson's hand.[37]

What made the Reynolds claims so dangerous was that they revived scrutiny not only of Baker's dealings but of Johnson's personal fortune. Johnson and Lady Bird had built their wealth through KTBC, a business subject to extensive federal regulation. In March 1964, CBS president Frank Stanton told Jenkins that *Wall Street Journal* reporter Louis Kohlmeier was preparing an exposé. A few minutes later, Jenkins told the president that Jesse Kellam, the man who ran the station for the Johnsons, said "Kohlmeier's now calling him. He started calling last night."[38]

Kohlmeier's two-part article made national news. While he found no evidence of regulatory interference, he painted a picture of cronyism and blurred lines between public office and private enrichment. Among the people listed as having worked for both KTBC and Johnson's campaigns were John Connally, Jake Pickle, Jesse Kellam—and Walter Jenkins. The piece noted that Jenkins had served for years as Lady Bird's corporate treasurer while also working as Johnson's top aide, stepping down from the private role only after Johnson entered the White House.[39]

By spring, Democrats on the Rules Committee had largely circled the wagons. They agreed to limit the inquiry to Baker and avoid subpoenaing Jenkins. But press coverage continued to grow. The *Evening Star* assigned two reporters to the Baker case full-time—what an observer later called a harbinger of "an increasing emphasis on investigative reporting."[40]

Rumors about young women became a minor part of the Baker scandal, but one treated cautiously and under a sexist double standard. "Every vigilant newspaper office in Washington has a list of names of those implicated with Baker and his lobbying friends and his girls," wrote *New York Times* columnist James Reston. The *Saturday Evening Post* called it "an American 'Profumo case,'" invoking the recent British scandal that had forced War Minister John Profumo to resign over an affair with a young woman.[41]

The press protected male but not female participants—labeled "girls" or "beauties"—in illicit heterosexual encounters.[42] Reynolds himself admitted lending out his apartment to powerful men for extramarital trysts, but balked at naming them to the Rules Committee, saying it "might embarrass" men who had merely been "escaping from the drudgery of marital life." Baker admitted his affair with Carole Tyler, writing in his memoir that he felt "the guilt of a longtime family man with a loyal wife and five children," since he "did little to conceal" the romance. But, in a testament to his own supposed moral rectitude, Baker wrote that while he loved Tyler, "I refused to leave my family for her."[43]

For Jenkins, the danger lay not in sex but in his role in Johnson's business endeavors and personal finances. The Baker scandal had placed him, however unwillingly, in the crosshairs of a press corps newly attuned to political corruption and increasingly willing to name names.

All the Way with LBJ

Jenkins's year in the White House entangled him in the era's most troubling domestic surveillance. He later acknowledged that, as the president's liaison to the bureau, he reviewed and passed along reports from Hoover's deputy, Cartha "Deke" DeLoach, on the wiretapping of Martin Luther King Jr., the nation's most prominent Black civil rights leader.[44] These reports, authorized by Attorney General Robert F. Kennedy, reached Jenkins by January 1964. By one scholar's count, Hoover wrote Jenkins eleven times about King from February through April. After the FBI used both wiretaps and a hidden microphone to surveil King during his two-day stay at a Los Angeles hotel that July, Hoover forwarded Jenkins a three-page memorandum marked both "obscene" and "top secret." Jenkins scrawled an instruction to his secretary, Mildred Stegall, in pencil to file the memo under King's name.[45] The man who handled some of the White House's most sensitive secrets—and who cooperated without apparent hesitation in surveillance of another man's sex life—would soon fall victim to similar scrutiny himself.

At the Democratic National Convention in Atlantic City that August, when Black Mississippians tried to challenge their exclusion from that state's party organization, Jenkins became Johnson's on-site agent and strategist. A group of insurgents calling themselves the Mississippi Freedom Democratic Party (MFDP) sought to unseat the state's all-white delegation. Johnson feared that racial conflict—including unrest in Harlem and white rage over the Civil Rights Act—could fracture his fragile political coalition. He also believed allies of Robert Kennedy were scheming to wrest the presidential nomination from him, and at times he seemed to believe that the MFDP was a vehicle for that effort.[46]

As the MFDP mounted its challenge at the convention, Jenkins worked furiously behind the scenes to prevent other white

Southerners from joining white delegates from the Magnolia State in walking out. He passed on frank assessments of Johnson's options, even when they clashed with others' advice. After hearing a claim that delegations from Texas, Georgia, Florida, and North Carolina would remain if the MFDP challengers were seated, Jenkins added, "I don't agree with much of that. I don't think any of them would stay." In the end, party leaders allowed two MFDP representatives to serve as symbolic, nonvoting "at large" delegates. When most white Mississippians walked out in protest, Jenkins—working with John Connally and others—pressed other Southern delegates to register their dissent by voting against the compromise while remaining on the floor and accepting the convention's decision rather than joining the walkout.[47]

Johnson confided in Jenkins in a moment of acute self-doubt. On the morning of August 25, as tensions mounted, Johnson phoned Jenkins from the White House, floating the possibility of withdrawing from the nomination altogether. "I don't think a white Southerner is the man to unite this nation in this hour," Johnson confessed. "I rather guess that if anybody's entitled to know, you are, to what I'm thinking." As Johnson ruminated about a potential floor fight over the nomination, Jenkins said at one point, "I don't agree with you on not winning" such a fight. While offering measured reassurance, Jenkins largely let Johnson talk. Johnson spiraled into fears about his health and mental stability, alluding to President Woodrow Wilson's stroke and breakdown: "I don't want to be in this place like Wilson." He asked Jenkins whether he should announce his withdrawal immediately or after a delay. Sensing Johnson's despair, Jenkins alerted Lady Bird Johnson, who wrote a private letter urging her husband to stay the course. Her intervention, combined with Jenkins's steady presence, helped Johnson recommit to the nomination.[48]

While Jenkins worked to manage Southern delegations and his agitated boss, he was also receiving FBI intelligence on the phone calls and comings and goings of King and other allies of the MFDP. Johnson's fear of a floor fight had produced a surveillance operation aimed not at the all-white Southern delegations threatening party unity and defying party leaders but at civil rights leaders pressing the party to seat the MFDP. Jenkins and Bill Moyers oversaw this surveillance for Johnson. Later on August 25, for example, again calling from Atlantic City, Jenkins read aloud from a detailed memo from DeLoach concerning Martin Luther King Jr.'s reaction to the compromise and other activists' dissatisfaction: "Martin Luther King is very, very unhappy about the way things have turned out." DeLoach sent such memos each morning and evening during the convention.[49] Hoover informed Jenkins that according to "a confidential source," Attorney General Robert Kennedy—Hoover's own nominal boss—would be staying on the Kennedy family yacht moored nearby.[50]

Jenkins also served as Johnson's intermediary with the two leading vice-presidential contenders, Hubert Humphrey and Eugene McCarthy. When Johnson finally arrived in Atlantic City, Jenkins oversaw the schedule, ensuring the convention's televised coverage unfolded on Johnson's terms. At one point Johnson leaned over and said, "Walter, this is going on too long," instructing him to postpone Humphrey's acceptance speech to the following day, "when people are watching."[51]

Despite Johnson's rousing convention speech and wide lead in polls over Barry Goldwater, the Baker scandal continued to loom. Throughout the fall, Goldwater's campaign sought to cast Baker as a symbol of moral and political corruption, linking Johnson to Washington's "wheeler-dealer" culture. Conservative publisher Regnery even printed 200,000 copies of *The Bobby Baker Affair: How to Make Millions in Washington*, though it sold poorly compared to a flood of self-published anti-Johnson books.[52] Still, Goldwater persisted, weaving Baker into his narrative of Johnson as a morally compromised president.[53] When Jenkins's own scandal broke, it would slot seamlessly into this existing storyline.

An Insecure Front-Runner

By the fall of 1964, Jenkins was clearly under strain. For years, Jenkins's doctor had noted his "florid face and red palms" and expressed concern about his persistently high blood pressure. That spring, a *Sunday Star* photo feature on Easter in official Washington showed Marjorie Jenkins dressed for the parade with five of their children on the front steps of their home—but without her husband. Walter was, as always, at work.[54]

As the general election approached, Johnson remained haunted by the specter of Bobby Baker. In private, he worried that the scandal would resurface, that Goldwater would make "morality" a campaign issue, and that as a result of the Baker inquiry the public would begin to blur the lines between Baker and Jenkins: two trusted aides, both too close, both tied to money, both targets of suspicion. For Jenkins, this proximity was both a source of extraordinary influence and a deepening liability. He had become the public face of Johnson's inner circle—the aide who knew the most, worked the hardest, and stayed the latest. He was indispensable. He was also increasingly well known in Washington.

That fall, the First Lady left town for an extended solo campaign swing through the South, a testament to her growing role in the administration. She was steely and strategic, skilled at calming tempers and reading the mood of the country. Her instincts would soon be tested. In the weeks ahead, it would fall to her—not just as First Lady, but as a political operator—to manage a sudden crisis involving the man her husband called "the best man I've got."

CHAPTER 3

NO. 168287

In the separate cases of Jenkins's 1959 and 1964 arrests, Washington's vice policing produced sharply different outcomes for the same man, in the same place, on the same charge. In 1959, the incident in the G Street YMCA men's room was quietly handled—the record altered, his position obscured—in a way that spared him public exposure. More than five years later, amid a presidential campaign, another arrest in that same restroom unfolded very differently, setting off a chain of leaks, press maneuvering, and political damage.

The scandal's force lay in the distance between the two worlds Jenkins moved through that October night in 1964—from a blue-carpeted, cabinet-filled *Newsweek* party to a basement restroom coded as dirty, exposed, and policed. Police and journalistic discretion sometimes contained such incidents. This time they did not—reflecting not a change in the formal rules but the fragility of the informal arrangements that could shield certain men from the full weight of the law.

The Jenkins affair brought national scrutiny to the antigay policing system that had become entrenched in urban America since World War II. Together, his two arrests illuminate the rules and relationships that shaped their different outcomes. A series of chance events transformed the 1964 encounter in a YMCA restroom into a front-page story, revealing both the reach of antigay surveillance and its limits, complexity, and unpredictability. The first of those two arrests came on an unremarkable evening in 1959—the same cramped G Street YMCA men's room, a similar charge, but a radically different outcome.

1959: Discretion in Vice Policing

In 1959, Jenkins was arrested alone in a case kept out of sight through the exercise of discretion and record sanitizing that occasionally protected government officials, especially if they were married, from public exposure. According to the arresting officer's report, Jenkins cruised him, "went over to the other urinal and took out his penis and started to rub and stroke it," and then "reached over and grabbed hold of my privates twice. At that time I identified myself and placed him under arrest." Jenkins told the FBI he believed the policeman in this instance had "enticed" him.[1]

In 1959, he kept his job because specific protocols ensured the arrest would go no further. While the *fact* of his having been arrested was transmitted to the FBI, it did not draw attention during rushed security reviews, in 1961 and again in 1963, as his boss moved to the vice presidency and then to the nation's most powerful position. It was not simply chance or luck that led Jenkins's 1959 arrest to remain hidden from Lyndon Johnson, but Morals Division policy—one of at least two important patterns of nonenforcement that had arisen partly in response to the severity of punishment associated with morals charges.

One such pattern was the Metropolitan Police Department's practice of allowing arrestees to post a relatively small amount as collateral and avoid facing a courtroom. In August 1950, the Hoey committee objected to the practice and soon reported that the chief judge of the DC municipal court had agreed to require $300 minimum cash as collateral. But by 1959 the department had reverted to a lower amount and was once again allowing men to post collateral in return for forgoing judicial oversight. The procedure had multiple advantages from the police standpoint: it sidestepped judges who increasingly balked at vice-squad evidence; it generated a steady stream of forfeited collateral payments in lieu of judicial oversight; and it often avoided public exposure for arrestees.[2] After the 1964 scandal broke, police claimed this system had been instituted out of humanitarian concern for wives and children. The *Los Angeles Times* reported proudly that, unlike in Washington, local police in their city would not have permitted Jenkins to forfeit bail and go home.[3]

Buried in the FBI's report—and mentioned, albeit hazily, in some journalistic accounts at the time—is a second and more important factor: the Morals Division routinely sanitized the version of arrest reports shared with other government agencies, including the FBI. In part this policy reflected bureaucratic jealousy; for the recently retired Roy Blick, the Morals Division had long been his fiefdom, just as the FBI was J. Edgar Hoover's. But the policy also stemmed from the political sensitivity of one of the consequences of the elaborate postwar regime of antigay public policy: its tendency to sweep in otherwise "normal," upstanding men.

Police sanitized their records of the 1959 arrest, removing details that could have triggered official or public consequences. Jenkins's employer was changed from "Senate of the U.S.A." to "unemployed," graphic details replaced with a description of his behavior only as "loitering," and his charge altered from "Investigation (Pervert)" to "Investigation (Suspicious Person)." In a memo prepared at the FBI's request in 1964, Scott E. Moyer, then the new head of the Morals Division, explained that this was "standard procedure [in] cases of this nature."[4] Because the Identification Division records were publicly available, an FBI agent noted, they were "not considered sufficiently secure" to include the true facts about the arrest.[5]

This sanitization had direct consequences. In 1961, when Johnson requested a White House pass for Jenkins, the FBI provided the Secret Service with only the altered version of the 1959 arrest record. The agency charged with protecting the president and vice president learned only that Jenkins had been arrested as a "suspicious person," not for any sexual misconduct. Treasury Secretary Douglas Dillon later determined that the Secret Service "did not evaluate the FBI criminal report as involving a serious matter." No further investigation was triggered. The reason federal agencies were only haphazardly notified of arrests of their employees, officials claimed repeatedly during the inquiry into the Jenkins case, was that the police routinely shielded such information in the interest of protecting marriages.[6]

The effect was to conceal the nature of Jenkins's 1959 arrest from federal background checks. Jenkins's case thus exposed a routinized practice of selective nonenforcement and misrepresentation. The Morals Division kept detailed reports in confidential files while preparing sanitized versions, which went to the Identification Division and were made available to other officers and to the FBI. These edited reports often downgraded arrestees' occupations, recasting high-level officials as "ordinary" employees and sometimes also removing facts about their alleged crimes. Police later acknowledged they had routinely misrepresented arrestees' jobs and charges—not from indifference, they said, but out of "compassion, because of what disclosure might mean to the suspect's family and livelihood." While the claims of law enforcement officials are often unreliable, the fact that they framed the practice as a problem to be corrected rather than a point of pride lends their admission credibility. Jenkins's exposure in 1964 was therefore not only a political and personal crisis; it drew attention to and ruptured a longstanding regime of discretion that shielded married white men in white-collar government jobs.[7]

Jenkins's case unfolded amid a system of antigay police practices that was intensifying yet also increasingly drawing criticism from liberals. Saul Bellow's 1964 novel *Herzog*, published shortly before Jenkins's arrest and later awarded the National Book Award, captured this unease. In a courtroom scene, the protagonist, Herzog, watches as a "detective, a specialist in men's toilets," describes how he served as "a bait" to entrap a young German man. The officer testifies with practiced "speed and expertness." When the magistrate warns the defense attorney that a guilty plea will permanently bar the man from practicing medicine in the US, Herzog is outraged:

"You don't destroy a man's career because he yielded to an impulse in that ponderous stinking cavern below Grand Central . . . where policemen (perhaps themselves that way given) tempt and trap poor souls."[8] Bellow's depiction channels a central critique of tearoom policing: the disproportion between a momentary, private impulse and the irreversible consequences—including professional ruin and public shame—that it could trigger.

The growing prevalence of such cases, and the kinds of men they ensnared, strained the legitimacy of plainclothes policing of gay life. As Anna Lvovsky has noted, antigay policing "consistently captured white, middle-class suspects who otherwise rarely crossed paths with the police," prompting ambivalence from judges when cases reached trial courts.[9] This often generated pressure for leniency, especially when the defendant was married or professionally successful, as in Jenkins's own 1959 arrest. Although cruising could be dangerous, it was sometimes survivable even when the police arrived. The Jenkins scandal ultimately exposed not just the scope of antigay surveillance but also the uneven compassion baked into its enforcement. The system punished harshly, but inconsistently.

Even amid the harshness of antigay enforcement, then, there was also a recurrent leniency, particularly for men with families. In tearoom arrests, the state's interest in preserving the household often pulled in contradictory directions: punishing individuals while shielding their families from fallout. As Anne Gray Fischer has argued, legal liberalism in this period often translated into leniency for white women and intensifying scrutiny of Black women—a reminder that compassion, where it existed, was highly selective. For men like Jenkins, compassion often took the form of discretion. After his 1959 arrest, Jenkins was allowed to forfeit collateral and avoid court. So far as we know, he told no one, not even his wife. As one legal scholar observed, "Often when apparently respectable persons are arrested on charges of homosexuality, the officer will tell the arrestee that no notoriety will result from the arrest." In one such case, a man was arrested for soliciting sex, but when the officer "learned that the man had a fine medical practice in town," supported elderly parents, and was willing to see a psychiatrist, the charges were dropped.[10] Jenkins's experience in 1959 fit this pattern, disappearing into a file drawer. Almost six years later, a fall evening began in the same city with the same man—but this time, the consequences would be impossible to contain.

October 7, 1964: From Gala to Arrest

On the evening of October 7, 1964, Walter Jenkins left *Newsweek*'s glittering housewarming for the G Street YMCA, where plainclothes vice patrolmen were stationed in the lobby. The officers who arrested him did not initially realize they had detained Johnson's most indispensable aide. Jenkins worked day and night next to the most powerful man in the world, but saying so would have risked accusations of pulling rank, perhaps even guaranteeing the publicity he most feared. He was important, yet vulnerable. What gave the scandal its force was the gulf between the president's inner circle and spectacular disgrace. "In one awful, degrading rush, Walter Jenkins has plunged from grace and power," a *Life* columnist wrote.[11] And his fall occurred at a moment of intense public focus on Lyndon Johnson's character and authority.

Jenkins's October 7 schedule reflected his central role in orchestrating the presidency. Throughout the day a parade of powerful legislators and journalists had come to the White House to meet with him, among them Stewart Alsop and Senator Hubert Humphrey. At the bottom of his appointment list, he had scrawled in red ballpoint pen an evening obligation: "Go thru new bldg. of Newsweek." The cocktail party, hosted by Katharine "Kay" Graham, celebrated the magazine her late husband, Philip Graham, had purchased in 1961. *Newsweek*'s new Washington suite, upholstered in blue and looking south to the Washington Monument and the Mall, occupied the twelfth floor of a gleaming commercial building at 1750 Pennsylvania Avenue, a long block northwest of the White House. Ben Bradlee, the bureau chief, greeted guests at the door and later recalled Jenkins's arrival around 7:15 p.m.[12]

Jenkins's appearance at the *Newsweek* party reflected Johnson's insistence that he "be seen around town" on Washington's social circuit. Earlier that year, in March, at columnist Les Carpenter's invitation, he attended a screening of the presidential farce *The Best Man*, written by Gore Vidal.[13] Like *Advise and Consent*, the film dramatized the political weaponization of homosexuality as a present-day politician weighs whether to exploit an opponent's alleged same-sex activity during World War II. It underscored how memories of wartime license continued to animate Cold War fears and, unlike the earlier film, situated the allegation within a presidential campaign.

The *Newsweek* gathering, meanwhile, reflected the close intimacy between press and power in Cold War Washington. Six cabinet members attended; "Jenkins' Fall: Gala Before the Disgrace," ran a front-page headline in the *New York Herald-Tribune*. The *Post*'s own history illustrates the deference then afforded to powerful straight men in embarrassing matters. Phil Graham became the *Post*'s publisher through his marriage to Katharine Meyer, whose father owned the paper, and his rise and unraveling show how news organizations often shielded elite misconduct. Between his 1961 purchase of *Newsweek* and his suicide in August 1963, Graham's alcoholism, severe mental illness, and an extramarital affair produced public scenes in rooms full of reporters that nonetheless went unreported, even by rivals.[14] At the same time, *Newsweek* positioned itself as *Time*'s more progressive competitor, with attention to events unfolding among the radical right and in "Black America."[15]

Whenever the president and First Lady were away, the city's tempo slackened. As William Walton, a gay man who advised Jacqueline Kennedy on her White House restoration, observed, "When a president goes off for a weekend in Hyannis Port or to his Texas ranch, there is a noticeable lessening of tension." Johnson was airborne between Peoria and Chicago around the time of the arrest; Lady Bird Johnson was on a whistle-stop tour through the South.[16]

Contemporaneous reporting and eyewitness accounts indicate that intoxication did not explain Jenkins's trip to the YMCA. Although Abe Fortas and perhaps others appear to have floated that explanation to reporters, the surviving evidence points the other way. Hugh Sidey noted that "*Newsweek* had hundreds of candid pictures taken at the party and among them are several of Walter Jenkins and he is not drinking in any of them." A *Herald-Tribune* reporter who was present recalled that Jenkins "wasn't drunk, or even tipsy" when he left around eight. Ben Bradlee told the FBI that whatever alcohol Jenkins had consumed "could not have been much since he in no way showed any signs of intoxication."[17] And Jenkins's return to the White House, where he worked for several more hours after his release, reinforces the same conclusion.

Describing the scene to his editors, Sidey portrayed Jenkins not only as a political insider but as a well-liked family man at ease in Washington's social world. As in baby-boom America generally, children were an easy conversational bridge. Jenkins had chatted about his children and the PTA and was "tickled" by a story of his nine-year-old Lyndon's delivering the morning paper to an unnamed correspondent: Lyndon was bright, he said, but "because he was so quick he sometimes grew a bit uppity."[18]

Shortly after 8 p.m., Chalmers M. Roberts of the *Post*, who had recently written about Jenkins's role behind the scenes in resolving the dispute in Atlantic City over Mississippi's delegates to the Democratic convention, rode down with Jenkins in the elevator as they both departed. Roberts recalled that Jenkins doubled back to retrieve an umbrella.[19] Exiting the concrete-and-glass office building onto Pennsylvania Avenue, Jenkins walked around the block to the grimy brick G Street YMCA, crossed the lobby, descended a staircase, and entered a gray door stenciled "Men's Room" in black letters, where Andy Choka was already sitting in one of the stalls (see figure 3.1).[20] It was a space the American public did not see but would soon vividly imagine. Two police officers were nearby, waiting to spy on bathroom users by standing on a stool or chair and looking through an architectural transom over the door.

Like the comfort stations in nearby Lafayette Park, the YMCA's basement men's room drew men of disparate social classes, including strangers seeking sexual encounters, and was a focus of

FIGURE 3.1 Washington's G Street YMCA. National Photo Company Collection, Library of Congress, Prints & Photographs Division, LC-DIG-npcc-18890.

police attention. Jenkins was arrested at the YMCA for the second time—this time alongside Andy Choka, a Hungarian-born US Army veteran—by a four-man team from the Morals Division. The most senior officer, Louis Fochett, later told the FBI he had been speaking with the front desk clerk "when a man came in the front entrance"—Jenkins—whom he vaguely recognized but couldn't immediately place. "JENKINS walked straight to a stairway leading to the basement," Fochett recalled.[21] There, two other plainclothes officers were already in position. They watched Jenkins and Choka enter the restroom.

According to one of the arresting officers, Lamont P. Drouillard, "both men appeared slightly nervous" on their way in. Seeing this, he retrieved a stool—"similar to the type used by elevator operators," he remarked—which he routinely used to observe "immoral acts of individuals" in the YMCA bathroom.[22] Climbing atop it, Drouillard and his colleague, Robert Graham, took turns peering through the transom over the door, where they watched Jenkins and Choka engage in oral sex in a doorless toilet stall, though the sides of the stall blocked them from seeing the sexual act itself. The officers burst in and placed both men under arrest. With Fochett and the fourth officer, Thomas Herrity, Drouillard and Graham left the building and seated Jenkins and Choka in the back of a police cruiser.

The six men drove to police headquarters, not far from the Capitol. The arrestees were first brought to the Morals Division, where they were booked and the arrest was entered into a public ledger, accessible to anyone who asked. Jenkins's arrest report was assigned the identification number 168287. From there, they were brought to another unit for identification. Only Jenkins's thumbprint was taken, which was standard procedure for someone with a prior arrest. He was also photographed. Finally, they were led to the basement cell block, where each man paid fifty dollars in collateral and was released.[23]

Aware of Jenkins's high-level position, Officer Fochett told FBI agents that he first sought guidance before proceeding. He phoned Inspector Scott E. Moyer, head of the Morals Division, described the charge and Jenkins's role in the White House, and was advised to book him for "disorderly conduct." Fochett said he informed Jenkins that he could contact a lawyer, but also explained that a fifty-dollar forfeiture would avoid a court appearance. "JENKINS then said he would not call a lawyer in order to prevent publicity," Fochett reported. He also claimed that Choka admitted to the acts first, in Jenkins's presence. Jenkins, for his part, told the FBI that if Choka had confessed, he had not overheard it. According to Fochett, Jenkins "did not object to the arrest and made no claims as to innocence."[24]

Contemporary humor captured the perceived gulf in status between the White House and the YMCA. A syndicated editorial cartoonist showed LBJ slumped at his desk in the Oval Office as a Washington YMCA official leans over him, wagging his finger: "This sort of thing could give my organization a bad name!" (see figure 3.2). A Californian visiting Washington heard a similar joke: after a man "gave his business address as the White House executive offices," a hotel's desk clerk quipped, "'What's the matter? They throw you out of the YMCA?'"[25]

The site of Jenkins's arrest was part of a broader landscape of public restrooms targeted by vice squads nationwide. Built in 1903 as an emblem of uplift, the G Street Y offered cheap lodgings and athletic facilities and also served as a discreet meeting place for men seeking sex. Black Washingtonians were long excluded and relegated to a separate Twelfth Street branch. By the postwar era, disinvestment had left the downtown Y a symbol of decline—"The town center is a marble graveyard after dark," a former White House correspondent lamented. Still, even as highway rest stops began to take on a similar function, men in the 1960s continued to cruise in inner-city parks and public buildings.[26]

That landscape was actively policed by the Metropolitan Police Department's Morals Division, headed by Roy Blick, which targeted female sex workers and male cruisers. Vice units proliferated in the 1950s in American cities and were often pressured to justify their budgets and existence through arrests.[27]

What unfolded at the G Street YMCA formed part of a larger system of antigay surveillance and arrest. Mid-century public restrooms like the one at the G Street Y were places where class, race, and gender hierarchies were policed and transgressed under routine surveillance. As places where people exposed their bodies, associated with both contamination and cleansing, they became flash points in multiple cultural conflicts.[28] Johnson himself invoked re-

FIGURE 3.2 Editorial cartoon by Paul Conrad, *Los Angeles Times*, October 16, 1964. Used with permission of the Conrad estate.

strooms to dramatize the everyday humiliations of segregation; in July 1963, Katie Louchheim recorded him decrying in a speech "how women could not go to toilets cross-country if they were colored."[29] Understanding how those spaces were policed, and what was at stake for the men caught there, helps explain why a disorderly-conduct charge similar to one that vanished in 1959 could erupt into scandal in a few years later.

From Tearoom to Front Page

Arrests in public restrooms like the G Street YMCA, which were under steady police surveillance, usually made news only locally. For the men arrested, however, not knowing if the night would end in low-profile release, humiliation, or catastrophe was itself a form of punishment. In 1957, a Morals Division decoy arrest of an employee of the White House correspondence office led to investigations of two colleagues; all three resigned quietly and immediately. "His record is at that point blemished," Donald Webster Cory wrote in his 1951 book *The Homosexual in America*, describing what men seeking sex most feared, "and the arrest may become a permanent part of the police files." The fear that "he may, at any moment, be placing himself in a trap" shadowed even "marginal pleasures." Even when other institutions imposed punishments—as when Smith College professor Newton Arvin lost his job and was confined in a state hospital after postal inspectors searched his apartment and found physique magazines—it was often police action that launched the process.[30] In 1964, Walter Jenkins's arrest became the extraordinary exception that reached the national stage.

Public restrooms were the most common site of gay-related arrests in the 1960s on both felony and misdemeanor charges. *Life* reported that "Homosexuals everywhere fear arrest—and the public exposure that may go along with it." In a 1967 Chicago study, nearly a quarter of gay-identified men reported a police arrest "related to homosexuality," and half worried "often" or "sometimes" that their sex lives would lead to "being caught by the police."[31]

By the early 1960s, two techniques dominated the growing police practice of arresting cruisers: decoy stings, where plainclothes officers posed as available targets for advances, and clandestine surveillance, where officers watched men through vents, peepholes, and transoms. Jenkins was caught by the former in 1959 and the latter in 1964. Antigay policing was shaped by the postwar infusion of money and technology into police departments. One police journal explained how to conceal a motion-picture camera in a restroom;

Mansfield, Ohio, used such methods to charge dozens. The case for tearoom arrests was bolstered by a growing fear of homosexuals as predators. "Public restrooms can often be a hangout for the homosexual," warned a 1955 instructional film aimed at suburban schoolchildren. A San Francisco gay newsletter published a "partial list" of downtown tearooms "too dangerous even for the most daring inverts." As Margot Canaday has shown, postwar gay immigration cases followed a common trajectory "from bathroom to border," in which an arrest later was cited as the grounds for excluding someone from the country.[32]

Political reporters in 1964 often took for granted the necessity of tearoom surveillance; in his book on the campaign, for example, Theodore H. White called the G Street Y men's room "so notorious a gathering place of homosexuals that the District police had long since staked it out with peepholes for surveillance."[33]

Vice enforcement reflected Washington's racial order: a largely white, nonresident force patrolled an increasingly majority-Black city. The Morals Division arrested both white and Black men on gay-related charges, though its ledger for the day of Jenkins's first arrest, if representative, suggests Black women were hardest hit. By 1964, more than 80 percent of the department's 2,900 officers were white and living outside the district while the city's population was about 60 percent Black. On January 15, 1959, police arrested five Black women on prostitution charges; eight men—six white, two Black—on gay-related charges; and one Black man on a drug charge. The gay arrests were clustered near Lafayette Park.[34] As Kwame Holmes has shown, Black men faced sexual regulation not only from specialized units but also from precinct officers in Black neighborhoods.[35]

Public restrooms remained popular cruising sites both for men who did not think of themselves as gay and for those who did belong to a growing subculture. In St. Louis in the mid-1960s, a majority of tearoom participants were married and living with their wives. In 1967, 30 percent of 458 gay-identified men reported they had "gone looking for sexual partners" in a public toilet during the previous year.[36]

Arrest in the G Street YMCA's basement men's room could unleash swift and devastating punishment, both physical and professional. Gore Vidal wrote in *Esquire* about watching four policemen beat up a pair of suspects on the sidewalk in front of the building after such an arrest. The policemen, he wrote, "were, quite simply, enjoying their work," after which he "brooded on the curious horror of seeing our society at its most vicious two blocks from the White House." According to one reporter, police arrested eight men in that single tearoom during one five-hour period earlier in 1964, including "two college professors and several government employees." It was not the only tearoom in the area where officers had arranged "peepholes."[37] In Jenkins's case, the patterns of surveillance that had ensnared countless men now reached far beyond the confines of the restroom, colliding with the machinery of national journalism and partisan warfare.

In contrast to that of 1959, Jenkins's 1964 arrest quickly reached reporters, setting in motion the political and journalistic maneuvers that turned a private encounter into a national scandal. Leaks began almost immediately. A police reporter for the *Washington Daily News* received a tip about the arrest two days later, on Friday, October 9.[38] Senator John Williams of Delaware—already doggedly investigating the Bobby Baker scandal—also heard about the case when a Goldwater campaign staffer called his office on Tuesday afternoon to pass along a call from someone claiming to have "a lot of information on Walter Jenkins."[39]

By Tuesday night, the story was moving quickly through Washington's journalistic and political networks. Around 10 p.m. on October 13, John Barron, a staff reporter at the *Washington Evening Star*, received a tip about the arrest and relayed it to his editor, Charles Seib. He moved swiftly, dispatching two police reporters to check the arrest blotter early the next morning. "They took notes, learned from police sources about the previous arrest, and reported back to Assistant Managing Editor Charles B. Seib—all before 9 a.m. Wednesday, Oct. 14," according to David Wise of the *New York Herald-Tribune*. At 9 a.m., Seib called the White House in hopes of reaching press secretary George Reedy. With Reedy on his way with Johnson to campaign events in New Jersey and New York, Seib instead reached Liz Carpenter, Lady Bird Johnson's press secretary. Carpenter, in turn, called Jenkins's secretary, Mildred Stegall, and then Jenkins himself, who was still at home.[40]

As soon as Jenkins realized that reporters had learned of his arrest, he called the outside adviser Johnson trusted most with sensitive matters: the influential Washington attorney Abe Fortas. Jenkins had known Fortas since the 1940s, but even so, he struggled to explain the nature of his predicament. "I'm in terrible trouble," he said. Fortas told him to come immediately to his redbrick house at 3025 N Street in Georgetown—just four doors down from the home Jacqueline Kennedy had recently vacated. Jenkins took a taxi there, while Fortas walked home from his law office at Arnold, Fortas, and Palmer, eleven blocks away. Around 10 a.m., Fortas began coordinating a response on behalf of the White House: he phoned Seib and asked to see him, called Clark Clifford and invited him to join, placed Jenkins in the upstairs bedroom, and summoned Jenkins's physician, Dr. Charles Thompson. Then he drove to the *Star* offices, picking up Clifford on the way.[41]

Fortas and Clifford were central figures in a day of escalating newsroom intrigue. Both were prominent Washington lawyers in private practice who had long served as unofficial fixers and troubleshooters for Lyndon Johnson. Clifford, a patrician WASP and former aide to Harry Truman, had gradually earned Johnson's confidence. Fortas, born in Memphis to Orthodox Jewish immigrants, was even closer to the president. A former Yale Law School professor, he had worked in several New Deal agencies before entering private practice and had represented Johnson in the protracted legal battle over the 1948 Texas Senate primary, in which Johnson's eighty-seven-vote margin led to the nickname "Landslide Lyndon." Just months earlier, Fortas had stepped down as Bobby Baker's attorney, a sign of how entangled he was in Johnson's problems.[42]

They spent the afternoon moving from newsroom to newsroom, urging editors to delay publication on humanitarian grounds. (They also arranged to shield Jenkins behind hospital walls.) Their first stop was the *Evening Star*, where they met with Charles Seib and top editor Newbold Noyes Jr. The two emissaries, Noyes later recalled, said they had just seen Jenkins and "asked us in what seemed to me a very proper and low-key way to consider whether this was a story that we would want to print." Noyes agreed to withhold the story from that evening's edition. But he also revealed two critical facts that Jenkins had not disclosed: that he had been arrested previously, in 1959, and that police had taken a mug shot that clearly confirmed his identity. Fortas, reporting this back to Johnson, emphasized the seriousness: "They took a mug shot of him that they've got down there," he said, and "there's no doubt about the identity."[43] Alarmed, Fortas and Clifford moved on to the *Daily News*, leaving the *Post*—a morning paper that had a later deadline—for last.

Meanwhile, the city's rumor mill was whirring: by late afternoon, phones across Washington were ringing with anonymous tips about the arrest. The calls came from what the UPI described as "an unidentified tipster," while the AP referred to "tipsters, who were anonymous."[44] One such call came to the Washington bureau of the *New York Daily News* around 4:30 p.m. Wednesday; the caller identified himself as a member of the Republican Congressional Campaign Committee. When reached by a congressional correspondent for the *New York Times*, Republican committee spokesman Paul Theis confirmed that the call had been made, though he insisted the official responsible—whom he declined to name—had "acted without authority." *Times* reporter Tom Wicker, hedging only slightly, wrote, "Responsibility for the tips could not be pinpointed today, but there was some evidence to suggest that they had come from Republican sources."[45]

Some journalists identified the source of the tips as police officers, Republican Party officials, or both. "Police tipsters flushed out the Jenkins story," wrote *Time*'s correspondents in their comprehensive internal chronicle. Ted Lewis, a columnist for the *New York Daily News*, was more explicit: the story had "only [been] brought out into the open through tips from Republican Party officials." By midday Wednesday, Lewis wrote, officials at the Republican National Committee had decided it would be "smart politics" to let the story surface locally without any overt partisan involvement. But when neither the *Star* nor the *News* published anything that afternoon, "GOP sources passed the tip on to other newspaper correspondents."[46]

By early evening, Republican frustration boiled over. At 6 p.m., GOP national chairman Dean Burch, furious that the *Star* and the *News* had failed to run the Jenkins story, "took extraordinary measures to try to smoke it out." He called the major wire services—UPI and AP—and issued a provocative public statement: "There is a report sweeping Washington that the White House is desperately trying to suppress a major news story affecting the national security." The stakes were high. The Washington bureaus of both services were the largest in the country, each employing around a hundred accredited reporters—growth that had accelerated since the New Deal. The White House beat, in particular, had become "an extraordinarily grueling assignment in the Johnson administration," as the UPI bureau chief put it. Three-quarters of American newspapers relied entirely on the wires for national political news; the rest used them as a primary source of tips. If the wire services moved on the story, the national press would follow.[47]

The wire services hadn't uncovered the story themselves, but they had already been tipped off secondhand. "Reporters started tipping other reporters, and that's how UPI latched onto the story," wrote two *Time* reporters. Late Wednesday afternoon, a UPI reporter—who had heard the rumor from another journalist—called the UPI desk to ask if they knew anything about the Jenkins arrest. They didn't, but quickly assigned a different reporter to the story. A call to the White House confirmed that Jenkins had been hospitalized, and a brief item was drafted noting his admission for "fatigue and exhaustion." That story was still awaiting transmission when GOP headquarters called with Burch's inflammatory statement. Shortly after 6 p.m., UPI transmitted Burch's remarks, followed five minutes later by the prewritten item about Jenkins's hospitalization.[48]

By early evening, the full story was breaking. Around 6:45 p.m., a UPI correspondent called in from police headquarters with details of Jenkins's October 7 arrest. Just minutes earlier, bureau chief Julius Frandsen had phoned UPI's New York headquarters to alert them that a major story was imminent—one that would stand out among the tens of thousands of words transmitted daily by the Washington bureau's nine teletype circuits. At 8:09 p.m., UPI sent five paragraphs over the wire about the arrest of Walter Jenkins. Ten minutes later, a far more detailed account followed.[49]

The press's handling of the Jenkins case soon became a subject of debate within the industry itself. The *Bulletin of the American Society of Newspaper Editors* devoted the front page of its December issue to how Washington's three daily papers had approached the story and their October 14 meetings—by then widely reported—with Fortas and Clifford. The issue was framed around a pointed critique by UPI's top editor, Earl J. Johnson, reprinted in full from the *UPI Reporter*. The Jenkins case, he wrote, "became a major scandal in the end because five years ago the police reporters had failed to report." Editors at each of the three dailies penned detailed responses, each disputing Johnson's critique from a different angle. John T. O'Rourke of the *Daily News* defended the delay as a "bit of grace," which, he wrote, "made it possible for members of his [Jenkins's] family to brace themselves for a shattering disaster." Newbold Noyes of the *Star* rejected Johnson's claim that local reporters had grown "effete and sloppy in our handling of police news." In a pointed rebuttal, he noted that there had been 859,475 arrests in metropolitan Washington in fiscal year 1964 and argued that tracking down each arrestee would have been a waste of limited journalistic resources.[50]

Where O'Rourke and Noyes defended their decisions in humanitarian and pragmatic terms, Russ Wiggins of the *Washington Post* framed the issue more expansively, rejecting the charge that Jenkins had received special treatment from the press at all. If anything, he argued, prominent people often received *less* protection from publicity about their misdeeds. (Unlike the other two editors, Wiggins did not have to defend his own judgment in the case: as the city's only morning paper, the *Post* had a late-night deadline, so by the time he would have needed to decide to break the Jenkins story, the wire services had already made it moot.) Even the publication of a morals charge, Wiggins observed, was so harmful to a man's reputation that the *Post*'s policy was to avoid repeating unsubstantiated allegations, especially where the accused was an ordinary citizen. "The penalties inflicted by publication alone are beyond appeal and are not wholly removed by subsequent acquittal," he explained. That principle, he argued, also extended to prominent figures: the longstanding practice in Washington was to await court action before publishing such allegations if they were reported at all.[51] As for why Jenkins's first arrest had not surfaced sooner, Wiggins pointed out that it was not the press but police themselves who, by listing his occupation as "clerk," had shielded him in 1959.

Lyndon Johnson, too, saw the conduct of the police as the key issue: angered by widespread rumors that they had leaked the arrest, he ordered the FBI to trace how the story reached the press. The bureau homed in on two Metropolitan Police Department officers who, between October 7 and 14, had visited the Identification Division to withdraw Jenkins's arrest record. According to *Newsweek* editor Ben Bradlee, the FBI suspected—but could not prove—that a pro-Goldwater Park Police officer leaked the report to Dean Burch and the *Evening Star*. Bradlee summarized the bureau's findings for colleagues in a memo; although the FBI report is redacted and inconclusive, it tracks with his more pointed account. Two Metropolitan Police Department officers, he wrote, had made "mysterious withdrawals of Walter Jenkins['s] file at police headquarters between October seventh, the day of the act, and the day the story broke." One of them, Harry Lee Matthews of the Check and Fraud Division, said he pulled the file simply because "he had heard so much about Jenkins." The FBI reportedly believed him; Bradlee did not, "or at least, not necessarily."

Within the bureau's reconstruction of events, the second and more suspicious withdrawal of Jenkins's file came from Carroll

Shoemaker, a Park Police officer assigned to its Youth Aid Division. Shoemaker claimed he had requested the file because he had seen a man who resembled Jenkins in Lafayette Park one evening, though after viewing a photo of Jenkins, he insisted it was not the same person. The FBI, however, did not believe him. "They are convinced he is the leak to the Republicans and the *Star*," Ben Bradlee wrote in his internal *Newsweek* memo. Adding to their suspicion was the fact that the "immediate former chief of the Park Police" had recently joined the Republican National Committee—"specifically on the Bobby Baker case," Bradlee noted, "read: the Jenkins case." Shoemaker's sudden disappearance deepened the FBI's doubts. "Shoemaker went on sick leave yesterday, and is underground," Bradlee reported.[52] The FBI had to pressure the Park Police even to make him available for questioning. In the end, though they pursued multiple leads, the bureau failed to conclusively identify the source of the leak.[53]

The question of who had leaked the story remained officially unresolved. Who was responsible "may never be determined," wrote David Wise of the *New York Herald-Tribune* in a comprehensive account that weekend. James McCartney of the *Philadelphia Inquirer* noted that while "Republicans insist that the tips came from offices of the Washington Metropolitan police department," few Democrats in Washington doubted that the Republican National Committee had played a central role. One Democratic source told McCartney he believed "Republicans may have had a battery of phones operating, spreading the tip, before Wednesday was over." Dean Burch's decision to accuse the White House of suppressing a national-security story certainly fit that narrative. In the days that followed, commentators criticized Fortas and Clifford for having "tried to soft pedal" the Jenkins affair.[54]

That official mystery persisted until 2022, when Carl Bernstein—famous for his Watergate reporting in the 1970s—revealed new details in a memoir. According to Bernstein, then a young staffer at the *Star*, the original tip came from sources within the Goldwater campaign who had been "fed information" by Lieutenant Louis Fochett. Rupert Welch, the *Star*'s night crime reporter, told Bernstein the full backstory one night at a bar. Bernstein relates that on the morning of October 14, as part of the *Star*'s efforts to confirm the story, Welch had driven out to Fochett's suburban home in an unsuccessful attempt to interview the detective. By lunch, Welch was "furious" that Fortas and Clifford had dissuaded his editors from running the piece that day and "provided all the details" to a UPI reporter—an old Georgetown classmate—when he ran into him at the National Press Club.[55]

In short, Louis Fochett oversaw Jenkins's arrest *and* told someone in the Goldwater campaign about it. As we have seen, he was among Washington's most prolific officers in tearoom cases. He had personally arrested Norman Powell Heine in 1949 and another Senate aide in 1950. Over the following decade, Fochett frequently drew criticism from judges who questioned the propriety of his tactics. In a notable 1956 case, the US Court of Appeals overturned an assault conviction against a man who had groped Fochett in a movie theater, ruling that the detective's behavior had "let the suspect think there is consent in order to encourage an act which furnishes an excuse for an arrest."[56]

Fochett's tactics had already provoked confrontations with both gay activists and a Black uniformed officer. In 1961 he appeared in plainclothes at the first organizational meeting of the Mattachine Society of Washington, a new group founded to challenge federal antigay policies. When another attendee recognized him and organizer Frank Kameny announced that a vice patrolman was present, Fochett left. He had also figured in an earlier Lafayette Park incident in which a uniformed US Park Police officer, James E. Thomas—one of that force's few Black members—attempted to detain Fochett and two other plainclothes vice officers. (One of the perils of decoy operations was that uniformed police working for different police jurisdictions might mistake them for cruising homosexuals.) Thomas had *two* such encounters with Fochett, in fact; after the second, in 1960, Thomas was suspended, while the three white Morals Division officers, including Fochett, faced no consequences, a disparity

Thomas attributed to racial discrimination.[57] When he later read that Fochett had played a role in Jenkins's arrest, Thomas contacted an acquaintance in the executive branch, recounted the Lafayette Park episodes, and asked that the FBI be told he believed Jenkins had been entrapped.[58] That was likely not the case, but a morals charge carried such stigma that no legal defense could salvage an arrestee's public standing.

Bernstein's account is further supported by the FBI's own interview notes. When agents questioned all four officers involved in Jenkins's arrest, only Fochett was asked about contact with the press. He claimed to have paid "no particular attention" to the Jenkins case until a colleague informed him reporters were asking questions. Fochett admitted he had received "several phone calls from newspapers and news magazines" but insisted he had told all callers he had "no comment."[59] Bernstein's revelation means that Lyndon Johnson was right to wonder if a pro-Goldwater policeman had leaked the story to Goldwater campaign; in fact, it had been the very police lieutenant who oversaw Jenkins's arrest.

Damage Control

The day after the FBI released its summary report on the Jenkins case, Washington police officials announced a new crackdown: they would begin reporting cases like Jenkins's more systematically to the government agencies that employed the arrestees. The move marked a sharp reversal. Inspector Scott E. Moyer, who had replaced Roy Blick that summer as head of the Morals Division, explained that in the past the department had routinely downgraded the listed occupations of high-level officials for three reasons: "security," since arrest records were publicly accessible; "compassion," to shield families; and "space," a logistical justification. But while framed in part as a humanitarian gesture, the sanitizing of job titles amounted to unequal justice. It also clashed directly with the rationale of Lavender Scare policies. By obscuring the employment status of men in sensitive federal positions, the district police had effectively undermined federal security protocols—and failed to uphold the very standards those policies were meant to enforce.

Henceforth, the Metropolitan Police Department would notify all federal agencies "whenever one of their employees is arrested," and a full set of fingerprints would be taken from each suspect and sent to the FBI "whether or not the person has been arrested before."[60]

This promise may have gone unfulfilled. Instead of a crackdown, the Morals Division sharply reduced its use of decoys in public places between 1964 and 1965, probably in part because of Roy Blick's retirement but also reflecting a shifting political culture.[61] The Jenkins scandal had drawn elite attention to pervasive antigay surveillance. And that surveillance—policemen setting out to witness a sexual act in a public place—came to seem problematic.

The regime that had spared Jenkins in 1959 did not spare him in 1964. In a system where the aftermath of an arrest was never predictable, and could range from mere inconvenience to silent dismissal to brutal exposure, the same kind of arrest now became the highest-profile morals case Washington had ever seen. For Walter Jenkins, the damage was already done. For Lyndon Johnson, the challenge now was to contain the fallout.

CHAPTER 4

WEST WING, EAST WING

Walter Jenkins's arrest threatened to become a public spectacle—something without precedent in national politics, a morals case erupting in the middle of a presidential campaign—but the Johnson White House moved quickly to define it as a private matter, a misstep by a valued aide rather than a question of public trust. The effort unfolded mostly out of sight, in back-channel calls, carefully managed press interactions, and personal appeals. Lyndon Johnson relied on his closest advisers and said as little as possible. Lady Bird Johnson's visible and behind-the-scenes interventions, which highlighted family and household rather than state and security, would prove important in shaping how the affair was understood beyond the White House walls.

Between 9 a.m. and 4 p.m. on Wednesday, October 14, 1964, word of Jenkins's arrest reached men close to the president, setting off the first phase of the White House's effort to frame the affair as a private matter. Calls went out, arrangements were made, and messages were improvised and relayed in a hurried scramble. As it became clear the story would soon become public, the goal shifted to minimizing the damage.

In the span of half an hour that afternoon, Johnson's allies moved Jenkins out of sight and brought the president up to speed. At about 3:30 p.m. Jenkins left Fortas's Georgetown home for the short car trip to George Washington University Hospital. Fortas asked Jenkins's secretary, Mildred Stegall, to tell any reporters who called that her boss had been taken to the hospital. Clark Clifford told Lady Bird Johnson that Walter was "in the hospital for hypertension" and that there were "some other aspects of it but that she probably would be filled in later."[1] At 3:56 p.m., with those steps completed, Fortas telephoned President Johnson, then resting in the presidential suite at the Waldorf-Astoria Hotel in New York.

As Fortas briefed Johnson directly, he cast the arrest in terms that emphasized its sensitivity and the need for careful handling. At first, he was reluctant to give details. "Is it all right to talk on this phone?" he said.

"Yes, I think so," said the president.

"About a week ago Walter went to a party and at the end of the party he was picked up by the police and booked," Fortas said. What's more, the newspapers "had the story that it was a morals charge." He explained that he and Clifford had spent the day secluding Jenkins, then visiting the offices of the city's three daily newspapers in turn, pleading on humanitarian grounds for each editor to hold back the story long enough for Jenkins's family to be notified and the man stashed away out of the sight of journalists. Their aim was to present the situation as a private misfortune rather than a public scandal. They could not suppress many of the facts, but they could shape the story's tone.

Johnson was dumbfounded. "Just tell me: Could this be true?"

"Mr. President, I'm afraid so," came the reply.

"We thought under the circumstances that certainly Walter ought not to be around the White House," Fortas continued, "and that the best way to handle it was for him to go to a hospital, which has been done." Fortas had given "instructions to have no phone calls, no visitors, no nothing, and he'll be kept there under sedation."

Secluding Jenkins in the hospital bought time, but it did not resolve the political crisis taking shape. He remained a patient in George Washington University Hospital for twenty-six days—until after the election—and never returned to the White House. Johnson had made his steady control over the country's nuclear codes his leading argument for why voters should choose him over Senator Barry Goldwater. Now it appeared he had harbored on his staff a "security risk"—a man with access to government secrets whose homosexuality, under official US policy, made him vulnerable to blackmail by Soviet agents. Compounding the damage, Fortas told the president that police records showed Jenkins had been arrested once before, in 1959.

"Well, you don't foresee that you can keep this lid on for three weeks, do you?" said the president.

"No, sir," Fortas replied.[2]

With Election Day fast approaching and voters paying closer attention, the Johnsons and Barry Goldwater alike now faced the question of how to speak about a shocking event whose full facts were still unknown. The White House's initial answer took the form of a three-part response, completed by Thursday night when Johnson returned to Washington. First came a verbal statement from press secretary George Reedy at 10:30 p.m. Wednesday in the Waldorf-Astoria lobby, rhetorically shielding Jenkins behind hospital walls and the fact of his resignation.[3] Second was a rare written statement by the First Lady on Thursday, emphasizing Jenkins's dependent wife and children. Last was the president's own statement that night, framing the matter in terms of his commitment to national security. Meanwhile, LBJ began a series of on- and off-the-record efforts to cast Jenkins as a wayward member of his own family. Each statement, in its own register, steered reporters toward seeing the arrest not as a question for national judgment but as a private misstep.

Lady Bird Johnson's statement had the greatest public impact. In it, the First Lady cast Jenkins as a man in need of medical and pastoral care, figuratively returning him to his own marital household. She recast as sickness what police had labeled a crime, noting that he was receiving "the medical attention he needs." In so doing, she shifted the connotation of Jenkins's fall away from the West Wing and the president, linking it instead to the East Wing and the First Lady.[4]

After the president—and Mrs. Johnson, who had joined him in New York—spoke off the record with reporters during the Thursday evening flight back to Washington, Hugh Sidey wrote to his editors at *Time*, "The Jenkins[es] and the Johnsons *had* really all been family."[5] In the days that followed, the case slipped from the headlines, overtaken by the ouster of Soviet premier Nikita Khrushchev and a Chinese atomic bomb test. But outside events alone did not push it aside. Just as decisive was the White House's success in defining the affair as a private matter—an effort that succeeded precisely because it unfolded largely behind the scenes and because journalists were still inclined to take a First Family at its word.

The Hospitalization

Jenkins's hospitalization was a deliberate political tactic to frame his absence as medical rather than political and to remove him from immediate scrutiny. On the morning of October 14, when Jenkins tried to explain his predicament to Abe Fortas, he did not mention his 1959 arrest; Fortas and Clifford instead learned of it from *Evening Star* editors who had seen the police report. In a period when long hospital stays were common and illnesses often hidden, Johnson's advisers quickly arranged for Jenkins to check into George Washington University Hospital for "nervous exhaustion." Only after he was out of sight, as we have seen, did they alert the president to Jenkins's crisis by telephone from Bill Moyers's White House office. As another adviser put it, keeping Jenkins there would also buy time so that "after a period of time he can come out with some kind of a report," a statement "to the effect that whatever his difficulties were he's been cured, they've been overcome."[6]

Even before Fortas explained the situation to Johnson, he was already coaching the president about what to say. "If you're asked about it, you should say only that you have heard that Walter Jenkins is in the hospital on doctors' orders, you're sorry to hear it, and you hope to get more details." The real purpose of the hospitalization, Fortas said, was "first, getting Walter out of the White House on some plausible basis, and second, getting him to a place where we can protect him from inquiries and where there'll be a certain appeal to sympathy." Fortas summoned Jenkins's personal physician, Dr. Charles Thompson, who issued a statement to the press citing Jenkins's high blood pressure, though there is no evidence Thompson played a role in deciding to hospitalize Jenkins.[7]

Recent precedent underscored the special stigma attached to a gay-related arrest. Six years earlier, during the run-up to the 1958 midterm elections, sworn congressional testimony alleged that Eisenhower's top aide Sherman Adams accepted a vicuña coat and other expensive gifts from an industrialist and then intervened on the giver's behalf in disputes with two government agencies. The allegations were judged credible, and Eisenhower asked for his resignation. Even though Adams had used his public office for private gain, he nevertheless announced his resignation himself in a nationally broadcast address on radio and television.[8] By contrast, Jenkins's conduct bore no relation to his official duties—except under Lavender Scare policies—yet he became politically radioactive.

Fortas anticipated that reporters would soon ask how and when President Johnson had learned of his aide's troubles—and which troubles. For the time being, he suggested, the less said, the better. Perhaps Johnson had heard "things about the strain in the office or whatnot," but "I think we ought to play it down now." The president perhaps was "starting to hear," but "[you] don't know anything about it." Johnson instructed Fortas to retrieve some of Jenkins's most sensitive papers from his office safe. "Talk to him and talk to Mildred, so that what he has, goes over to you." Johnson did not explain why he wanted the documents secured. With an eye to press queries, he asked, "Who told me he was [hospitalized]?" Fortas said Stegall was a plausible candidate.[9]

It was true that Jenkins was exhausted, though this was not the reason for his hospitalization. In January 1964, a White House physician had warned him, according to notes taken at the time, that "he has got to learn to pace himself. That the job he is in now is going to kill him the way he is working night and day, seven days a week."

Fortas, however, left the newspaper editors with a more politically convenient account: that Jenkins had been drunk and could not recall what happened in the YMCA men's room. Recounting the conversation to Johnson, Fortas said, "Walter came over to see me this morning and that he has a complete blackout about the period involved, but he did go to this party and he had a couple of martinis. He was exhausted, he had a complete blackout about it, and that he couldn't remember anything." Then, to Johnson, Fortas admitted, "He *does* remember." Still, Fortas advised, they should stick to the blackout story: "I think our version of it is that he blacked out and he doesn't remember anything, and he won't be accessible to anybody."[10]

As the closest hospital to downtown Washington, George Washington University Hospital was a familiar refuge for the political elite. Six stories tall and built of limestone-faced reinforced concrete with federal Lanham Act funds, it had opened in 1948. Senators, Supreme Court justices, and cabinet officials were treated there; Jenkins himself had undergone hemorrhoid surgery there during the presidential transition at the end of 1960, and J. Edgar Hoover had prostate surgery there in 1962. In this era, average stays lasted nine days for all patients and seventeen for psychiatric patients, who made up about 6 percent of the hospital's daily census. That Jenkins's bill included a charge for "guard service" underscored the real purpose of his stay: to keep him out of the press's reach.[11]

Hospital stays in this period were often lengthy, and politicians commonly concealed them. After heart attacks in 1955, both Johnson and Eisenhower spent more than a month hospitalized; Nixon was confined for twelve days with a staph infection during the 1960 campaign. Kennedy's aides disguised his severe back problems in 1952, and although his 1954 surgery was impossible to hide, they attributed it and other ailments to wartime injuries or malaria. They also kept secret nine separate hospitalizations between 1955 and 1957, totaling forty-four days.[12] Johnson himself had earlier hidden hospitalizations in 1937 and 1948. Within the Johnson family, his brother Sam Houston Johnson was repeatedly institutionalized for alcoholism. The press also often remained silent about psychiatric cases, as in 1963 when *Washington Post* publisher Phil Graham was hospitalized.[13]

"Nervous exhaustion," roughly equivalent to what was colloquially called a "nervous breakdown," was frequently framed as a product of modern life or overwork. The phrase was used to explain canceled public appearances by figures as varied as Pope Pius XII, actress Rita Hayworth, baseball star Willie Mays, and Indian prime minister Lal Bahadur Shastri. A congressman argued that excessively long electoral campaigns was placing candidates at risk of nervous exhaustion, while the Pentagon claimed that overly zealous Senate probes into conflicts of interest in defense contracting were causing it in Air Force personnel.[14]

Both Johnson and Goldwater had themselves been hospitalized for nervous exhaustion. In 1946, Johnson's "flu" or "pneumonia," as reported in the press, was understood by aides, including Jenkins, to mask nervous exhaustion. In 1964, Peggy Goldwater told *Good Housekeeping* that her husband had suffered a "nervous breakdown" in 1937 and another in 1939. Columnist Drew Pearson seized on the revelation, calling for release of Goldwater's medical records and noting "reports" of a stay in a Flagstaff sanatorium.[15] While Democrats questioned Goldwater's fitness for nuclear command, Johnson's advisers avoided highlighting his medical history, aware that illness could also generate public sympathy.

In her landmark account of postwar masculinity, Barbara Ehrenreich observed that, by the 1950s, medical opinion was shifting from genetic to psychosocial explanations for men's supposed biological frailty: "There was something wrong with the way men lived, and the diagnosis of what was wrong came increasingly to resemble the popular (at least among men) belief that men 'died in the harness,' destroyed by the burden of responsibility." The belief that a uniquely lethal stress accompanied the breadwinner's role, she noted, was "so firmly fixed in medical opinion that it has withstood both the absence of supporting evidence and the presence of contradictory evidence."[16]

As word spread of Jenkins's hospitalization, friends and colleagues tried to reach him in numbers that reflected his deep ties across Washington. "I tried to telephone you this morning but gave up the attempt as impractical," one wrote in a Thursday morning note.[17] In Jenkins's personal papers, a folder labeled "Telephone Calls" bulges with seventy sheets documenting the outpouring. Thirteen are embossed "The White House, Washington"; ten say "Office of the Vice President, Washington"; two say "The George Washington University—Telephone Message." Callers included Senator Hubert Humphrey, House Speaker John McCormack, the Reverend Billy Graham, and the president's brother, Sam Houston Johnson. One note recorded that "Judith Moyers called about keeping Ann[e]," referring to the wife of Johnson aide Bill Moyers and the Jenkinses' youngest daughter. Others ranged from party officials and their wives to members of the large Texas House delegation, a top AT&T lobbyist, Walter's priest, columnist Jack Anderson, and the chief public relations officer for Lockheed Martin. Together, the calls formed a cross section of the political and social worlds in which Jenkins had moved.[18]

On Thursday at 11:40 p.m., President Johnson phoned Jenkins in his hospital room—a moment that, despite a reporter learning about it almost immediately, never reached the public. A *Time* reporter heard of the call from a hospital intern on the same floor, along with other telling details: "a uniformed guard is in the room with Jenkins," and doctors on rounds had skipped his room, "a most unusual event."[19] None of it appeared in print.

Although Jenkins's hospitalization was arranged for political reasons, he did receive genuine medical care during his stay. His blood pressure was monitored, and his hospital bill included charges for an electrocardiogram, an electroencephalogram, and a surgical procedure, possibly related to treatment for the bursitis that troubled him periodically. Among his personal papers is a card from a nurse who cared for him: "To one it has been my great honor to serve. A most cooperative patient."[20] Yet the hospital would not be only a place of rest and treatment. In the days ahead, it would become the backdrop for the most serious test of his long friendship with Lyndon Johnson.

"Somebody Goes Wrong in Every Family"

The news of Jenkins's arrest reached Johnson late in the afternoon of an exhausting campaign day. His voice was hoarse and his hands chapped after a morning of stops in New Jersey and Pennsylvania. Arriving at LaGuardia Airport in early afternoon, he was met by his bitter rival, Robert F. Kennedy, who had resigned as attorney general to run for the New York Senate seat held by Republican Kenneth Keating. The two rode together in a motorcade through Harlem on their way to the Waldorf-Astoria, where Johnson would speak that evening at the Al Smith Dinner, a white-tie fundraiser for Catholic charities.

"He and his family were close to the President's family, and this very intimacy is now the heart of the President's problem," wrote the *New York Times*'s James "Scotty" Reston. Unable to deny the bond, Johnson set about making it intelligible to the public. On the phone, he peppered Fortas with questions: Did Jenkins and Andy Choka know each other? (No.) Was "a fee" involved? (No.) What else had Jenkins offered by way of explanation? (Not much.) Skeptical that the arrest was routine, he asked whether it might have been "a frame deal." "No, sir," Fortas replied. "I hate to tell you that I don't think it was. I just think the man went off the rocker." Finally, mindful that the new scandal would be seen in the light of the Bobby Baker affair already shadowing the campaign, Johnson asked, "What does this do to your Baker angle?" Fortas acknowledged that it would likely intensify the focus on morality that Goldwater had made his campaign's primary line of attack.[21]

Almost as soon as the first inklings of the story came over the UPI wire, Lyndon Johnson—as if clinging to the reassuring iconography of his presidency's first minutes—abruptly left the hotel at 6:30 p.m. for an unscheduled visit with Jacqueline Kennedy. Only two reporters followed the unmarked presidential limousine to Mrs. Kennedy's

FIGURE 4.1 President Lyndon B. Johnson after visiting Jacqueline Kennedy at her apartment in New York City, October 14, 1964, shortly after wire services reported Jenkins's hospitalization. AP Photo/Matty Zimmerman.

new Fifth Avenue apartment. Emerging from the building, Johnson was photographed at Jackie's side (see figure 4.1). He told her nothing of the Jenkins news.[22] Whether deliberately or not, the visit offered an appealing answer to the inevitable questions about how the Jenkins story had reached him. He soon instructed George Reedy to tell reporters on background, "We heard about it just as I went to Mrs. Kennedy's this evening," later revising this to "when I got back from Mrs. Kennedy's." At 7:30 p.m., Reedy confirmed to reporters the UPI story that Jenkins was in the hospital.[23]

At 8:02 p.m., back from Mrs. Kennedy's and determined to minimize any threat to his reelection, Johnson concluded that Jenkins had to resign. "He's out, but we've got to *say* that he's out," he told Fortas. The 1959 police report made it impossible to chalk up the events of October 7 to some sort of misunderstanding. "We've crossed a bridge here; we can't ever come back on it," he said. "I think the presidency is something that we've got to protect, and you can't protect it by procrastinating." Johnson wanted the resignation announced in the same morning papers that would carry news of Jenkins's arrest and hospitalization. Someone, perhaps Reedy aide Malcolm Kilduff, "ought to say that he has resigned and we've appointed Bill Moyers in his place." Moyers—a thirty-year-old Texan who first worked for Johnson in 1954, when Jenkins hired him for a summer job—was a former Baptist seminarian and thus presented a reassuring "morals" profile. Fortas left for the hospital to secure Jenkins's resignation.[24] At 8:09 p.m., UPI reported Jenkins's arrest.

When Fortas returned to the White House, he and Clifford spoke again with Johnson to lock in a public statement on Jenkins's departure. Johnson said that Eddie Weisl, an entertainment lawyer and his closest ally among New York Democrats, "feels very strongly against using the word resignation." Johnson disagreed: "I don't think in light of the '59 record that you can do anything *except* say the word resignation." Johnson then put Weisl, who had come to the Waldorf's presidential suite to help him strategize, on the line. Clifford urged avoiding "a contest or controversy over whether or not the charge was a proper one. That's over. We're going to lose that fight." When Weisl persisted, Clifford was blunter: "Walter says that some activity was taking place. Walter's not in a position to deny it."[25]

Johnson was careful to stress that he had not known of Jenkins's 1959 arrest—a claim borne out by his recorded surprise when Fortas told him—and thus had not knowingly kept a security risk on his staff. Yet ignorance carried its own dangers. The greater political risk lay less in what happened on October 7 than in the fact that police records showed it had happened before. Indeed, Johnson grasped immediately that the most damaging issue was the "security angle," the idea that a man with access to sensitive information had been exposed as vulnerable to blackmail. Late on the night of October 14, he told Fortas, "They're playing this security angle very big, that here's a man that sat in the highest councils, privy to everything."[26] In the eleven months since Dallas, Johnson seemed to feel that his legitimacy as president, and even his right to the office, was at stake in every public utterance. Jenkins had been in the room when Johnson met with congressional leaders about the Gulf of Tonkin incident. He had attended National Security Council briefings. He was Johnson's man, not a Kennedy holdover. Having elevated Jenkins and empowered him to manage the flow of information to and from the Oval Office, Johnson could blame no one but himself for Jenkins's access to Cold War secrets.

The 1959 arrest posed a direct challenge to Johnson's credibility. Under Lavender Scare rules it should have disqualified Jenkins from sensitive work. Johnson had to explain how neither the FBI nor the White House had learned of it as Jenkins rose to become the top aide first to the vice president and then to the president. Whose fault was it? Should Johnson emphasize that the crucial error was made in 1961, when the buck stopped at John F. Kennedy's desk? Or would that approach only underscore that Johnson was merely an accidental president, elevated by a hideous crime? On the heels of the Baker scandal, how would the public receive this news impugning the character, or at least the "morals," of a second top Johnson aide? The episode distilled Johnson's deepest political fear: that the public might view his succession not as the rightful continuation of Kennedy's presidency but as tainted by questionable associates and unearned power.

Jenkins's presence in National Security Council meetings, Johnson feared, lent credence to Goldwater's charge that the incident was a "clear indication of lax security" in the administration. Either the White House's procedures had failed to screen out a potential risk or an exception had been made for someone personally close to Johnson—damaging either way. The vulnerability was compounded by Jenkins's role in determining personnel policy: only weeks earlier, he had warned department and agency heads against announcing federal appointments until after FBI checks were complete. Had Jenkins somehow used his position to shield his own conduct from scrutiny? Given the complexity of the clearance system, disproving such suspicion would be difficult. Johnson even floated to Fortas the idea of appointing a special investigative body modeled on the Warren Commission.[27]

As he monitored early coverage late Wednesday night, Johnson's mind leaped to an early Cold War spy case that had fused homosexuality with treason in the public imagination. Speaking with Fortas, he wondered aloud what secrets Jenkins might have been in a position to give away and "who else" he might have been involved with, likening the situation to "the Burgess and Maclean thing." Guy Burgess and Donald Maclean, British diplomats in Washington who vanished in 1951 and later surfaced in Moscow as Soviet defectors, had become notorious not only for espionage but also for Burgess's flamboyant homosexuality, cementing the mid-century association between queerness and disloyalty.[28] Like other Democrats of his generation, Johnson's reflexes had been shaped by such scandals and by the damage they inflicted on the Truman administration and the party.

Ever wary of being branded "soft" on national security, Johnson recalled the price Democrats paid after Secretary of State Dean Acheson's 1950 remark about a friend accused as a Soviet spy: "I do not intend to turn my back on Alger Hiss." Shortly after 1 a.m. on Thursday he told Fortas, "I don't think it does much good to talk compassion. I think you just get into kind of a Dean Acheson turn-my-back statement." Any "semblance of being protective or defensive" had to be avoided.[29] His phrasing revealed how deeply the early Cold War had scarred him and how determined he was to show no softness in the face of one of the most discrediting accusations imaginable.

With reporters pressing for comment and Johnson still scheduled to speak in the Waldorf ballroom, he left it to Reedy to deliver the formal statement. At 10:15 p.m., in a makeshift press room off the

Waldorf lobby, an emotional Reedy stood on a chair before some seventy-five journalists and read: "As I told some of you earlier today, Walter Jenkins, who has been suffering from fatigue, went into the hospital this afternoon on the orders of his doctor. Walter Jenkins submitted his resignation this evening as special assistant. The resignation was accepted and the president has appointed Bill D. Moyers to succeed him." Asked when the resignation and Moyers's appointment occurred, Reedy said "shortly before this briefing." Speaking only on background, he declined to address reports that Jenkins had been arrested, on the ground that his "sole source of information was the UPI report."[30]

At 11:20 p.m., Johnson took the ballroom dais. He trimmed his prepared remarks—centered on the need for steady leadership in the Cold War—and offered an aviation metaphor to voters weighing whether to extend a presidency that began aboard a Boeing 707: "Strength and courage are essential, but they are like the fuel in an airplane." To reach the desired destination, he added, one also needed "a sense of direction, caution in the cockpit, and an experienced pilot." A reporter observed that he "slashed his statement to nine minutes, part of which he raced through so fast his audience had no chance to applaud."[31] Johnson then returned upstairs to spend several more hours with a small circle of confidants, debating how to manage the affair.

As he puzzled over how to explain his tie to Jenkins, Johnson considered off-the-record remarks portraying him not as a political ally but as family. "Now is there something we can say that's good?" he asked. "If none of you have ever had anything like this in your family, why, you wouldn't understand it, but nearly every family has had some problem and we regret it very much." He floated analogies: "Some of us have mentally retarded brothers and some of us have alcoholic brothers and somebody goes wrong in every family," and he returned more than once to versions of the "every family has had some problem" line.[32]

The formulation echoed language Johnson had long used to describe his closeness to men he worked with and whose flaws he accepted. In 1958, speaking of Senate caucus members who were potential presidential candidates, he likened himself to a father: "A father loves his sons, though one son may drink a little too much, another may neck with the girls a little too much." Fortas may have brought such wayward-family tropes to mind in their first conversation that afternoon. "You know, Abe," Johnson said, "I just—I swear, I just can't believe this." Fortas replied, "Isn't it fantastic? I wouldn't believe it of my own brother or myself." Clifford, however, pushed back: "Of course every family has problems, but they don't happen to have *this* kind, and I believe it would not be wise to attempt to deprecate it." The less said, the better; needless elaboration would only cause trouble.[33]

Against Clifford's advice, Johnson repeatedly invoked the language of kinship to describe his aide's fall in the ensuing hours and days—a framing that also deflected scrutiny from his own judgment. Folksy analogies and family references had served Richard Nixon well in his 1952 Checkers speech. On Thursday, Johnson told Attorney General Nicholas Katzenbach that he had been as shocked as if "you and Lady Bird had been living together every night" or "my daughter committed treason." That evening, on the flight back to Washington, he told reporters off the record that it was "as if his wife had run off with another man or one of his children had come home pregnant."[34]

He soon made the analogy a recurring off-the-record line, and on October 24 he used it publicly. In a paid telecast where members of the Young Democrats posed questions, Johnson was asked specifically about Jenkins, prompting his first direct comments on the case on broadcast television. Calling Jenkins's plight "very unfortunate and unpleasant and distressing," he said it "probably resulted from intense overwork." But, he said, "I was as shocked as if someone had told me that my wife had murdered her daughter."[35]

The truth was that familiarity *had* placed Jenkins above suspicion—even to the FBI. Pressed by Johnson on why there had been no FBI check on Jenkins in 1961, Deke DeLoach admitted, "We didn't feel there was any need to because we knew him real well, of course, and everything was fine."[36] Before agents had interviewed a single witness, in other words, DeLoach acknowledged that Jenkins had simply been so well known to the bureau that his arrest record was ignored. To the Johnsons, he was family, as the First Lady herself would soon signal in an unusual public statement that figuratively returned him to his marital household.

"My Heart Is Aching Today"

The Jenkins case became front-page news nationwide because of the threat it posed to Johnson's reelection. A few papers, including the *Baltimore Sun* and *Los Angeles Times*, splashed it across the full width of page 1.[37] "Mr Jenkins has gone into hospital," reported the *Economist*. France's *Le Monde* ran it on the front page of its Friday edition, prefacing the story with an editorial warning that "it is impossible, in the land of militant puritanism, to underestimate the reactions that this affair could set off." The news reached as far as Cuban state television and Egypt's domestic radio.[38]

On Thursday at 9:12 a.m., as the president waited aboard his plane to take off at LaGuardia, Lyndon and Lady Bird Johnson spoke by phone about Walter Jenkins's fate. The First Lady urged giving Jenkins a job at the LBJ Ranch or her Austin television station—shifting him, in effect, from their public household to their private one, beyond the reach of Lavender Scare restrictions. The president recoiled. The station, he noted, could risk losing its license if someone with Jenkins's record were put in charge. More to the point, while she could "let them know" privately that the family would ensure that Jenkins could provide for his own, "I don't see any reason to 'know' publicly." That, for Johnson, marked the line between sympathy and sanction: help in private, but no public act that might signal an ongoing connection to the former aide.

Mrs. Johnson told her husband she had spoken to Marjorie Jenkins, who believed the arrest was "a put-up job" and felt "her life is ruined, that their life is ruined, and it's all been laid at the altar of working for us." Lady Bird worried that other staff might see their failure to rally behind Jenkins as a betrayal. (In January, she had written in her diary after a luncheon for Queen Frederica of Greece, "I was so happy to have Walter Jenkins there from our office, and I hope it was at least an hour's respite from the turmoil he's living in now," likely a reference to publicity over Don Reynolds's allegation that Jenkins had pressured him to buy advertising on KTBC.[39]) Lyndon, however, focused on what he, as president, could "know" or sanction publicly. At stake, he said, was the "whole ball game." The risk was that you "confirm it, you can prove that you're a part of it, everything else. You just can't do that to the presidency, honey." He said she should promise only private financial support, avoid visiting the Jenkinses herself, and send an emissary—such as fellow Catholic Tommy Corcoran—instead.

Lyndon Johnson's language during this call echoed the Truman-era associations he had invoked with Fortas the night before. "The average farmer just can't understand your knowing it and approving it or condoning it," he told Lady Bird, "any more than he can Acheson not turning his back." Secretary of State Acheson's archetypal blunder of fourteen years earlier was clearly never far from Johnson's mind. Lady Bird stated firmly that she planned to comment on the case. The president did not clearly assent, but—unlike the idea of a public job offer—he did not advise against it, instead stressing that she should run it by Fortas and Clifford, which she said she had already done. She thus secured his tacit acquiescence to a statement of support for Walter.[40]

The First Lady—whose unprecedented solo whistle-stop tour through Deep South states the previous week had drawn national attention and, at times, a hostile reception from local whites—now issued a rare, eighty-six-word statement under her own name. "My heart is aching today," it began, "for someone who has reached the point of exhaustion in dedicated service to his country." She stressed that Jenkins was a father of six and a man of religion. Calling him a family man who "has been carrying incredible hours and burdens since President Kennedy's assassination," she evoked a nervous breakdown from overwork, making no reference to the arrest. She invited the public to respond with sympathy, not censure. She predicted that his "recovery" would be aided by the fact that he was "now receiving the medical attention that he needs" and also by "his wife and six fine children and his profound religious faith."[41]

By speaking before her husband, the First Lady cast the Jenkins matter as private sorrow rather than a question of public consequence. Her invocation of November 22, 1963, aligned the aide with Johnson's campaign themes of service, sacrifice, and patriotism. Emphasizing his role as head of an ordinary household with vulnerable dependents underscored his respectability. Her faith in the redemptive power of the family shaped how Americans thought and talked about the episode. For many who had never heard Jenkins's name and knew nothing of his White House role, the image of a family man placed his sexual deviance in a new and more sympathetic light.

The fourth of Lady Bird Johnson's five sentences was the most important: "I know our family and all of his friends—and I hope all others—pray for his recovery." It was the statement's only prescriptive note. By invoking the First Family, she used her ceremonial standing to invite the public into an open-ended circle of concern. Prayer, she suggested, was the proper response to the shocking news, and Jenkins was a fitting object of sympathy.

Lady Bird intended the statement to register as an unusual act of independence. Her public gentility masked a firm managerial hand: within weeks of moving into the White House, she installed Liz Carpenter as both press secretary and staff director—a first for a First Lady. The White House chief usher recalled that she commanded White House operations "rather like the chairman of the board of a large corporation." Julia Sweig aptly describes the Johnsons' substantive partnership as "more New Deal than New Frontier."[42] By linking Jenkins to the gendered trappings of her unofficial office and to the Johnsons' private household, Lady Bird pursued a purpose that was both personal and political.

She also took steps to ensure the statement would be noticed. The editor and publisher of the newspaper she knew best were invited to the White House and asked to print it in full. J. Russell Wiggins of the *Washington Post* later recalled that he and Katharine Graham were summoned from a George Washington University board meeting to the family sitting room, "that little blue room way up on the top floor." The First Lady, he said, "was like a vessel under full sail" as she read her statement aloud and requested its publication.[43]

Her remarks drew wide broadcast coverage on Thursday and prompted an AP story that appeared in many Friday editions.[44] Some applauded. "I want to thank you for your statement on behalf of Mr. Jenkins which I have just heard on television," a Washington civil servant wrote that day. Many Americans "were waiting for a word of assurance," she added, "and since Mr. Johnson could not, for good and sufficient reasons I am sure, speak as yet, a word in defense of Mr. Jenkins from you was comforting." Others recoiled. A Connecticut woman wrote the next day, after Lyndon also issued a statement, that it was "unbelievable that both you and the President have both publicly condoned the actions of Mr. Jenkins," and said the statements had "lost our family's vote."[45]

In the early edition of Friday evening's *Washington Post*, Mrs. Johnson's statement was woven into the front-page coverage. Laurence Stern reported that "President Johnson made no immediate comment on the incident. However the First Lady said her heart is 'aching' for a man who 'has reached the end point of exhaustion in dedicated service to his country.' " He quoted her next two sentences and then, at her request to Wiggins, reproduced "the full text of Mrs. Johnson's statement."

Lyndon Johnson's own statement, released Thursday evening upon his return from New York, stressed that J. Edgar Hoover would get to the bottom of what happened. Echoing his wife, the president noted that Jenkins "has worked with me faithfully for 25 years" with unusual "personal dedication, devotion and tireless labor." But he centered his remarks on the fact that he had received "no information or report of any kind" about "his personal conduct" and that "within moments after being notified last night" he had both asked

Jenkins to resign and ordered Hoover to "make an immediate and comprehensive report promptly to me and the American people."[46]

In later editions of the *Post*, Stern led with the president's statement and its national-security implications, though the full text of the First Lady's remarks still appeared.[47] In the *New York Times*, a morning paper, Tom Wicker likewise led with the president's statement and quoted only the first sentence of the First Lady's. Washington's two evening papers, many other dailies nationwide, and UPI followed the same pattern. Some papers—in cities as far-flung as Boston and Honolulu—ran the president's statement while also carrying, under a separate headline, the earlier AP story on Lady Bird's remarks.[48]

The First Lady received a flood of mail, mostly from women, about her decision to use her platform. Some judged her harshly. "Instead of wasting your grief on some damn old pervert," a Cleveland woman wrote, "why don't you grieve for some of the people you and your fake, phony husband are trying to make suckers out of," evidently referring to voters she believed would be better served by Goldwater. But the vast majority praised her. "I was really touched when I read in the paper about your wonderful Christian attitude regarding the illness of Mr. Walter Jenkins," wrote one. Another thanked her for "a sympathetic statement about not only Mr. Jenkins' family, but a kindly comment about Walter Jenkins himself." A third, a block captain in her Baltimore precinct, linked her praise to the First Lady's recent tour of the former Confederacy: "I was very proud of you on your trip south, but I think I am even more proud of you now."[49]

"Curious Crew"

Goldwater's campaign also worked to shape perceptions of the Johnsons' closeness to the Jenkins family. Publicly, the candidate told reporters in Denver on Thursday that he would not exploit the tragedy and would speak of it only in national-security terms: "I don't intend to comment on it at any time." Yet the wire services broke the story on October 14 immediately after a press conference in which his handpicked Republican National Committee chairman had demanded that they do so. And Goldwater himself repeatedly tarred Johnson by invocation—using the phrase "curious crew" seven times in one speech and pausing for effect after mentioning the president's "companions." His campaign also aired a television spot that pointedly called Jenkins "Johnson's closest friend."[50]

These winking denunciations were echoed at the grassroots. Signs at GOP rallies and hastily printed bumper stickers read "Lyndon Baker Jenkins." Voters in Cleveland received "shocking pink cards on which is printed, 'Go Gay with LBJ.'" On October 20, William F. Buckley predicted the episode "will be iterated and reiterated coast to coast day in and day out until November 3rd." Even so, while one prong of Goldwater's case against Johnson was a supposed decline in public morals, his campaign struggled to tie that theme directly to the specifics of Jenkins's arrest. Bishop Gerald H. Kennedy, the United Methodist bishop for Los Angeles and a Republican, said the episode ought not decide the election, adding, "You find this sickness in many parts of our life now, even among teachers and preachers. It seems to be growing." Even for those who saw Jenkins as part of an increase in gay visibility, the case did not necessarily signify a larger moral collapse.[51]

Goldwater's running mate, Congressman William Miller, denounced Jenkins frequently and blisteringly. "We know a person of this type is the easiest prey for any agent of the communists," he said in a Friday television interview. To a *Time* reporter he added, "It's the break we've been waiting for. I think it lends substance to what we've been saying all along—that there is a lack of morality in the highest places in government." Richard Nixon, campaigning in Indiana for Goldwater, likewise urged Johnson to "come clean" about both Jenkins and Baker, warning that Americans would "not stand for immorality in the White House." As for Goldwater's own restraint, early the following week he issued a public statement complaining, among other points, that the FBI agents who interviewed him about Jenkins failed to ask "my opinion of the subject's loyalty to the country."[52]

Journalists had already noted that Jenkins belonged to a special Air Force unit founded in 1961 and officially commanded by Barry Goldwater. The 9999th Air Reserve Squadron, made up entirely of members of Congress and their staffs, met on Tuesday mornings. Goldwater, a decorated pilot, was an Air Force enthusiast who spent weekends at Andrews Air Force Base flying F-18s. Critics charged that the squadron functioned chiefly as a lobbying vehicle for Air Force projects.[53] In a statement, Goldwater said of Jenkins, "His unit of assignment is headquarters command, so I was not required to give him an efficiency rating." Records showed that both men often missed the weekly Tuesday morning meetings. FBI investigators ultimately concluded—though not publicly—that there was indeed no evidence Goldwater had ever evaluated Jenkins.[54]

Conservatives quickly used the moment to revive the Baker scandal. Columnist David Lawrence complained that Jenkins had never appeared in person during the Baker inquiry and urged the Senate to reopen it before the election. The Goldwater campaign received a barrage of letters urging a harsher tone. Several supporters pressed the candidate to link Jenkins to Lyndon Johnson's skinny-dipping with newsmen at the White House, a practice revealed in January by the *Chicago Tribune* columnist Walter Trohan and repeatedly denounced in right-leaning publications. "WAS WALTER JENKINS THE INSTIGATOR OF THE NUDE MALE SWIMMING PARTIES WHICH SO DELIGHT THE INTERIM PRESIDENT?" one Floridian's telegram demanded. Others wondered whether the Jenkins case was connected to the dismissal of accused Russian spies without trial, reflecting the Republican right's taste for conspiracy. "PURSUE NEW MATTER VIGOURSLY [*SIC*] THE WAY LABOR PARTY HANDLE PROFUMO CASE," urged another, invoking the 1963 British scandal in which a cabinet minister resigned over an affair with a woman linked to a Soviet spy.[55]

Some correspondents exulted that talking about Jenkins "will pick up thousands of women votes now—clean-cut family vs. LBJ +

Jenkins." Others predicted the opposite: "So many people, women especially (and these, I am sorry to say are allowed the vote) are 'sorry for Mr. Jenkins' and think Mrs. J. and Mr. J. are such 'tender hearted' people." Still another wrote that the campaign needed to explain more clearly why Jenkins was dangerous. "We have tried out the 'security' risk aspect of the Jenkins matter on our office force," wrote this Washingtonian, "and were amazed to discover that most of the women did not understand that all perverts are the prime targets of the Soviet apparatus. In other words, we had to explain to them how suspect Jenkins must be, as a pervert." He urged that "all efforts be made to get across to the public an explanation of why this is true." Another gendered take came from a Republican who demanded, "get rid of all homo-sexual flossies in government and make the running of this country a 'he man's world' and a 'she woman's world.'" Yet in a sign of the party's deep divisions, moderates urged Burch and Miller to rein in their attacks lest they backfire. "Congressman Miller's attack on Jenkins," a North Carolina man wrote to Burch, is "ugly and repulsive. It will cost the G.O.P. more than votes than it will win. Stop him."[56]

In his 1988 memoir, Goldwater devoted ten paragraphs to the Jenkins resignation, portraying himself as having virtuously refused to exploit the opening it presented. The historical record of his handling of the crisis has been obscured by selective recollection. Goldwater correctly recalled that he had "said the only matter which concerned the campaign was the national security aspect." More self-servingly, he added, "It was a sad time for Jenkins' wife and children, and I was not about to add to their private sorrow." Taking what he called the high road, he claimed to have learned something that "never got through to Johnson and Moyers—that winning isn't everything." He further contrasted Johnson's allegedly having "said nothing publicly about the case" [*sic*] with Lady Bird's "finest hour—doing what her husband should have done immediately instead of stalling and having his pals trying to suppress the story." In fact, Johnson commented publicly on Jenkins the next day and again several days later.[57]

Goldwater's account of restraint has since been cited approvingly by some liberals, who contrast it with the antigay rhetoric of Republicans in later decades. At the time, however, many liberals saw the Republican campaign quite differently. To James Reston of the *New York Times*, Goldwater's initial vow not to exploit the case quickly rang hollow: the candidate, he wrote, "has not been faithful to the higher morality he has invoked," noting that the Republican National Committee was circulating bumper stickers reading "Light Bulb Johnson. No Wonder He Turned Out the Lights in the White House." Thirty liberal clergymen—including Reinhold Niebuhr, Thomas Merton, and Abraham Heschel—issued a statement condemning "smears" that used Jenkins's arrest "as a weapon." The document avoided partisan language, but at a New York press conference the president of Union Theological Seminary made clear that the target was the Goldwater campaign. An editorial cartoonist for the *St. Louis Post-Dispatch* depicted Goldwater and Miller whipping the skeletal remains of a horse, under the caption "Giddap Critter—The Polls Will Be Closing Soon."[58]

A Scandal Contained

In 1964 there was no policy debate about gay rights. Goldwater's caution was read less as tolerance than as a recognition that pressing the attack carried risks. "There is no doubt that the Republicans have a weapon which could help them if used skillfully," wrote John Steele of *Time*, adding that mishandling it could backfire, just as partisan criticisms of Nixon's finances collapsed after his 1952 Checkers speech.[59]

By and large, the White House effort to emphasize Walter Jenkins's wife and children worked. It helped that Jenkins had no male lover, no effeminate traits, and no visible tie to the gay male subculture. In Washington and Texas, he was known as quiet, conventional, and—above all—a hard worker, fitting the notion that strain had pushed him to the brink. In an age of consensus, testimony from those at the apex of the political order, especially the First Lady's rare public statement, represented him as the family man he was. Voters did not seem to blame Johnson for Jenkins's arrests. Late on October 14—the day the story broke—Johnson ordered a telephone survey from his pollster Oliver Quayle; it found voters cared deeply about Nelson Rockefeller's divorce and remarriage to a younger woman, but not about Jenkins or Baker.[60] Rockefeller's actions spoke directly to his own character; Jenkins's troubles, by contrast, could be cordoned off as an aide's misfortune. What mattered was whether the man on the ballot was a family man, not whether his aides had stumbled.

For Americans unfamiliar with Jenkins, the White House's statements were not the only influence. Many filtered the news through what they already "knew" about homosexuality, drawing on a growing repertoire of public images, sometimes observed, often stereotyped. Increasingly in the 1960s, the gay male subculture, overlapping with the world of men cruising in public places, had been shown in paperback exposés, newspapers, and radio and television programs. "Having worked in Hollywood in the studios and in San Francisco," an Orange County woman wrote to Dean Burch, "I know when there is one, there is always one more or groups of them." By contrast, the Johnson-Humphrey chairman for Santa Barbara County told a reporter the news could even help statewide: "Well hell, if we can carry the homosexuals in southern California, we've got it made." The remark was not for attribution, and in 1964 the idea of courting a gay or lesbian vote was still literally a joke. Yet it revealed a small but telling shift: an assumption that gay people existed in significant numbers, that they were visible—and that they were part of the electorate.[61]

In the public eye, the Johnsons had met an aide's misfortune with compassion, casting it as a domestic sorrow rather than a public concern. Quayle's poll findings suggested that the framing had worked: the story seemed unlikely to alter many votes, and few believed it reflected on Johnson's own character. Behind the scenes, Lady Bird's quiet authority had been essential to keeping the narrative on those terms.

The Jenkins affair might have spiraled into an open-ended scandal; it did not, and that was not accidental. The Johnsons, especially Lady Bird, kept the story within the bounds of private misfortune, summoning empathy and personal credibility to foreclose other narratives. What the public saw was a wife's humane response to a trusted friend and colleague's crisis; what it did not see was the orchestration that helped give such compassionate responses a prominent place in the coverage the arrest generated.

CHAPTER 5

THE COLUMNISTS

The Jenkins story was an unprecedented and shocking intrusion of sexual deviance into national politics. Even with Jenkins whisked out of sight just before his exposure, the American press had never before described so graphically the private sexual behavior of a public official. The news spread that the president's closest aide had left the White House under a cloud. It was shocking enough that many assumed it might alter the trajectory of the presidential campaign.

Many of the first to hear about Jenkins's arrest did so by radio. "I was driving home from work, and I heard just a sort of a snatch of a radio broadcast and I wasn't sure what I had heard," recalled an aide to House whip Hale Boggs and former advance man for Johnson in the 1960 campaign. "And I got up to the apartment and turned the radio on." In the diary of Katie Louchheim, a Democratic socialite and fundraiser, "JENKINS NIGHT" was written in pencil across the top of the page. In a telephone survey of 327 Iowa City residents completed the next day by social scientists, 42 percent had learned about Jenkins's arrest—usually from the radio or television—within five hours of the first news report; most of the remainder read it in the next morning's paper.[1]

The news of Jenkins's resignation was followed sixteen hours later—midday on Thursday—by another shocking and perplexing news flash: Nikita Khrushchev, the Soviet premier, had been overthrown. The liberal columnist Drew Pearson wrote in his diary, "Never has so much happened to turn the tide of history in a single day," but concluded nonetheless that Jenkins "is really going to hurt Johnson." By Friday morning, still more news broke: the British Labour Party defeated the Tories, the St. Louis Cardinals won the World Series, Hurricane Isbell hit coastal Florida, and China tested its first atomic bomb: "such is the luck of Lyndon Johnson," sighed the conservative syndicated columnist James Kilpatrick.[2] Departing from its traditional cover drawing of a single newsworthy individual, *Time* used photographs of the Chinese, Soviet, British, and American leaders with diagonal text summing up four nations' top stories: "The bomb; the overthrow; the squeaker; the scandal."

While the initial disclosure anticipated the media's growing willingness in the late twentieth century to report on officials' private lives, the Jenkins story unfolded in accordance with a postwar Washington pattern in which a small group of syndicated columnists had enormous power to shape stories. All of Washington's major syndicated columnists wrote about Jenkins, but his hospitalization created a cordon that only two journalists broke through. Just twice, news slipped out from behind the door to his hospital room, numbered 2017A, and appeared in a column by a well-connected journalist close to the White House.

It was the wire services that broke the Jenkins story, but columnists, especially William S. White and Betty Beale, shaped its trajectory. Each column had a dramatic emotional effect on readers, and each strongly reinforced the administration's preferred narrative without seeming too overtly to do so. The first was an opinion column by White, a Texan and the journalist closest to the president, who brought the reader into Walter Jenkins's hospital room and offered a counterintuitive snapshot of the scene by comparing Jenkins to a combat veteran. The second column, by Beale, described an outpouring of "understanding, affection and compassion" by friends of the Jenkinses. It also disclosed an act of public approbation from the nation's premier symbol of both law enforcement and anticommunism: J. Edgar Hoover himself had sent a bouquet of flowers to

Jenkins in the hospital. This startling fact—the existence of these flowers—was quickly confirmed by the wire services and deemed to have major news value and thus lost its association with Beale. Many Americans learned it directly from other trusted sources like David Brinkley, the Washington-based coanchor of NBC's nightly *Huntley-Brinkley Report*.[3]

Republican chairman Dean Burch later said that White's column and Hoover's flowers together destroyed any chance for Goldwater to reap a political benefit from the Jenkins story. As Hoover sending flowers passed into the lore of the 1964 election, Burch was not alone in treating it as a baffling accident. Over time, the fact that the scoop first appeared in a society column faded from view. In reality, the story's origins lay in the network of newswomen that had emerged in Cold War Washington—professionals whose exclusion from the National Press Club drew them together in a professional association of their own and whose embrace by the Johnson White House gave Beale crucial access. It was the most important single development in news coverage of the Jenkins case after his resignation. Beale herself knew well the impact her disclosure would have: "Such support from Hoover, of course, put an end to talk of security risks," she wrote in her 1993 memoir.[4]

The Pileup of News

"As this campaign started," said Dan Rather to CBS News viewers, it seemed that one of three things must happen "if Senator Goldwater is to have a chance: a foreign upheaval, a government scandal, and/or an economic crisis. Now in the space of twenty-four hours, not one but two of these possibilities have materialized." Rather thought that the international news would outweigh Jenkins: "The Jenkins affair certainly figures to cost President Johnson some votes, but Khrushchev's downfall may gain him more."[5] Still, nothing guaranteed the foreign crisis would keep Jenkins off the front pages.

Journalists struggled to think of a comparable instance of a homosexual being purged from the public sphere so spectacularly. "I've been trying to think of a parallel to the Jenkins case and I cannot," wrote John L. Steele, the *Time-Life* Washington bureau chief, to his editors in New York. "The Cleveland bastardy case was quite different; the Vandenberg case never hit the prints and besides Ike already had been elected." In any case, neither instance—a forgotten nineteenth-century scandal and the decade-old case of a gay aide whose nomination was withdrawn quietly—would have been familiar to many readers. "This one is more of a fiction story," Steele continued, "reflecting a little of the theme of the play 'The Best Man,' or Allen Drury's 'Advise and Consent.'" A columnist recalled that at the height of public interest in Drury's novel, "the question put most often to Washington newsmen was whether the city is really like that. The answer, in the light of the Walter Jenkins case, seems to be yes."[6] While Washington journalism tiptoed around the subject, prominent fictional works had dramatized the Cold War capital's surprising preoccupation with male homosexuality. Only now was the news beginning to catch up.

As with any major news event, reporters wrote follow-up stories. In a televised debate the night the story broke, the national leaders of groups of young Republicans and young Democrats clashed about the meaning of Jenkins. Similar debates followed when district and county party chairmen appeared together. Reporters covered statements from the Secret Service and Treasury Secretary Douglas Dillon about why the White House had not learned of Jenkins's 1959 arrest, and from the Pentagon announcing that Jenkins's top secret clearance had been suspended. The *New York Herald-Tribune* science editor used Jenkins as the hook to explore scientific puzzlement about what caused homosexuality and whether it could be treated. Editorial cartoonists portrayed the campaign as unusually dirty. One showed an elephant with a camera and a donkey with a tape recorder, each holding a flashlight and each holding rolled-up "campaign secrets," peering at one another through a keyhole, with the caption, "Why, the Dirty—!"[7]

Seeking a local angle, a *New York Post* reporter tracked down Andy Choka's estranged wife in a German section of Queens where she lived with her two children and her mother. In "a thick German accent," she complained about the many telephone calls she'd received, adding that she had long been separated from her husband. "We know nothing about politics, scandals or what he's been doing," she said. A local newspaper in Southern California even ran an article—"Jenkins Arrest Shocks Friends in Ventura"—about a friend of Jenkins's from their World War II service who, though shocked by the arrest, said he would always remain his friend. The man clipped the article and sent it to Jenkins.[8]

As the Jenkins scandal broke, insiders privately noted the divergence between how the press handled it and how they handled the private life of John F. Kennedy. A woman whose husband had created campaign films for John F. Kennedy now wrote to Jenkins, "We know very well there were areas in [Kennedy's] personal life which if known to the Great American People, would have considerably damaged him." *Time* reporter Murray Gart saw immediately that the Jenkins case was "in some ways not unlike equally low-level issues in bars and at cocktail parties during past campaigns," such as "Mamie Eisenhower's 'illness'" in 1952 and "Jack's way with women" in 1960. But where those matters remained "gossip circuit fare," the Jenkins case by contrast was "page one news."[9]

Reporters fanning out to gauge the public response found that most voters were startled but did not connect it to their own voter preferences. After speaking to seventy people in the Los Angeles suburb of Sherman Oaks, a *Time* reporter suggested the pileup of presidential-election stories would actually make Jenkins's resignation more forgettable than that of Eisenhower aide Sherman Adams in 1958, which happened in October of a midterm campaign. He quoted Olivia Meridia, identified as a Black maid, as saying, "If you condemn this one thing, you can condemn the whole world." The columnists Rowland Evans and Robert Novak polled voters in three locales about the Jenkins affair—Lansing, Michigan; Owensboro, Kentucky; and Pomona, California—and found "only 11 of the 102 voters did not know about it." Few said their votes would change;

an Owensboro housewife said, "Why should it? I never was going to vote for Jenkins." Still, the reporters concluded, the "phenomenal awareness around the country" about the case indicated "some success" by Republicans.[10]

Some journalists read the mood and predicted regional differences in the public reaction. The pollster Samuel Lubell's syndicated column suggested, "The arrest will also strengthen the disgust with both candidates that already exists and is particularly strong in the South." The Black-owned *Chicago Defender* reported on the fears of Black government employees in Washington that the scandal would help Goldwater, who had opposed the 1964 Civil Rights Act. The unsigned story expressed a concern shared by Johnson himself that it might hurt Johnson in "the unsophisticated Midwest, and other farm areas where it is easier to understand man-animal relationships than man-man relationships." Such predictions were widespread within campaigns too. A New England Democrat wrote the White House that Rhode Islanders' opinion would be particularly affected because of its high proportion of Italian and Irish Americans. The Jenkins matter, he said, would be "a bitter pill for them to swallow."[11]

Coverage of the scandal in at least some of the Black press reflected a distinctive skepticism toward the police version of events. *Jet* magazine, from the Chicago-based publisher of *Ebony*, drew an analogy that few white readers would have understood: "While the nation was shocked over the arrest of top White House aide Walter Jenkins on a morals charge, the Supreme Court quietly turned the spotlight on police tactics used in arresting Mississippi NAACP leader Aaron Henry on similar charges," referring to Henry's conviction by an all-white jury of charges based on allegations made by an eighteen-year-old white hitchhiker. This was followed by four paragraphs on the Supreme Court taking up "Henry's questionable arrest" after a possible illegal search by police. As Jennifer Dominique Jones notes, in the context of the push for civil rights legislation, the Jenkins and Henry stories tightened a connection between Blackness and "morals" cases.[12]

Echoing the Goldwater campaign, conservative columnists saw in Jenkins a further sign of apocalyptic moral decline. Holmes Alexander conceded that Johnson hadn't known about Jenkins's 1959 arrest but could not resist a conspiratorial assertion that Jenkins "has had another sort of protection which, in this town's atmosphere, shields the homosexualist, the disloyalist and the common criminal under the same umbrella of tolerance." For the arch-segregationist James Kilpatrick, the element of disgust made Jenkins's offense even worse than more ordinary and understandable crimes. He wrote that, faced with Bobby Baker's corruption, the typical voter "silently loves a crook," that most people have "a latent urge to swindle," and thus the case generated "no perceptible revulsion." In the case of Jenkins, by contrast, "One imagines the offense. And one is revolted." Raymond Moley charged in *Newsweek* that "Mr. Johnson lives in a community in which such derelictions as Jenkins' have been common for years" and that "the cover-up failed," concluding that "if the moral tone set by government and the policies it follows erode the fiber of our people, the loss is total, irrecoverable, absolute."[13]

Liberal columnists lacked a single angle of approach. Murray Kempton denounced Johnson for abandoning Jenkins and for his "false masculinity" and "need to drive cars at 85 miles an hour on public roads while drinking beer." By contrast, he said, John F. Kennedy "was a combat soldier and never talked about it"—a remarkable assertion, since Kennedy's campaigns had spared no expense to inform voters about his wartime heroism. Walter Lippmann denounced Goldwater's emphasis on morality. Drew Pearson tried unsuccessfully to find adequate evidence for his suspicion that New York ad man Lou Guylay, who worked for Goldwater, had set up Jenkins. Eventually Pearson published a column revisiting his coverage of the 1954 suicide of Lester Hunt following his son's morals conviction. Pearson also advanced the view—likely wrong—that Jenkins could have won at trial contesting either his recent charge or the 1959 one.[14]

Combat Fatigue

While many in the Washington press corps had known and liked Jenkins, none did more to reframe his deviation than William S. White, who invoked his experience as a war correspondent and replaced the YMCA restroom with the figure of the injured combat veteran. A Texan and University of Texas graduate, slightly older than Johnson at fifty-nine, White had worked for the Associated Press from 1926 to 1945, much of that time in Washington, where he met Lyndon Johnson in 1933. Later he covered the liberation of Paris and the Allied advance across Europe. His 1986 memoir includes admiring tales of Churchill in wartime London, a briefing by a British naval commander on the coming plans for D-Day, and encounters with Hemingway in liberated Belgium. In 1945 White moved to the *New York Times*, where he covered the Senate and rose to chief congressional correspondent. At key moments, his reporting had helped Lyndon Johnson's quest to position himself as a national rather than merely a sectional leader.[15]

White's reporting relied on his access to top senators and other officials, whom he tended to portray as great men.[16] He believed reporters ought not report on the private behavior of public figures. He recalled in the 1980s that his column aimed to have "a clear point of view," not "to rummage in Washington's moral trash bins." The reporter's job was not "to enforce the criminal code or even especially to assist the Church in its sublime mission to fight the sin and admonish and reclaim the sinner"; he sneered at latter-day investigative reporters and their "midnight meetings with shadowy informants in a cloaked if not daggered way," perhaps a reference to coverage of the Watergate scandal. He had no compunction about reviewing a book by his close friend Dean Acheson. White left the *New York Times* in 1958 to write a column for United Features Syndicate that appeared three days a week in as many as 175 newspapers.[17]

Passionately anticommunist, enthusiastic about postwar affluence and political moderation, White was also notably sympathetic to the racial views of most Southern whites. He praised Senate traditions including the filibuster, criticized John F. Kennedy for moving too fast on civil rights, and red-baited Bayard Rustin in his account of the 1963 March on Washington, which he called "undeniably orderly and moving but nevertheless unwise." During the Senate debate on the Civil Rights Act of 1964, White made clear he thought its public accommodations and private hiring provisions went too far. He wrote a *Harper's* column in 1960 about women officeholders and their irritating tendency to moralize.[18]

Johnson's ascension to the presidency was also an elevation of White, who by mid-1964 was widely seen by other journalists as the President's mouthpiece. At Johnson's first address to Congress after the Kennedy assassination, Lady Bird Johnson sat between her daughters on one side and June White on the other. In an April 1964 diagram in *Esquire* that arranged the "Washington press establishment" from left to right, White was near the center and labeled "The Court Oracle." "White's column is now read avidly by other Washington newsmen watching for nuances in the President's thinking," wrote Charles Roberts of *Newsweek*; "it is regarded on most issues as a true reflection of the White House 'line.'"[19]

White pegged his new column to a profile of Jenkins he had written ten months earlier, in December 1963 when Jenkins was new to the White House. That column called Jenkins a modest and "moral man," implicitly contradicting Johnson's wheeler-dealer image. "I am glad that you read Mr. White's article about me," Jenkins replied to a friend's note. "It was generous of him, and he is a fine gentleman." A few months later White profiled George Reedy, when he replaced Pierre Salinger as White House press secretary, again suggesting that the aide's virtues reflected favorably on LBJ. Now he wrote a new essay—and quickly.[20]

In one of the first columns on Jenkins to appear, White invoked his status as a war correspondent. "A human tragedy of measureless pathos, a tragedy to tear the heart as few things have ever done in my 50-odd years of rather urgent living, is the story of Walter Jenkins," began the first of thirteen paragraphs. Like Lady Bird Johnson,

White argued that Jenkins had worked too hard since the Kennedy assassination, but he offered more detail, confiding in readers that Jenkins had recently "developed a red and frightening flush that told even a layman of a dangerously high blood pressure."[21]

The column's pivotal sentence came in the opening of White's fourth paragraph: "I have just come from the hospital room of Walter Jenkins." This generated public attention because no other journalist had been permitted, or would be permitted, to write about visiting Jenkins. Maximally invoking his own reportorial credentials, White fixed the physical space of the hospital and projected it indefinitely into the future: "It is a scene that will burn forever in the memory of one whose own profession has caused him to see so much of human suffering—the death of so many in battle, the death of hope for so many others." Four paragraphs later, he declared that Jenkins was suffering from "combat fatigue," which he certified as medically correct. "At the hospital I told this to his doctor. The doctor replied softly: 'Yes, you are right. Except that for this kind of combat fatigue they give no medals.'" He suggested that what Jenkins had faced since the Kennedy assassination would "break any man."

By comparing Jenkins to the singularly celebrated figure of the combat veteran, White worked to lock in as the definitive interpretation that Jenkins had buckled under stress, a victim of overwork. Reordering the relationship between Jenkins and his reported action, he wrote, "If there has been a slip it has not been from the real, the true Walter Jenkins." He recalled that in his previous column about Jenkins, "after another tragedy just short of 12 months ago," he had labeled him "one of the most conscientious and most truly moral men I ever knew," a statement he now reaffirmed—"every word of it."[22]

White did not so much downgrade Jenkins's offense as remove him from the scene of the crime. There is no vice cop, no YMCA, no police station, only a fleeting mention that Jenkins resigned "in dreadful circumstances." The column left open the possibility of police error while implicitly labeling as improper any curiosity about the details: "I do not know precisely what in this shattered state he may have done. I do not intend to ask." White evoked ascendant concerns with the effects of stress on male breadwinners. He medicalized Jenkins, but he invoked not cure but "rest to regain his true self."[23]

With extraordinary economy, White made Jenkins's sexual transgression off-limits for polite discussion, confirmed the First Lady's portrait of a man buckling under strain, and replaced the disturbing image of the YMCA restroom with the combat veteran and all of the culturally sanctioned virtues he embodied in postwar America. No other journalist had breached the walls of George Washington University Hospital. With you-are-there directness, White's column offered readers the sense that they might now possess maximal understanding of the situation. Whatever there was to know from actually being present with Jenkins and his doctor, as White had been, the reader would now know as well. And White's interpretation was given the solemn imprimatur not only of a medical man but of one involved in treating Jenkins.

The column drew in part on the genre of the eulogy; White called Jenkins a man forced to "bury a lost career." A colleague of Jenkins's wrote to White that he had "the very highest regard for this wonderful man you have so appropriately eulogized." But it also drew on the genre of declaring one's loyalty to a friend in trouble, a genre with which White was familiar from covering Washington during the early Cold War. He stood by, he declared, his previous column portraying Jenkins as "one of the most honorable, most conscientious, and most truly moral men I ever knew."[24]

The column, which first appeared in Friday's *Evening Star* roughly forty-eight hours after the first wire-service bulletins about Jenkins's arrest, had a strong impact on the reception of the scandal, generating letters to the editor in newspapers across the country, as well as letters to White himself, which he collected and forwarded to Jenkins. The column moved people of all ages and many walks of life. A college student wrote to White from his dorm room at the University of North Carolina at Chapel Hill, "You tried in your editorial to lift him up, wipe some of the dirt out of people's minds. With me, you have succeeded." A woman wrote, "I'm eighty one years of age, your article was one of the finest I have ever read. I have read much in my life."[25]

Since White was widely thought to speak for Johnson, the public and the powerful alike lined up alongside him. When the column ran on the front page of the *New York Journal-American*, Richard E. Berlin, the Hearst Corporation's president, sent a copy to the Johnsons with a note saying, "This is the way we like to treat our friends." Jesse Kellam, the longtime KTBC station manager, wrote to White, "Thank you so much for having put into words the substance of my thoughts concerning our mutual friend Walter Jenkins." Friends and colleagues told Jenkins that White spoke for them, too: "now I do not know how to express my feelings—but Mr. White has done so in his article which I know you have read, but which I attach," wrote one, concluding that "you can and must regain your true self, and your friends believe you will."[26]

A particularly powerful response to White's column, postmarked in New York City, observed that White's role as a columnist seemed to give him a "license to speak that others lack." Though implicitly, the author hinted at his or her own deviation. "The climate itself, a tragic commentary on our world, is such that most of your readers who support your views in this case cannot afford to risk publication of their names without in turn risking the setting in motion of severe repercussions." The writer added, "But we can let you know there are those who support you by remaining anonymous as we do so," concluding by proposing the collection of donations to help Jenkins get back on his feet and for his children's college fund.[27]

White changed readers' minds. "I no longer am inclined to wonder if his doctor is covering up for him," wrote one woman. "Mrs. Johnson's plea for our prayers for his healing is truly justified, as you have made me see. And if me, then surely many others." An anonymous writer said, "I had no way of understanding the situation until your brilliant and touching column appeared in the *Los Angeles Times*."[28]

Some criticized White for failing to mention the 1959 arrest. The *Tampa Times* ran an "editor's note" with White's column saying "we feel obligated to point out to our readers that Mr. White totally ignores the arrest of Walter Jenkins in 1959 on a morals charge." In a letter to the *Los Angeles Times*, which published eight diverse responses, one reader complained, "Mr. White's tear-jerker about Walter Jenkins (Oct. 20) overlooks the fact that he was arrested for a similar dereliction five years ago. How many such acts would Mr. White consider as par for the course?" Another reply called it a "maudlin defense of a twice-arrested man," *maudlin* being a favorite word of the pro-Goldwater right for what they considered the sentimentality and emotionalism of Democrats. According to White, a hostile stranger called him after the column appeared to ask if he, too, was "a homosexual." A contrasting letter in the roundup praised White for recognizing "the difference between a minor lapse of a fundamentally decent man, and the habitual lewd conduct of these deviate-types."[29]

Another syndicated columnist, Marquis Childs, perhaps inspired by White's column or envious of his access, was eager to know what Johnson wanted written about Jenkins. Childs asked for an appointment in a note suggesting there might be "far more to it than meets the eye at the present moment" and saying he would like "some guidance at some point during the next three or four days" from the president. Johnson met Childs the same day. Two days later, Childs published a column that revealed little new beyond the fact that Johnson "follows from day to day, almost from hour to hour, the inquiry into the Jenkins case" and that "The President is convinced that the charge came not because Jenkins was involved, but because he was a bystander."[30]

Needless to say, White's unasked-for favor delighted Lyndon Johnson. On Saturday evening, the president phoned White to praise the column. It was, he said, "the best I ever read. Everybody in town cried about it." He suggested as well that if White was available, he might drop by the White House. "Come by and have a drink," he said. "Come in the southwest gate. I'll leave word." White's column evidently meant a great deal to Marjorie Jenkins as well. In a message to Lyndon and Lady Bird, secretary Mary Rather wrote that Marjorie "praises Bill White every time I talk to her."[31]

Say It with Flowers

Betty Beale, the only syndicated society columnist in the nation's capital during the early atomic age, defined her subject matter as "politics after six."[32] A banker's daughter, congressman's granddaughter, and Smith College graduate, she began writing columns for the *Star* in 1945. An early triumph came one week into the Eisenhower administration, when she broke the news that foreign ambassadors attending a Tuesday afternoon reception were "surprised and delighted" that, for the first time anyone could recall, "whiskey was offered in an undisguised state before 8 o'clock in the evening" at the White House. After other reporters pressed the White House press secretary in vain for further details, the Associated Press put the story out on its wires and quite a few papers ran it on the front page.[33] Seldom, if ever, had a scoop first appeared on the society or women's page and then jumped to front pages nationwide, a pattern that her story about Hoover's flowers would repeat.[34]

Two months after the whiskey story, the Post-Hall Syndicate offered Beale a weekly column, which eventually ran in over 100 newspapers. Beale later credited Elizabeth and Leslie Carpenter—married columnists for Texas newspapers—with persuading the syndicate to extend her the offer. In the 1950s, Beale became a Washington icon. She criticized Eisenhower for the fact that his state dinners were "dominated entirely by big businessmen" while artists, writers, and intellectuals were overlooked—and was vindicated when the Kennedys took her advice to bring in the latter, for which they received much favorable press.[35]

Beale's bread-and-butter topic for columns was parties, and she had a gift for rendering social life into narrative prose. She wrote an impressive 1961 column on the "lonesomeness" of the new African ambassadors in segregated Washington. As mentioned in chapter 2, she had covered a January 1964 wedding shower at the Jenkins home that was attended by various Texas congressmen and the legendary hostess Perle Mesta. "The Walter Jenkins household the other evening was a happy mélange," she had begun that account, which went on to describe fifteen-year-old son Walter Jr.'s "impromptu concert in the living room," then declared that nine-year-old Lyndon "looks like a mischief maker if I ever saw one" and included the names and ages of the other four Jenkins children. Beale concluded that "Father Jenkins remained calm through it all. You could see why being around LBJ, the dynamo, is no problem to him." Later in January, covering a White House party for a group of senators in the East Room, Beale wrote that Jenkins worked so late that he arrived "halfway through dinner."[36]

Beale's syndicated column, "Exclusively Yours," offered readers a window into the social lives of the nation's leaders. Its "meat" was "scoops" about the powerful, as two fellow Washington newswomen put it, "and the potatoes are the chitchat." Beale's summer 1962 report that Ethel Kennedy had pushed the historian and presidential aide Arthur Schlesinger into the pool at a dance at Hickory Hill—Beale had not attended, but pieced together the events afterward—became, like her earlier scoop about the Eisenhowers serving whiskey, a wire-service story and the talk of the capital. While waiting in the corridor to enter President Johnson's first address to a joint session of Congress, Beale asked the Johnsons' "Negro cook," Zephyr Wright, what would be on the menu for the Johnsons' Thanksgiving dinner. In the spring of 1964, she reported on the Washington preview of the Hollywood adaptation of Gore Vidal's play *The Best Man*, attended by playwright and screenwriter Vidal and White House notables including "the president's close assistants, Walter Jenkins and Bill Moyers, and their wives." She reported that Luci Baines Johnson would be taking a summer job as an optometrist's assistant.[37]

Beale was close to the Johnsons (see figure 5.1). She had known them in the 1950s, and stayed overnight at the LBJ Ranch, and she wrote later that the Johnson presidency gave her "my very best entrée into 1600 Pennsylvania Avenue." By her account, "The soci-

FIGURE 5.1 President Johnson and columnist Betty Beale, March 1964. LBJ Library/ Photo by Cecil Stoughton.

ety press had never seen the liveliest Kennedy parties—which were strictly private—and there were no really lively parties during the Truman and Eisenhower years." In August of 1961, *Newsweek* ran a photo of Vice President Johnson, who loved to dance, dancing cheek to cheek with Beale.[38]

Crucial to Beale's entrée at the Johnson White House was her close friendship with Liz Carpenter, whom Lady Bird Johnson had made the first ever press secretary to the First Lady. Liz and Les Carpenter's reporting had helped Johnson win the 1948 Texas Senate primary, even before they helped Beale get her syndicated column in 1953. Beale and Carpenter became friends and collaborated on various Women's National Press Club events as officers in that organization. In 1955, for example, Carpenter was president and Beale was on the board of governors of the organization. Writing on club letterhead, Carpenter addressed Beale as "Ike" to thank her for playing Eisenhower in a skit at the group's annual banquet. During the fall 1960 campaign, Carpenter went to work for Lady Bird Johnson as her press aide.[39]

Beale and Carpenter had supported one another professionally. The two women sat down for a meeting on the afternoon of November 28, 1963, the day after Johnson's speech to a joint session of Congress. Beale subsequently suggested it "would be of great help to the First Lady if an able, qualified woman who understood the Johnsons' personal and political needs were made The Assistant to the First Lady, or, perhaps, Assistant to The President and First Lady." That person, she said, should be Carpenter herself. Three days later Beale wrote a column on the Johnsons' inner circle that included both Carpenter and White.[40]

Carpenter was known for her attention to social graces. She sent women reporters flowers and cards on White House stationery knowing the impact this would have on recipients. In her memoir Beale stressed Carpenter's savvy and generosity: "Having been a newswoman herself, she knew what would make news and how to dispense it. If she had an item particularly suited to my column she would give it to me, even pointing out the best or most amusing angles." When Beale traveled abroad, Carpenter wrote her letters of introduction to US ambassadors on White House letterhead. The unmarried Beale appreciated that the Johnsons dropped a prior rule that unmarried newswomen could only attend White House functions unescorted.[41]

Knowing that Beale's column about Hoover sending flowers to Jenkins would be major news, editors at her syndication service attached a rare cover note to the copy that went out to subscribers. "We have every reason to believe," said the note, "that the lead item on Walter Jenkins in the enclosed BETTY BEALE column for this week-end is exclusive. Because of its importance and the possibility that it may become public before the release date of the column, we suggest that you release that portion of the column immediately."[42]

Her reporting on the flowers was sound, but the typescript of the column in Beale's personal papers suggests the column underwent edits at a late stage to correct a misstatement about Hoover's intentions. An otherwise-final draft originally stated that a "note" had come with the flowers stipulating that Hoover had sent them "only with the understanding that you show this card to everyone who comes to your room," but this was not in the published version. In that draft, this part of the text was struck through and replaced with new language that called the stipulation a "verbal one" that "came . . . along with" the flowers. The version of the column published in the *Star* on the evening of October 21 indicated that this "verbal" message "according to Mrs. Jenkins . . . coincided with the delivery" of the bouquet.[43] Sometime after transmission to the syndication service, "verbal" became "oral" and "according to Mrs. Jenkins" was deleted. Thus, as the column appeared in nearly all newspapers, the request for visitors to be shown the card bearing Hoover's name was called "an oral one that came to his sickroom along with the bouquet of flowers."[44] Hoover wrote to many correspondents that there had been no such message, and no other evidence confirms Beale on this point.

As her editors anticipated, Beale's scoop captured the imagination of the public, who rarely received any unfiltered information about Hoover. "Last night I could have collapsed," one angry Southerner wrote Hoover, "when I heard David Brinkley say on his news broadcast how well the Jenkins family is taking their 'tragedy' and 'why, even J. Edgar Hoover sent a message and flowers.'" Noting that Hoover was the only federal official trusted in Bible Belt areas, the writer was horrified by the implications—"The very thing that we used to call black sin is now called sickness"—and called on Hoover to "rebuke the Jenkins family and the news media" for making Hoover's gesture public.[45]

The news of Hoover's floral gift signaled to Americans that Jenkins was ill and also that he was not dangerous. Beale's scoop mattered because, in the context of the discussion of the nature of Jenkins's transgression, it suggested that Hoover was aligning himself with the First Lady's narrative of Jenkins as recovering from nervous exhaustion. In early 1960s Washington, the sending of flowers to hospitalized friends and rivals alike was routinely done and sometimes publicized by the recipient. The previous week, Goldwater had sent former President Harry Truman flowers after he had a fall with a note saying "Get well. No campaign is worth the name without you."[46] Nor, of course, was Hoover unusual in having sent flowers to Jenkins.

From one tantalizing piece of independent evidence, we know that the bouquet from Hoover meant a great deal to Jenkins himself—and that people in the Johnsons' inner circle, including Abe Fortas, knew about it. A few days before Beale's column, Deke DeLoach memorialized an 11 a.m. meeting on Friday, October 16, with Fortas, who had just seen Jenkins in the hospital. Fortas reported that although Jenkins was still very distressed and "under heavy sedation," and indeed feels "he will never again be able to hold his head high in meeting people," he was feeling much better as a result of a phone call from President Johnson the night before and "the receipt of flowers from the Director with the Director's card on the flowers." According to DeLoach's memo, the card accompanying the flowers read "J. Edgar Hoover and Staff" and these were "the only flowers that Jenkins would allow to remain in his room."[47]

Beale protected the identity of her source. In a draft of her 1993 memoir, Beale suggested that someone got in touch with her to let her know about the flowers: "Somebody—I don't recall who—tipped me off." In the memoir as published, Beale's alleged lack of recollection was excised: "somebody tipped me off."[48] In theory, Marjorie Jenkins could have been the leaker; the column begins, after all, "Mrs. Walter Jenkins now believes that her husband will pull through," and Marjorie is the only person quoted by name describing the outpouring of support. (In Beale's tenth paragraph, a series of unnamed friends—"a Washington man," "a family friend from Texas," "a fellow Texan," "the wife of a Congressman," and "a Capital newsman"—each briefly praise Walter's character.)

It seems likelier that a third party, not Marjorie Jenkins, gave Beale the scoop, quite possibly someone in the White House. Many people in the White House would have seen the advantages of such a leak; given Liz Carpenter's closeness to Jenkins and her probable access to the information that Hoover had sent flowers, she seems a plausible candidate. The column was a major scoop for Beale and aided Jenkins by informing Americans that Hoover respected him. Probably no one benefited from it as much as Lyndon Johnson, for whom it was especially convenient that, since it appeared in a column devoted to "society" and "women's news," the White House press secretary and the president were unlikely to be pressed for comment on it. Beale would have known that the column would reinforce Lady Bird Johnson's framing of the Jenkins resignation and render the matter "women's news" and thus not something for George Reedy or Lyndon Johnson to address.

"We Are Having Problems with Mr. Hoover"

Once Beale's column appeared, the women who covered the First Family for the nation's two wire services each sought to confirm it. The AP's Frances Lewine called the hospital seeking confirmation of Beale's story. A similar message on another scrap of paper said, "Helen Thomas U.P. asking about Betty Beale's article." Both Lewine and Thomas, media scholar Maurine Beasley notes, had initially been assigned to meet the insatiable demand for news about Jacqueline Kennedy, but in time they "won the opportunity to cover the president as well as his wife." Both wire services soon ran their own stories confirming Beale's scoop. The front page of the *New York*

Post, then a liberal tabloid, screamed, "FBI Source: Hoover Did Send Flowers to Jenkins in Hospital." The *Washington Post* ran its own story about the sympathy of neighbors on the Jenkinses' street, including four who together sent Mrs. Jenkins "a large house plant."[49]

The story was tricky for Hoover: while his position in Washington was widely considered untouchable in part because of the many secrets he knew, he was notably sensitive about the subject of homosexuality. In the postwar decades, Hoover responded aggressively to the merest hint of speculation about his private life and "often tried to avoid the homosexual issue." "Upon hearing even the most idle gossip, he dispatched Bureau agents to interrogate the offending parties and trace the allegations to their origins," Beverly Gage observed, recounting several vivid instances. When Drew Pearson wrote that Republicans "don't seem to realize that Hoover has been in the same category with Jenkins for some years, only has been careful not to use the YMCA," he did so only in his diary—not his syndicated column.[50]

The reaction to Beale's scoop diverged sharply along partisan lines. At the Republican National Committee it was certainly unwelcome news. "As you can imagine," chairman Dean Burch wrote a supporter, "we are having problems with Mr. Hoover, especially with his report on the Jenkins case and the beautiful bouquet of flowers to the individual." Liberals and progressives by contrast warmly praised Hoover for his reported action. In the *Village Voice*, David McReynolds called it "the first and only human action I ever knew him to take." A law professor in Manhattan and a Unitarian Universalist pastor in Queens each wrote to praise Hoover.[51]

A few Republican-leaning press outlets offered relatively gentle criticism of Hoover for jeopardizing their evident hope that the Jenkins scandal would hurt LBJ electorally. William Loeb, conservative publisher of the influential *Manchester Union-Leader* in New Hampshire, expressed dismay that Hoover had endangered public confidence in the FBI. Ted Lewis, Washington columnist for the conservative *New York Daily News*, wrote that Hoover "has left himself open to criticism." Other conservatives defended Hoover's rectitude: one columnist even wrote that if *Hoover* were to come under suspicion, "then we might as well begin to suspect our children, our other relatives and our oldest friends of secretly plotting against us."[52]

Hoover found himself in an unusual position: he had certainly played no role in publicizing the story, but he could not deny its truth. Bureau spokespersons admitted that Hoover had sent the flowers but claimed he did so before Johnson ordered him to investigate the case—or even, somewhat less plausibly, before learning the reason for the hospitalization. Loeb released Hoover's reply telegram, which acknowledged the director had sent flowers but explained, "Neither I nor the florist issued instructions that my card, which read 'J. Edgar Hoover and Associates,' was to be prominently displayed or shown to everyone who came to Jenkins' room." Hoover included identical language in his replies to many other letters from the public about the flowers, both before and after the election.[53]

Across the country, the story about Hoover's flowers enraged conservative Republicans at the grassroots. A vast amount of angry mail poured into FBI headquarters. One compared the news to "finding out there is no Santa." Another wrote that "not since our cowardice in connection with Hungary, the Bay of Pigs, and the Berlin Wall, have I been so staggered." One writer enclosed Beale's column and noted, "The Washington 'socialites' may dismiss this sordid thing but that doesn't mean the rest of the country does."[54] A similar vocabulary permeated much of this correspondence: Hoover had undertaken a "whitewash," he had "condoned" deviant behavior, he had pinned a "medal" on Jenkins, the gesture was "maudlin," and presumably worst of all, the director's own reputation was now "tarnished." Several took a sarcastic tone: a letter suggested Hoover open a flower stand in the YMCA basement "to have handy a bouquet for every deviate arrested," and a telegram read "YOUR GIFT OF RED ROSES TO JENKINS VERY APPROPRIATE NOW HOW ABOUT A KISS."[55]

Some of the angry letters to Hoover denounced what they considered Hoover's implied support for medicalizing deviance. Americans "don't turn to perversion when we are exhausted," one wrote. To some, the action threatened the nation's moral standards: "any pervert or sexual deviate will be encouraged to display their avocation more publicly because if they are caught they will receive the accolades of our government leaders and may also receive an OSCAR."[56]

Others saw a more immediate consequence that might flow from it: "If Lyndon Johnson wins another four years you, Mr. Hoover, must share part of the blame."[57] The fact that the Hoover story limited Barry Goldwater's ability to benefit politically from the fall of Walter Jenkins clearly animated a significant proportion of the grassroots anger aimed at the director.

No critic was more vocal than Walter Judd, an ultraconservative former Republican congressman who had lost his seat to a Democrat in 1962. In an October 26 appearance in Minneapolis, Judd criticized Hoover in terms that vaguely hinted at his queerness. Judd declared that the bureau was "compromised" by Hoover's action and demanded to know if the bureau "is involved in such a way that it fears being hurt by some revelation Jenkins could make." Some wrote to the Minnesotan with gratitude; in the words of one woman, "our confidence in the FBI has been shaken for the first time in our lives." Another voiced "disbelief and literal horror" at what Hoover had done.[58]

Judd's attack was almost without precedent. "The unusual twist in the Walter Jenkins case," Irv Kupcinet observed in his syndicated column, "is that G-man J. Edgar Hoover now is coming under attack for one of the few times in his laudable career." The FBI responded forcefully. Clyde Tolson himself—Hoover's top deputy, with whom the director had long socialized and traveled in a de facto though unacknowledged spousal capacity—wrote to Judd denouncing his statement as, among other things, "evil-minded and base."[59]

Judd also received angry mail from a number of FBI agents. "I challenge you to show that in Mr. Hoover's lifetime, he has ever once given implied or actual approval of moral decay or in any way has approved of or sympathized with homosexuals," wrote one. Another said he had long "admired your forceful and knowledgeable exposure of communist duplicity," but Judd's latest remarks "must make the communists jump with glee." An FBI agent wrote to Judd that his question was "completely disgusting to me," and that "In asking such a question, you indict yourself." Another wrote that he does not believe "even one pervert has ever been a member of our organization." Judd seemed genuinely tortured by this angry response. He drafted and revised a detailed apology to DeLoach, in which he claimed to have been misconstrued, and mailed copies to many of those who wrote him.[60]

Hoover sent replies to nearly all mail he received about the flowers, whatever its tone—except if the writer articulated unorthodox views about sexuality. Thus, one letter praising Hoover's "simple beautiful gesture" did not receive a reply because the writer also stated, "I further think every human being possesses latent homosexuality." (On the letter, someone at the bureau handwrote, "no ack[nowledgment] because of views re homosexuality.") Further, the bureau punished reporters whose handling of the flowers story Hoover did not like. The day after the election, he ordered bureau staff to remove any critics of his gesture from the FBI's list of "special correspondents" perceived as friendly to the bureau and thus favored with leaks: "I want all persons on our mailing lists who have improperly construed the action I took in sending flowers to Jenkins removed."[61] The bureau's director had weathered a disconcerting episode. With Johnson reelected, he had an important ally in the White House—and one for whom he had done an important if inadvertent favor in the home stretch of the campaign.

"The Trouble Your Flowers to Me Caused"

Though a few people suggested he do so, Lyndon Johnson gave no Checkers speech in defense of Walter Jenkins. Since Senator Richard Nixon's nationally televised speech in 1952 defending himself against financial disclosures that imperiled his place on Dwight Eisenhower's presidential ticket, the name of Nixon's cocker spaniel—a gift to his children from supporters—had become shorthand for overcoming damaging news in a clever fashion. In the Jenkins case, however, American voters encountered potent defenses of Walter Jenkins, elaborating on the First Lady's support, in the testaments by the columnist William S. White and, as given voice by Betty Beale, the iconic FBI director himself. White and Beale were both creatures of Cold War Washington, traditional reporters who curried favor with politicians. They looked down on what they considered "snooping" and aggressive investigative methods.[62] Many other journalists followed their cues.

In an interview shortly after the election, Dean Burch, the Republican chairman, acknowledged that the Jenkins episode had not significantly affected its outcome. "As it turned out," he said, "because of the peculiar logic employed by William White and the accidental fact that J. Edgar Hoover sent flowers to Jenkins," any chance of Goldwater benefiting politically "was practically nullified."[63]

On election night, while Lyndon and Lady Bird Johnson gathered at the Driskill Hotel in Austin, Liz Carpenter attended a party at Katie Louchheim's Georgetown home. In her diary that night, Louchheim wrote that Carpenter had said to her that "the N.Y. analysts call Walter's malady a Samson syndrom [*sic*], a sub-conscious wish to destroy oneself completely, pull down the temple, etc." Later, she wrote, "Bill White and June came from seeing Walter Jenkins." They had spent some time with him in his hospital room and reported, "He was so happy to see the totals mount." A few weeks later, home from the hospital, Jenkins typed out a letter to Hoover. "Considering all the trouble your flowers to me caused you," he wrote, "the least I can do is to tell you of my deep and sincere gratitude."[64]

CHAPTER 6

THE MAIL

During his twenty-six days in George Washington University Hospital, Walter Jenkins became the focus of an extraordinary outpouring of letters. Hundreds of Americans wrote to him and his family. Some pieces were sent care of the White House, others to the hospital, and still others to the Jenkins home address. Items addressed to "Walter Jenkins, Washington, DC," found their way to him. Civil servants affirmed their high esteem for him, Catholics promised to pray a novena for his family, and Republicans praised his public service. Countless strangers wished his children well. Some confided private thoughts or even secrets. "Were it not for the fact that many eyes will no doubt read this letter before it reaches yours, I would not remain anonymous," one woman explained to Marjorie.[1] Amid the flood of sympathy and advice were also letters from gay men who saw something of themselves in Jenkins and his plight. He preserved this avalanche of mail along with carbon copies of his replies, most of which he wrote in the early months of 1965.

The torrent of letters Jenkins received in those weeks also illuminates the meaning that Americans gave to the stories they read and discussed. As the sociologist Ari Adut has observed, "scandals occur when publicity endows actual, apparent, or alleged transgressions with significant effects," and "the key to understanding scandal" is "the lived experience of its disruptions."[2] Read this way, the mail offers a window into how Americans in 1964 thought about sexuality and family life—an x-ray view of what was otherwise hidden. They addressed Jenkins less as a deviant than as a man in crisis, and in that role, many saw their own struggles reflected. "I write this note to you as one average American to another," explained a married woman in a Cleveland suburb, observing that everyone has at times acted "impulsively" or done something they regretted. "I know *I* have and I know I'm not alone, nor are you."[3]

In 1964, Americans saw Walter Jenkins as a family man facing a morals charge that had become shockingly public, not, in Robert Self's phrase, as a "rights-bearing member of a sexual minority."[4] The homophile movement, as it was then called, had yet to launch a sustained public challenge to the federal employment ban, an effort that would begin in earnest in 1965. Half a decade before "coming out of the closet," a concept that emerged only at the turn of the 1970s, most Americans assumed that the key question for Jenkins was how to repair and preserve his marriage and family, not whether he was a homosexual.

In a nation poised between conformity and liberation, Americans still looked to the marital household as a reliable framework for containing deviance and rehabilitating even men who strayed far from sexual norms. Many believed a stable marriage could absorb a man's same-sex tendencies—and many men with such tendencies hoped the same. A Long Island man wrote Jenkins that his own marriage had been strengthened after a morals arrest; "in spite of the fact that my wife had to appear with me three or four times in court, my marriage survived . . . not only survived, I would say, but grew into a union of greater happiness." Americans had accepted the message of postwar marriage experts, as Kristin Celello aptly summarized, that "with enough effort, any marriage could be saved, if not from unhappiness, then at least from divorce." One letter, set aside with a few others in a slim folder marked "Mean Letters," called Marjorie's predicament "very sad but *he is to blame* + he should never have married."[5] But this was the lone suggestion that the Jenkins marriage had been a mistake.

Again and again, Americans cast marriage itself as the crucial solvent. Staying married was a panacea. It was not only virtuous for a wife to stand by her husband; Marjorie herself was imagined as the one who could nurture Walter back to health. "In time," a friend assured her, "family, love, and care and medical assistance can mend the pieces into a whole, healthy, happy man, husband, father and citizen again." Some even looked ahead to the possibility that medicine might one day offer a more modern approach to Walter's problem. Postwar science had already conquered disease with antibiotics, eased parents' fears with the polio vaccine, and solved contraception with the Pill. In the words of a California woman, "Medical authorities are still working on the 'pill' for this." In the meantime, Jenkins's identity as a married father of six mitigated his deviance in the eyes of many. "If as they imply, you do have [a] suspect tendency," a Bronx man wrote Walter, "then thank God you at least tried to have a family."[6]

Back into the Sun: Marriage as Cure

Most Americans who wrote to Jenkins expressed concern for his health and wished him a speedy recovery. "I was slow in writing," a friend admitted, "but Mildred said you were deluged with mail." Of ninety-seven store-bought greeting cards with preprinted messages in the Jenkins hospital correspondence, nearly half (47) were get-well cards, like one whose senders urged him to follow the doctor's orders so that "soon you will be home fit as a fiddle." The rest offered religious blessings of various stripes (33), "thinking of you" sentiments (12), and sympathy cards (4), along with a single congratulations card, from a Washington couple unknown to Jenkins, saluting him for having such a "fine FBI report."[7]

Some correspondents, especially in Washington, may have shown kindness to the Jenkinses because he mattered to the president and First Lady, so that their offering support seemed politically prudent. The Democratic fundraiser and Washington socialite Katie Louchheim sent Jenkins flowers in the hospital even as she expressed disgust in her diary over Jenkins's behavior.[8] Yet many letters to Jenkins conveyed more than store-bought sentiment; they offered serious ideas and personal reflections.

In the immediate aftermath of the arrest, it was members of the Johnsons' official family, not Walter or Marjorie's blood relatives, who were on the scene to help. On October 18, four days after Walter entered the hospital, his secretary Mildred Stegall wrote to Walter's mother-in-law in Wichita Falls with updates on his condition—he was "improving every day" but "still very, very tired"—and enclosing paperwork related to renewing his Texas vehicle registration. (Later, Mrs. Whitehill traveled to Washington to help watch the children while the Jenkinses vacationed in the Caribbean.) Dorothy Nichols, a longtime Johnson aide, stayed at the Jenkins home with two other women to help Marjorie. "We'll stay here as long as we're needed," she told a reporter. "Then more will come." Neighbors offered practical help with meals and childcare.[9] Around them, others began to present recuperation as the means of restoring his public standing.

Correspondents with public relations experience understood intuitively that a narrative about the restoration of Jenkins's health was essential to salvaging his reputation. Charles Luckman, once chief executive of Pepsodent and Lever Brothers, wrote Jenkins, "The single most important thing is to regain your health. You will then find, if you have not already, that there will be no problem in maintaining the stature which you have built by doing so much for so many throughout the years." Luckman offered to speak to him on the phone or in person to discuss how he might be able to help. A South Carolina woman wrote Marjorie that "The important thing is that your husband will get the necessary help to rid him of the affliction."[10]

Americans understood that the Jenkins household was undergoing a process of being restored to normal conditions. They wanted to help. "I envy the people who took time to give you not only sympathy but also assistance in keeping your household operating smoothly," wrote one stranger to the couple. Sargent Shriver, the director of the

Peace Corps, wished that the Jenkins family "will all manage to find the courage to sustain you as a family during these first, most difficult weeks and months." Ben Bradlee, the editor of *Newsweek*, wrote Marjorie, "we pray for the strength and courage that will bring your family together back into the sun."[11]

Health and Household

The letters to Marjorie cast her as the essential agent of Walter's rehabilitation. One woman, acquainted through her husband with Walter but not Marjorie, urged, "Please remember that he needs you now more than ever before." A family friend on the Interstate Commerce Commission offered a long list of reassurances that culminated, "Compare your 'incident' to the sorrows of Mrs. Kennedy—either Rose or Jackie!" Others stressed that recovery depended on a steadfast spouse: "Over the years I have had two friends who had and survived catastrophes worse than Walter's. In both cases they did so only because their wives stood like rocks." Friends and acquaintances also held the Jenkinses up as a model household. "If and when Tom and I start a family, I hope that I can come up to my estimation of your success," wrote Carolyn Kellam Curtis, the daughter of KTBC's Jesse Kellam. A young Texan who had known the couple in Washington recalled that "your home was a genuine oasis to me and you were both an extremely stabilizing influence on me as the young adolescent that I was."[12]

Friends and strangers alike worried how the Jenkins children would weather the blow. "Louden Wainwright in the Oct. 30 issue of 'Life' mentions your six children. May I say that were my name Jenkins, I would have much to be proud of." A similar reassurance, focused on how his children would regard him: "I am sure your children, when the cruelties of others have ceased will, and probably do now, see their father as all children do—as a loving person and a dedicated public servant."[13]

People recognized that the widespread reporting on the scandal would make it difficult for Jenkins to move beyond it. One California man suggested that Walter "for your own convenience substitute your middle name (or compound one) in place of using your current first name." More commonly, those who wrote recognized that Jenkins would need to learn to live with stigma. "When the hubbub wears away with time," wrote a Massachusetts couple, "you will be faced with the problem of guessing people's reaction when you mention your name. We and millions like us will, if given the chance, extend a friendly hand and our best wishes for renewed success." In a similar vein, a student at Purdue University in Indiana wrote, "I'd be proud to have a fine American and his family for neighbors, such as you and yours, any day."[14]

One correspondent invoked the suicide of Senator Lester Hunt. Now a union organizer in California, this man had been in Washington "at the time of the Hunt case," he wrote, working for the National Education Association. "I recall Mrs. Agnes Meyer [the philanthropist and journalist whose husband Eugene had bought the *Washington Post* in 1933] referring to the senators now gone, thank God, as 'thugs.'" Now, he saw a similar turn of events in Republican efforts to exploit the Jenkins arrest: "Obviously we have not gotten free of thugs in the political field," he wrote, "something we should really work hard on, in the next few years, if any decency is to survive."[15]

In another notably thoughtful letter, a Protestant minister in Honolulu explained how his own view of homosexuality had changed. The impetus for the shift was the fact that "a young man who served as my organist took his own life some years ago. He was a splendid person and a true blessing to the church and humanity. It came out that he had suffered from the same, apparently, orientation emotionally as you had revealed in the recent publicity." This awareness led "some of us to inquire and do some reading," and as a result, the pastor wrote, "I do not hold the same point of view that I once did. . . . I do not ask you to change your natural self, but somehow so act as to keep hurt from those you love and who love you." The pastor had, in short, become aware that there were queer people hidden in his congregation and indeed on his staff. Jenkins, he asserted, might have a certain "orientation" that cannot or need not "change," but even if so, he could protect his wife and children from "hurt" by staying alive.[16] His goal was to discourage despair.

Of all the letters Jenkins received in the hospital, that of a thirty-four-year-old Barnard College alumna named Mab Ashforth Goldman stands out both as the longest—at 1,305 handwritten words—and for bluntly comparing Jenkins's sexual secrets to those of John F. Kennedy. "My husband is a Princeton man," she explained, "and we have had many close friends in common with the late President." Without using Kennedy's name, she noted that her husband had worked for his presidential campaign. "We knew of the failure to keep certain vows (which are given lip service today), certain failings that would have cost him dearly" had they become known. However much "we loved him" and "feel unequivocally that he deserves his place as a great hero," they knew, too, that "there are others who, armed with certain proofs, would not feel so." She added, "I do not for a moment, nor I think do most Americans believe Lyndon Johnson to be a truly honest man," and yet millions would vote for him because, as with Kennedy, "his ability outweighs his failures."

Goldman's letter offered a series of philosophical meditations on the theme that it was society's treatment of Jenkins, rather than his character, that was immoral. "It is the tragedy for you," she wrote perceptively, "that your 'failures' have been too graphically depicted for people to disregard them." She placed those so-called failures in context—"Though there is a natural revulsion, in most people, to homosexuality, nonetheless the world should know and remember that this tendency is world wide"—and associated it with "some of our great geniuses" and with "ancient Greece, which we applaud and revere." She emphasized the circular logic of the Lavender Scare: "yes you could have been" vulnerable to blackmail, "but only because of *our* conditioned thinking in those areas." Americans imagined themselves to be free yet were, in fact, "imprisoned by Calvin and the Puritans (not to mention others)." Jenkins wrote back with thanks for her generosity in writing him "at such length and so understandingly."[17]

Unblemished

Closer to home, longtime friends and colleagues struck a plainer note: undimmed loyalty, and a readiness to accept the account of a nervous collapse. "It was clear to me he was heading for a collapse, for a complete nervous breakdown," James Rowe, a New Deal veteran, wrote "Margie" on the night of Walter's resignation. "Now it has come. I hope only that it will be brief and temporary."[18]

Many promised that their friendship would not change despite the sudden change in his public standing. "I hope the events of the past few hours have no effect on our friendship"; "[I] have always been a Walter Jenkins man"; "Please know that we will always remain your friends." One friend wrote, "I know how bleak the future must look to him now, but both of you will come through this with colors flying because Walter and Marge are the same people they were yesterday with the faith, admiration and respect of the same friends." A former employee, on White House letterhead: "Last May I completed eleven years of working for you with an unblemished personal regard for you. Now here it is Oct. 21, 1964 and it's all the same—unblemished."[19]

Americans thanked Jenkins for his service. "Although I'm on the opposite side of the political fence (a Goldwater Republican)," wrote a Minnesotan, "I'd like to add my thanks for your 25 years of government service." A group of St. Louis residents circulated a petition praising his work. Another correspondent thanked him for "the enormous contribution which you have made to good government in America during the past twenty-five years."[20]

A chorus simply said they were "with you." "Your friends are still with you—so keep your chin up," urged Fred F. Smith, a veteran of the all-Black World War II regiment in which Jenkins was an officer and now president of the Urban League of New Haven. Variations piled up: "My heart is with you"; "millions of Americans are with you in your fight"; "Everybody's with you"; our family is "with you all the way." Strangers, too, hoped to "share with you in some way this great hurt." From Wichita Falls, a neighbor of Marjorie's parents wrote, "We are all 'pulling for you'—even a few Republicans."[21]

Others insisted that, whatever had happened, they did not care. Liz Carpenter wrote, likely on the morning after Jenkins was hospitalized, "I was so proud last night when the dozens of calls that came in were all—'*What can I do?*' Not, 'Is it true?'" Others echoed the sentiment: whatever occurred was "an insignificant detail"; "most people—and not only your friends—consider this much less important than you undoubtedly think they do"; or "events of the moment don't bother your friends one god damned bit!"[22]

Those less close to the Jenkinses sometimes imagined that this might not "have more than a passing effect on your career." More typical inside government was White House colleague Lee White: "Your present pack of trouble is pretty good-sized, I'll admit," he wrote, before adding the perhaps less than reassuring counterpoint that "the high regard in which all of us who have worked with you hold you is far greater."[23]

Male friends sometimes reached for familiar banter about seeing him once he recovered. An employee of the Democratic National Committee, saying his doctor had doubled his blood-pressure medicine, urged Jenkins to "get well fast" so they could play golf on an even basis after the election. Another friend told him to "discuss conditioning your shoulder for golf with your doctor" and hoped to "play a round before long." A colleague wrote, "I look forward to the first opportunity to get together and drink to the perdition of our enemies."[24]

Human fallibility was a constant refrain in letters to both Walter and Marjorie. "Walter, none of us are perfect," wrote a friend. "Please believe me that these things can happen in the best of us," wrote California governor Pat Brown. "We are all human and none of us is without faults," a friend told Marjorie. "In times of fatigue how many of us do things which later on we regret," a nun wrote her. Another friend added, "I am very certain that I do not know *one adult person* who doesn't have *something* in his or her life that he or she would really hate to see blown up in headlines."[25]

A single New Testament phrase recurred, one that cast Christian forgiveness as the proper response to sexual transgression. In the Gospel of John, as rendered in the King James Version, Jesus intervenes to spare a woman accused of adultery, admonishing her accusers: "He that is without sin among you, let him first cast a stone at her." The line was familiar to many not only from church or school but from popular culture; postwar Hollywood repeatedly recycled the episode in biblical epics. "Let he who wishes cast the first stone," William S. White wrote in the last paragraph of his column—a version that conveniently omitted the word "sin."[26]

The biblical injunction was elastic enough to accompany differing views of same-sex desire. It could serve as a reproach, as when a housewife in Woodside, Queens, wrote, "I don't approve of what you've done, but as our Lord said, 'Let the stone be thrown by the one who is without sin.'" It could also be stripped of the word sin and any hint of disapproval. "To recognize homosexuality as a syndrome that cannot be wished away is not to make a moral judgment either way," observed an Episcopal priest in a small Connecticut city, "but I can see no better reason for casting stones in this direction than in many other areas of human predilection." In his letter, he appended the phrase to a primarily medical view of homosexuality.[27]

Quite a few correspondents—especially Jenkins family members, hometown acquaintances, and those writing to Marjorie—said they simply did not believe the accusations. Marjorie's mother wrote that "no one believes a word about the scandal they are trying to capitalize on," adding that "even the Republicans say it is just a vote getting idea." A Wichita Falls friend close enough to have telephoned Marjorie insisted, "Bill and I do not believe it." Another hometown resident called it the "boldest lie . . . that could ever be imagined. No one here believed it except a very few queer thinkers." A woman in Norfolk told Marjorie, "I do not believe all of the awful things I've heard about your husband," while allowing that "a lot of evidence points out that he's guilty of certain things." A married woman in Kansas wrote, "I and many like myself, don't believe the charge against your husband," and, hedging slightly, "If the charge was true you would still have our sympathy and understanding, since it could only be caused from illness."[28]

Others reached for explanations. A Protestant minister listed nearly every possible excuse, including that "your previous arrest had occurred during the term of a republican [*sic*] president." An Iowa woman invoked the era's catchall bogeymen: "I have a strong conviction that your husband is a victim of organized crime in America, and, perhaps, Communism. . . . They seem to use sex a great deal in their work." A Californian who said he had been falsely accused by a policeman offered "heartfelt sympathy for the communistic activities attempting to destroy your good name." From New York, a man implied that ordinary domesticity itself acquitted him: "I feel your Honor nor any one else that has a comfortable Home + Etc would do it in Public."[29]

Many blamed the press for inflating a private matter. "You must also know, Marjorie," one friend wrote, "that the press & the news media have enlarged upon this tragedy far beyond what should have been; that the matter got unduly out of hand because of newsmongers." Strangers likewise called the coverage "unfair"; one said the general public "resents that this was made public and has only contempt for those immoral enough to permit its publication."[30]

Others stressed the disproportion between offense and punishment. Jerry Voorhis, the former congressman best known for losing to Richard Nixon in 1946, reflected on the special power of a morals charge to disgrace. "Even assuming that it is all true—which I do *not* assume—what it all adds up to is that you had *one* fault," he wrote in longhand on American Airlines "in flight" stationery, "and that it was the kind of fault which, for some reason, in our present society seems to be regarded as a frightful thing—and almost unforgivable. Society can be cruel." Strangers, too, were troubled. A woman wrote Jenkins from Toronto, "It is criminal that what you have done should be so dreadfully punished."[31]

A few framed the damage as unworthy of the nation. A Marianist priest argued that Republicans' willingness to "take away the good name of a man to use it for its political ends" harmed the nation's standing: "America humiliates itself before the nations of the world!" A Bronx man contrasted Marina Oswald, the widow of presidential assassin Lee Harvey Oswald—"coddled" and able to "live out her life in a comfort she could only dream about in her native Russia"—with Jenkins, who after twenty-five years of service was branded for "suspect" homosexual tendencies and told "to dig his early grave." Unusually for a letter to Marjorie, he also invoked Andy Choka: "What really was the crime these two men committed? . . . Human frailty—that's what his crime was."[32] Few minimized Walter's offense so bluntly, but the letter captured a wider sense that the punishment outstripped the act.

"I Walked in Your Shoes Once Myself"

A smaller but striking portion of the mail went further: This is my story, too. In the fall of 1964, the Jenkinses received letters from twenty Americans and one Canadian who saw in their ordeal a direct echo of their own. Among them were fourteen men who wrote about their own same-sex desire and described how morals arrests had ruptured their lives. "I walked in your shoes once myself," wrote a man from Alexandria, Virginia, "being also married with a growing family and a responsible job in the Federal Service only to have it blow up in my face following an arrest for disorderly conduct." Six women identified with Marjorie's experience—often humiliation, grief, or confusion in the face of a husband's behavior.[33] "I have experienced exactly what you are going through—a husband who was high in government, who lost everything because of disorderly charges," wrote a woman from Washington, DC. The correspondence arrived from across the United States—from greater Washington and New York City to California, the Midwest, and the South—with one letter from Canada.[34]

Taken together, these letters illuminate queer experience within mid-century marriages, unmediated by later recollection or the retrospective frames of the post-gay-liberation era. These contemporaneous first-person accounts, written with no judge or psychiatrist in mind, bear witness to the state's intrusion into private life. Notably, many came from men who remained married and may or may not later have embraced a gay identity. In this sense they complement queer oral history projects, which tend to feature those who did assume LGBTQ identities and, if married, "eventually divorced and began new lives."[35]

Men felt that Jenkins had endured a more public, more extreme version of their own nightmares. "I have had a problem much like yours, and solved it," a man typed on a postcard, without saying what the "solution" was. Mailed from Philadelphia and bearing a Flemish oil painting of the Flight into Egypt, it concluded: "My tragedy was only personal; yours is much greater and will take greater courage to face and solve, but it can be done. I hope you can do it. It will be the real test of your manhood." A Cleveland father of four counted himself among the "thousands" who "have lived your torture but who have had the good fortune to escape public notice." A man from Long Beach said he'd been falsely accused by a local police officer—"My conditions were identical to yours—YMCA and all"—and that he had "never committed an act of perversion in my life."[36]

Seven of the men explicitly indicated that they were married. From Tennessee, a Baptist minister wrote that until a year earlier he had led a large church: "Then there was a circumstance similar to yours in which I was relieved." From Arizona: "I was forced to resign my job with the Department of the Interior last July." From Canada: "I have a personal understanding of your problem." From New York State: "I, too, was in a similar position nine years ago this past February."[37] If any of the men had had any same-sex romantic relationships, they did not say so.

The writers did not experience the exposure of their deviance as an impetus to come out; they often remained in their marriages just as Jenkins did. Indeed, government policies encouraged men with same-sex desires to marry in part so that family life might keep such impulses in check, a pattern Lauren Gutterman has shown was also true for women. Courts, too, sometimes refused to grant divorces or alimony to wives who discovered their husbands' encounters with men, assuming that "marriage itself could cure them," as Alison Lefkovitz put it.[38] Postwar society pushed Americans into marriage, confident it was not only the foundation of social order but also the cure for personal failings.

An arrest was a crisis, hidden from wives if possible or, if not, concealed together from others outside the family. Men wrote to Jenkins about their own experiences of starting over with their wives and children after an arrest. A New Jersey man wrote, "Get a good psychiatrist, also be more religious, and discuss relocation with your wife and children, as you will get the 'cold shoulder' from many former very good friends." The Tennessee pastor, just over a year after his arrest, was no longer preaching full-time, but "I came back and have a small church and am teaching here in our high school." He said he was "happier than I have ever been" and that his wife and six children "are well adjusted to our new way of life."[39]

Married men arrested on disorderly charges had every reason, and in some ways more reasons than ever, to stay married. Marriage could be insulation from some of the worst potential consequences of arrest because officials and bystanders tended to sympathize with the collateral harm to dependent wives and children. Police, judges, bosses, journalists, and extended family frequently shared that instinct. And many men also felt genuine concern for their wives and children and wanted to spare them further suffering.[40]

Not everyone endorsed reform or concealment. "As one who also has your tendencies," a Staten Island man wrote, "I sympathize with you. It is very unfortunate that you were caught. I hope I never do [*sic*]." In his office, he said, the "men who talk about your case the most" are "all latent homosexuals, although they don't realize it." Thus, he cast himself as a homosexual—not a "latent" one. Though he appeared to see nothing wrong with cruising, he kept his sexuality from coworkers: "I'd love to tell them a thing or two about themselves but cannot give myself away."[41]

Standing in Marjorie's Place

Many readers—especially wives—saw themselves in Marjorie, even when their own crises involved infidelity or divorce. From a New Jersey suburb, a woman assured her, "It will be a rough road, but I am sure you must be a strong American woman who will be able to handle this newest problem. (I did.)" A woman in Kentucky wrote Walter that her family had faced "a similar experience," though in her case it "cost me my home, and my children's home for life." She hinted that her husband had left for another woman. She wrote, "my prayers for you have been answered—your wife is True Blue," a pointed contrast to her ex-husband, now living with his second wife.[42]

Some men recognized in Jenkins a familiar fight with compulsion. One, eleven years sober, wrote, "I myself have had the experience of misfortune and this misfortune was aided and corrected only through the wonderful friends and fellowship of Alcoholics Anonymous." Another recalled being "a compulsive gambler—it was the hardest task I ever had to give up this vice. Keep your chin up and don't ever give up."[43] They offered no theory of sexuality, but they connected queerness with other "sins" or addictions and gave straightforward testimony that change was possible.

A woman from an Appalachian steel town wrote Marjorie about the public disgrace that followed her husband's embezzlement conviction. A respected local lawyer, he began a one-to-ten-year term in a West Virginia state prison that year. The family lost everything, including their home. She and their daughter moved in with her sister across the Pennsylvania line; their son borrowed money to finish college. "Both love and adore him even though he brought this disgrace upon them," she stressed, and so did she herself. She pinned hope on parole after 365 days: "If parole is granted, we will begin again. I still love my husband very much and I am sure that he will once again be able to be a proper member of society."[44] Blindsided by his secrets, she chose to stand by him and rebuild their household.

Some men, too, said desire could be mastered. One man from Manhattan's Upper East Side wrote, "I eventually put myself in the care of a psychiatrist, and, after nine years of psychoanalysis, I can safely say that I have come through the ordeal rather well." A married man in Los Angeles County, a Catholic convert, credited a psychotherapist and the sacraments with helping him avoid acting on same-sex desire; he called "the so-called tendency to perversion" a "turning away from love to a counterfeit of love." A former federal employee in Alexandria recommended a self-help book called *Prayer Can Change Your Life* (1957).[45]

None of the correspondents faced the national glare the Jenkinses did, but a Connecticut woman had endured three times what she called "the hell of public exposure." The third time, she and her husband could not hide it from their two children. After years of struggling to adapt to her husband's risky behaviors, she added, she had chosen to separate from him, unlike the other wives who wrote. She offered Marjorie hope that the suffering need not be lasting. "My children seem strengthened, rather than broken, by the ordeal of their poor father's exposure," she wrote. "Their lives have not been warped; instead, their human sympathies seem to have been developed in a way that is deeply satisfying to me, their mother." She framed separation as compatible with steadfast mothering.[46]

Only one of the letters to Marjorie came from a writer who identified as homosexual: an Ohioan who praised her resolve. "A woman of your great strength to stand by her husband 'through sickness and death' certainly deserves recognition," the writer added, describing life as one of the "thousands of homosexuals in the U.S. alone" as a burden defined less by misery than by fear.[47] Of the fifteen writers who disclosed same-sex desire, this is the only one whose gender is not indicated; the rest were clearly men.

The novelist Charles Jackson—known for *The Lost Weekend* (1944), the bestseller that shaped modern understandings of alcoholism—knew this terrain. After his second novel, *The Fall of Valor* (1946), was published, strangers had written him about private marital crises rooted in same-sex desire. Jackson hinted only briefly at his own marriage and encounters: "I happen to know a good deal about these matters, from my own experience with people and with myself." Instead, he stressed his role as a writer: Jenkins might take comfort from "the hundreds of puzzled and disturbed letters I received from *both* husbands and wives after my novel 'The Fall of Valor.'"

Jackson did not suggest that Jenkins read *The Fall of Valor*, in which a couple's fading marriage cracks on a vacation to Nantucket when the husband, an English professor, becomes obsessed with a young Marine. It was just as well, given the novel's denouement; in a trope common in postwar gay fiction, the Marine kills the protagonist after he makes a sexual advance. Rather than invoke the plot, Jackson closed by reflecting on the letters: "my first reaction is always: such suffering and misunderstanding is always so unnecessary—and wasteful and wrong. There but for the grace of God go I—and I *was* there."[48]

Marjorie and Walter

Amid these vivid confessions the Jenkinses' own voices can seem distant. Of the clippings, prayers, and advice that reached him, one form of comfort stood out to Walter: Tucker Ashworth, an actor who had starred in a hit Broadway comedy for two years in the mid-1950s, copied by hand eight sentences from an 1883 Henry James letter to Grace Norton. The lines, Ashworth said, "help me when I am feeling bad—I hope they will help you." James had counseled his friend, struggling with depression: "Remember that every life is a special problem which is not yours but another's, and content yourself with the terrible algebra of your own. Don't melt too much into the universe, but be as solid and dense and fixed as you can." Jenkins thanked many well-wishers, but his reply to Ashworth was unusually effusive: "at the time I received your letter last Fall, in the hospital, and many times since, Henry James' letter written in 1883 has been most helpful to me; I know I shall re-read it many times in the future, and with great profit." It is one of the few moments when he hinted at his own suffering.[49]

Marjorie's voice is harder to hear. Only her early-1950s letters to Walter survive—likely from before her alcoholism worsened—and the FBI never interviewed her. Others described the strain to bureau agents: his relentless work for Lyndon Johnson, they said, left her lonely. The connection between their "afflictions" remains uncertain, but it seems possible that her drinking pushed Walter toward even longer hours. The report quotes two men—including Paul Popple, his close friend and White House colleague—saying she had a drinking problem. A third witness, LBJ's military attaché Howard L. Burris, described two occasions when she drank and cried. The most recent, on October 4, just three days before the arrest, was a small anniversary party at the Jenkins home. "Mrs. Jenkins cried at the party," the agents reported, "but stated that for the most part the nineteen years had been 'good.' She also commented that her husband worked all of the time and her only comfort was her religion and if she had not been a Catholic she might as well be divorced because she never saw her husband."[50]

One of the few places Marjorie's perspective appeared in print was Betty Beale's column, which was an effective salvage job in part because it fit the facts to mid-century marital norms. The opening words—"Mrs. Walter Jenkins now believes that her husband will pull through"—cast Marjorie as the supervisor of Walter's recovery, echoing postwar advice that made it a wife's duty to work on, improve, and save her marriage.[51] Beth Jenkins Bromberg later described her mother as status-conscious; perhaps Beale's framing offered her a sense of dignity. Marjorie's severe alcoholism progressed after the move back to Texas. The only written replies that survive to letters sent to her in 1964 are in Walter's hand.

"I Can't Hide My Head in the Sands"

On the one hand, the mail that poured into the Jenkins household in the fall of 1964 reaffirmed an older sexual ethic that made marriage the cornerstone of adult life.[52] Yet the very act of writing about such private troubles so openly marked a change: the Jenkins scandal had pulled these topics out of the shadows. People's responses displayed the familiar tension between sympathy and disgust that long accompanied debates over homosexuality; in this case, sympathy quickly prevailed. "There is much warm feeling and sincere centering on your speedy recovery," one friend assured Walter. Another woman, confronting a similar crisis in her own family, explained, "I can't hide my head in the sands."[53]

Taken together, the letters capture the "lived disruptions" of scandal that Adut describes. Freed at last from Lyndon Johnson's demand that his staff answer every letter on the day it arrived, Jenkins replied to most of his hospital mail in early spring 1965. By then he had news: "We are living in Austin now and are just moving today into our new home," he told a Wichita Falls friend on April 9.[54]

The mail clearly mattered to Jenkins, and soon it became part of the story told about him. He answered nearly all of it, skipping only anonymous notes and the handful of hostile ones; White House staff helped draft replies and also drew the volume of the mail to the Johnsons' attention. In the published edition of Lady Bird Johnson's *White House Diary* (1970), her entry for November 17, 1964 adds: "An interesting and heartening note is the barrage of mail he has received in the aftermath, much of it from the general public, which seems so understanding of a man who had, indeed, reached the end point of exhaustion." That sentence is absent from Lady Bird's contemporaneous audio recording and appears to have been inserted during manuscript preparation. Six years later, then, out of the same loyalty that marked her 1964 statement, she took a small liberty to be sure readers knew about the "barrage of mail." She understood that her words would shape how Americans remembered Jenkins—until, in another era, the letters were reopened and read.[55]

CHAPTER 7

LBJ'S LOSS

Walter Jenkins disappeared suddenly, silently, and permanently from the public eye. A name ubiquitous for decades in the official correspondence of Lyndon Baines Johnson, after October 14, 1964, was relegated to the White House "social file," the First Lady's files of holiday greetings, condolences, and official functions. He continued to correspond occasionally with staff, but often by routes that kept his name out of government records. For Johnson, the absence was both personal and political, removing from his side the aide he trusted most.

For the FBI, October 14 marked the start of a sweeping inquiry into every aspect of Jenkins's life. Its official purpose was to determine whether his actions posed a security risk. Johnson also pressed the bureau to learn exactly how the arrest had unfolded and whether political enemies were involved. The inquiry cleared Jenkins of any security violations. The FBI report crystallized the sexual politics of postwar Washington, revealing a world governed by the fear of exposure. The investigation also marked the moment when Johnson had to find his way for the first time without Jenkins at his side. Jenkins's departure altered the presidency he had helped run, depriving it of one of its steadiest figures—a loss Johnson could neither remedy nor publicly acknowledge.

This chapter traces the intertwined consequences of that rupture: an investigation and political aftershocks that forced Johnson to govern without his closest aide, and Jenkins's forging of a new life beyond Washington.

The Investigation

J. Edgar Hoover's handling of the Jenkins inquiry largely as a favor to Johnson reflected what his biographer Beverly Gage called "perhaps the greatest political alliance of his career." Jenkins and Deke DeLoach, both Catholic, often acted as go-betweens; on March 9, the two bosses and aides had lunched and swam at the White House. That summer, Hoover had, at Johnson's insistence, investigated the disappearance of three civil rights workers by infiltrating and sabotaging Mississippi's Ku Klux Klan; aided in the illegal wiretapping of Black activists in Atlantic City; and, in September, issued a pre-election report blaming summer riots in Harlem and elsewhere on "underlying economic and social conditions" while—unusually—ruling out any communist planning.[1]

Johnson, expecting the Jenkins report to clear his team, micromanaged the process, dictating interview lists to Nicholas Katzenbach, urging selective press leaks, and, ironically, insisting the only instruction was to "get equal and exact justice." He urged that the bureau question Jenkins about the Baker case during his hospital stay, a request Hoover overruled. He pressed DeLoach on October 20 to wrap up the inquiry: "When are we going to be able to say that there's no security involved here?"[2]

The final FBI report named seventy-two interviewees—including five senators, eight House members, and the First Lady—and noted that another 363 were questioned. Friends told Jenkins they had praised him to agents; his high school teacher Helen Grace Gould described "several sessions" with an FBI investigator. Agents interviewed Norman Heine about the 1949 morals arrest Jenkins had helped resolve.[3] The report confirmed that Jenkins's arrest, though sensational in its political impact, had been entirely routine in its circumstances. In the preceding six months, forty-four other men had been "picked up on morals charges" in the same restroom. Agents also examined why "Pervert" had been added in blue ink to Jenkins's 1959 arrest log entry, concluding it was standard procedure, and, as we have seen, determined that morals arrest records were routinely sanitized for outside access.[4]

The report confirmed that Jenkins had unrestricted access, in the words of National Security Adviser McGeorge Bundy, to "any and all data available in the White House" with "no restrictions whatsoever." Jenkins had attended eleven meetings of the National Security Council. The national-security review was brief; agents found little to investigate. As the report summarized, Jenkins "would rather die than be a conscious participant in the compromising of information," and no evidence suggested otherwise.[5] Johnson wanted Hoover to learn how Republicans and reporters had learned of Jenkins's arrest. Agents chased leads suggesting that Goldwater or the Republican National Committee might have played a role, but the trail proved fruitless, and the bureau eventually dropped the matter.

The Jenkins report listed ten men under the heading "Alleged Association With Other Persons With Possible Homosexual Tendencies," drawn from interviews in Texas and Washington. Several had seen their careers derailed by morals arrests, such as a Texas judge who withdrew from a statewide race after being "caught" with a young man. Jenkins told the FBI he had heard that this man, "who originally appeared to possess great promise and potential for future accomplishment," had been rumored to be involved in homosexual activity. Others were quietly barred from federal employment, as when a man Jenkins had recommended for a job was rejected because of a prior Lafayette Park arrest. The files also recorded evidence about gender nonconformity and hearsay with little effort to separate rumor from fact.[6] The purpose, more than probing Jenkins's sexuality, was to show that the bureau had pursued every lead.

Some cases involving these ten men ended without dismissal. One man had worked for Senator Eugene McCarthy and, like Jenkins, forfeited collateral after a tearoom arrest in 1963. He remained in his job, where no one learned of the arrest. Such an arrest record, however, was a sword of Damocles, likely curbing his career ambitions since any job application risked a background check that could bring it to light.[7] Federal agencies were inconsistently notified of arrests, even as hundreds of men were charged with morals offenses each year.[8] Like Jenkins's surviving correspondence with Norman Heine, the variety of outcomes described offers a rare picture of the range of ways men maneuvered through the Lavender Scare—resigning, changing careers, or avoiding detection altogether.

Another avenue of inquiry was to investigate Andy Choka, the man with whom Jenkins had been booked. FBI agents trying to locate him learned to their amazement that CBS had already flown him to New York for an exclusive interview in which he denied knowing Jenkins, said he was not entrapped, and offered to take a lie-detector test. The footage of that interview apparently never aired. A retired Army enlisted man on a veterans' disability pension, Choka had a record dating to 1948 for indecent exposure and related offenses, including a court-martial in France and later convictions in Pennsylvania. He told the FBI that his encounter with Jenkins was his only homosexual experience.[9]

At the Soldiers' Home in Washington, where he had been living, Choka was admitted to its hospital on October 16 as a psychiatric patient but was soon dismissed and moved to the Westminster Hotel. The manager of the Army and Navy Club, where he worked as a timekeeper, initially told *Time* he would be kept on if he continued showing up for work; within five days, he was out of a job. After the bureau released its report, Johnson asked DeLoach to have Choka reinterviewed about possible contacts with Dean Burch or another official of the Republican National Committee. By then Choka was living at another hotel under the name Andy Andrews and working under his real name at a store in Lanham, Maryland. He denied knowing the Republican leaders and volunteered that he had voted absentee for Johnson.[10]

FIGURE 7.1 Robert Waldron (*center, facing camera*) with (*from left*) unidentified woman, Marjorie Jenkins, and Walter Jenkins. Courtesy of Beth Jenkins Bromberg.

Only one other federal employee was discovered and let go as a result of the FBI's eight-day investigation. Bureau agents learned that Bob Waldron, a former 1960 campaign "advance man" for LBJ who remained close to the Johnsons, had had various same-sex liaisons, gay friends, and perhaps a roommate or two (see figure 7.1). Unlike Jenkins, Waldron was a bachelor whose marked effeminacy led many to assume he might be gay. The FBI report noted that "Mrs. JENKINS likes him much more than JENKINS does, inasmuch as WALDRON is an excellent dancer and is charming with the ladies." In 1964, Waldron was on the staff of J. J. "Jake" Pickle, the newly elected congressman from Johnson's former House district. Under questioning, Waldron admitted to "active homosexual activities" since "approximately 1959," though he said these were "limited to the privacy of his own residence." Pickle accepted his resignation on October 19. For Waldron, the discovery of his sexuality by the

FBI ended his federal career, but the matter was handled without public exposure.[11]

The FBI report stressed Jenkins's sexual indecipherability: no one interviewed had known, or had any inkling, that he had same-sex inclinations. Classified at the time, with only an eight-page summary released on October 22, the ninety-four-page report noted that no one who knew Jenkins suspected homosexual tendencies; Deke DeLoach was quoted saying he was "an above average golfer" who never displayed "sissy" mannerisms. Air Force colonel Howard L. Burris, a longtime friend, probably spoke for others close to him in lamenting that he had taken such a risk "so close to election day." Burris wished Jenkins had chosen "a private place where he would not have been detected" instead of the YMCA.[12]

As the FBI's short public summary neared completion, Johnson intervened to have references to Jenkins's sexual history removed. Acting on Johnson's behalf, lawyer Ed Weisl revised a draft that quoted Jenkins as saying he had "first participated in an act of homosexuality as a child" and had done so "on extremely rare occasions" on an adult. Weisl phoned Hoover to request that this be replaced with a statement that Jenkins did "not recall any further indecent acts" and, if any occurred, he would have been drunk or fatigued and unable to remember. Hoover noted that agents were "very definite" about Jenkins's admissions—including oral sex with Choka—but agreed to make the change. After confirming the wording with Weisl, Hoover inserted the sentence Johnson wanted.[13]

Despite the changes Weisl requested, Jenkins responded to the FBI's summary report with outrage over the details that remained. Released on October 22 and quickly picked up by wire services, the summary opened by stating the inquiry had "disclosed no information that Mr. Jenkins has compromised the security or interests of the United States in any manner." Yet it also asserted that Jenkins had admitted the "indecent acts" for which he was arrested in 1959 and 1964—a detail repeated in an 11 p.m. local news broadcast.[14] Around 11:30 p.m., Jenkins called the White House press room to have the release read to him, then vehemently objected to the sentence and threatened to hold a press conference disputing it.

That night, Abe Fortas was called in to calm an enraged Jenkins—"on the verge of a fit," Fortas wrote—who protested he had never said "this and that" before a psychiatrist arrived. Both men praised the bureau's "magnificent, compassionate job," the doctor sedated Jenkins, and Fortas went home. By morning, with the FBI report leading newscasts and unaware of Weisl's edits to the summary, Jenkins awoke furious again and prepared to call a press conference. Fortas hurried back. Further sedatives failed, and at 8:30 a.m. a nurse, on the psychiatrist's orders, administered "some sort of 'knock out' drug." Jenkins also phoned Deke DeLoach to denounce the report as false, claiming his psychiatrist urged him to make a statement. DeLoach cut him off, saying he "got off better than he was entitled to" and the bureau could have been "rough." Hoover asked Fortas to consider removing the hospital room's telephone and worried Bobby Baker might visit, perhaps to share in the praise Jenkins was receiving for his service.[15]

In his only written account of how he understood his arrest, Jenkins drafted—at least four times—a memorandum responding to the FBI's October 22 summary. He listed three objections. First, he disputed that he had "admitted having engaged in the indecent acts," explaining that in his sedated state he had said only that he did not know whether he had had sex with men in the YMCA toilet. Second, he rejected the claim that any such experiences had occurred after "extreme fatigue and imbibing in alcohol," insisting instead that he had "no recollection of such instances." To a modern queer reader, such denials may feel disappointing but understandable: a man whose secrets had been ripped from him might not willingly disclose whatever remained.

Jenkins's third and strongest objection concerned not the Choka incident but an implication about his work. The report stated that he had "limited association with some individuals who are alleged to be, or who admittedly are, sex deviates." In an early draft, Jenkins wrote, "I suppose this sentence could be said with truth about many employees of the United States Government," but he later deleted it. What remained was a formal protest: "I am particularly disturbed that a person reading this report in the future may be led to believe that I have knowingly associated with Government employees who, to my knowledge, are or were sex deviates." On the contrary, "in every instance where any file I received provided [a] basis for suspecting the applicant engaged in homosexual practices, I recommended against the appointment of the applicant." While Jenkins accepted his hospitalization and seclusion, in short, he rejected any suggestion that he had tolerated homosexual colleagues.

He made only one exception—Bob Waldron. In January 1964, an FBI background check had turned up allegations that Waldron had engaged in homosexual acts. Jenkins recalled that he "did not know, and I do not know at this time, whether he was or is in fact a homosexual," but nonetheless recommended against his appointment. Even so, "on a few occasions, I was present at social gatherings where this person was also present."[16] Waldron's continued presence in Johnson's circle was indeed striking; Bill Moyers, Luci Baines Johnson, and Beth Jenkins Bromberg all remembered him as the only "obvious" gay man in Johnson's orbit. That he resigned after Jenkins left was, of course, inevitable given what the FBI already knew; what is more surprising is that he was tolerated for so long, even at the height of the Lavender Scare. Johnson and DeLoach, eager to move on, brushed off Jenkins's complaint; DeLoach told the president he had "let him think" it was being added to the files—suggesting it was not.[17]

Six decades later, it may seem strange that Jenkins's sole formal response was to affirm his diligence in enforcing the very policies that destroyed his career. Yet few in 1964 wanted to be on record about same-sex acts. Even Frank Kameny, later a champion of coming out, had not yet told his own mother he was gay and would throughout his life avoid discussing his own two arrests in public restrooms.[18] In any case, if the FBI episode closed one file, it opened another one in the court of public opinion. Very few Americans shared Kameny's view of antigay policies as unjust discrimination. There was little reason to think those policies would be dismantled anytime soon.

Learning to Stay Silent

For a few days, Johnson believed he had managed to put the Jenkins affair behind him as a public controversy. The October 24 broadcast of his taped interview went off without a hitch. In private, though, he continued to lament the loss. To Robert McNamara he sighed that "Walter Jenkins is gone" and "he helped a lot." To Dick Goodwin he complained that no one around him knew how to craft news releases that would produce headlines. "Walter Jenkins knows how," Johnson observed, before abruptly ending the call: "But he's not here."[19] Though he lacked Lady Bird's expressiveness, the repeated mentions in his recorded phone calls make clear how intensely he felt the loss.

Needled by pro-Goldwater placards, Johnson inadvertently reopened the subject. On October 28 in Southern California, amid otherwise friendly crowds, demonstrators held signs declaring "Lyndon, Baker, Jenkins—our YMCA welcomes you" and "Immorality—the wages of sin is death."[20] At the San Diego airport, a reporter pressed him about Republican attacks on "the morality problem." Johnson answered that errant employees were dismissed and then, fatefully, added that Eisenhower had faced "the same type of problem" with his appointment secretary. "The only difference," he said, "is that we Democrats felt sorry for him and thought it was a case of sickness and disease and we didn't try to capitalize on a man's misfortune. So I never, we never mentioned it."[21] He was alluding to Arthur Vandenberg Jr., Eisenhower's would-be appointments secretary, who withdrew after an FBI check uncovered evidence of homosexuality—information never publicly reported at the time.

Headlines like "LBJ Says Ike Had Own Jenkins Case" quickly revived the scandal. Eisenhower denied any knowledge. Republicans seized the opening. Chastened, Johnson admitted to Clark Clifford, "We want it to die, and we don't want to revive it, and we don't want to be debating Walter Jenkins with them. And I guess the best thing to do is when they ask you is to say, 'no comment.'"[22] The San Diego episode made clear that, however deep his personal sense of loss, Johnson could never again speak of Jenkins in public. He was too likely to blurt out more than he meant, or to let his emotions show.

Johnson's landslide reelection only hardened his determination to keep Jenkins out of the news. A week later, a brief comment from Marjorie Jenkins to a reporter—"He is coming along just fine"—sent him into a fury. He asked Abe Fortas to warn Walter, "please don't make a five-column headline," adding, "If I were you, I'd cut off that phone some way." When Fortas pointed out it had been Marjorie, not Walter, who had spoken, Johnson snapped, "Maybe he can do something about that. Maybe he can cut off the phone." He instructed Fortas to drive home the point by invoking Bobby Baker's failure to settle Ralph Hill's lawsuit in 1963 after ignoring Jenkins's advice: "Just say, now, Bobby didn't listen to him, and if you don't, I can't help you. Just tell him that, that bluntly."[23]

Lady Bird Johnson, by contrast, treated the Jenkinses more gently. On November 17, a week after Walter returned home from the hospital, she visited the Jenkins family. "We talked about the office," she recorded in her audio diary, "and I told him very simply that no army of men could take his place." Speaking of the presidential election, Walter "said he felt like an anvil had been lifted from his chest when it was clear, about ten o'clock, that Lyndon had certainly won." They spoke about the children: the teenage Walter Jr. "was just being a model boy," while "the twins were still full of deviltry." She suggested the Jenkinses move to Austin, offering land on the Johnson ranch and the family's private accounting business. She concluded, "There is no estrangement between us three—none at all—but there is a complete understanding that everything has changed, or so it seems to me." The episode, she reflected, was "one of the two or three most painful things in my life—more painful than the death of many close to me."[24] Lyndon Johnson, meanwhile, remained fixated on the possibility of entrapment. In a 1969 oral history interview, he referred to the *Newsweek* party's waiters as possible Republican operatives. "The waiters they had there were waiters from the Republican National Committee," he said, referring to a possibility that the FBI had examined and rejected.[25]

Though official Washington was now largely closed to him, friends helped the Jenkinses. They spent Thanksgiving with Hobart and Lynette Taylor; Hobart, a Black lawyer and Johnson equal-employment adviser since 1961, had joined the White House staff that spring. A lobbyist took Jenkins to his first public meeting since "the doctor had strongly advised me to do some things like that." Marjorie's mother cared for the children while the couple traveled to Puerto Rico and Mexico. Work remained uncertain. On December 29, he declined an invitation because he had set up "a series of job interviews," adding that he and Marjorie were headed to Mexico City "to check out a thing or two." In New York in February, a University of Texas banker friend let him use his office and phones; he had cocktails with pollster Oliver Quayle and joined Eddie and Alice Weisl for drinks.[26]

The scandal ruptured and stigmatized the longtime friendship between the two men and their families, forcing elaborate steps to disguise their continued bond. The Johnsons hid their loyalty so well that outsiders assumed they had abandoned Jenkins. In January 1965, one of Walter's brothers wrote in outrage that the president had failed to "clear your good name" by telling the nation "this terrible thing is not true." Walter quickly responded, "I can assure you that the President has done everything possible to be helpful and will continue to do so." Even so, the appearance of estrangement hardened. Columnists Evans and Novak concluded in their 1966 biography that "Johnson resolved the conflict between friendship and the election by coming down on the side of the election." In reality, Johnson kept Jenkins on his payroll, still preparing the president's annual tax returns. And while Walter was dropped from KTBC's rolls, Marjorie remained on them.[27]

The Johnsons also found discreet ways to support the family financially. At Johnson's request, Mary Lasker, a wealthy Democratic donor and close friend of Lady Bird, sent Jenkins a generous Christmas check with a note explaining, "I know how expensive your illness must have been and want to send you this gift in order to help with the costs of it." Lasker, heir to her husband's advertising fortune, was a leading advocate for medical research and national health insurance and had championed the massive postwar expansion of federal research funding. She told Johnson she was glad he had suggested the gift. That same Christmas, Johnson's conservative Texas patron George Brown gave Walter and Marjorie $3,000 each. For the larger sum, however, Johnson turned not to a Texas loyalist but to Lasker—a liberal New Yorker, a woman, and a friend identified with Lady Bird. Money and discretion bought time, not a path back to Washington; for Jenkins, the next months were about starting over in Texas.[28]

Reinvention in Austin

Publicly, Marjorie assured reporters that her husband had many job offers, but in reality, prospects were limited. "I would like to see you stay in Washington," a friend wrote in January, noting that "the President has a 16 million majority to comfort him." Jenkins admitted that his closest friends were in the capital but added, "I have to make a living, though, you know, and know of nothing I can do in Washington without taking on assignments that I do not care to handle." He had no interest in becoming a Washington lobbyist, and "nothing else here has been offered me." Fortas told Johnson that his efforts to place Jenkins in banking or accounting posts were going nowhere: "it's not going to be easy, actually, to get the right thing underway for him."[29]

Other pressures also pointed the family toward Texas. Marjorie wanted to return to Texas; Lady Bird had urged it during her November 17 visit; and it may have been what Lyndon Johnson preferred—or what Jenkins believed best for himself. What is clear is that Jenkins found his private-sector options in Washington limited, and the move to Texas suited both personal needs and political calculations.

As inauguration week unfolded, Jenkins made a few low-profile appearances in friendly Washington settings. He skipped the swearing-in itself, watching it on television with Luther Holcomb, who remembered it as a sad moment. Soon afterward, however,

Jenkins appeared at the Texas State Society's biweekly breakfast, where some sixty men greeted him with a standing ovation, and with Marjorie at a party for inaugural committee chairman Dale Miller—what Betty Beale called "their first Washington appearance" since his resignation.[30]

Meanwhile, the press turned his next move into a guessing game. The Associated Press first reported he was moving to Austin, then that he was not. A syndicated column claimed the "inside word around the White House" was that he had a "good-paying job" lined up there, raising unanswered "questions" about whether it would be at KTBC. The same column pointed to the Jenkinses' vacation in Puerto Rico and their "rested and hale appearance" at inauguration parties—evidence, it suggested, that he was fit to testify in the Bobby Baker probe, which Senate Democrats had stalled. The *Austin American-Statesman* ran a front-page story that his twin sons had been placed in school in the city. By mid-March, the *Houston Post* confidently reported that Jenkins himself was living in an Austin apartment.[31]

Some coverage slipped into sensational insinuation. When Walt Jenkins Jr.'s car broke down on the road between Washington and Baltimore in January, police traced the abandoned vehicle to the LBJ Company—a holding company for family assets—and found a gas receipt in the glove compartment bearing Walter Jenkins's credit card. Syndicated columnists Robert Allen and Paul Scott pounced on the "mystery," claiming Senate Rules Committee members intended to question Jenkins about it. Half a century later, Walt vividly recalled his father showing him the article: "It's all innuendo, all suggestive: It's *Jenkins's* car. What was the *Jenkins* car doing abandoned on the Baltimore-Washington expressway in the dark of night? That kind of phraseology."[32]

Walter's departure from Washington was delayed until March by the continuing Baker investigation. Although the Jenkinses' longtime housekeeper left her job around January, through late January and early February Jenkins remained in Washington while the Senate Rules Committee debated whether to compel his testimony. The

Democratic-controlled committee ultimately issued a subpoena, but Leon Yochelson, a psychiatrist at George Washington University who had treated Jenkins, appeared in his place, warning that Jenkins's health—and perhaps even his life—would be in jeopardy if forced to appear. Jenkins's attorney, Peyton Ford, also spoke, insisting that his client very much wished to testify but was prevented by his doctor's strong objection.[33]

Ultimately, the Rules Committee allowed written answers instead. In his forty responses, Jenkins acknowledged arranging for the LBJ Company to buy a life insurance policy from Don Reynolds and perhaps alerting Reynolds that a competitor sought to purchase KTBC ad time, but insisted, "Certainly I did not 'pressure' him to do so." Years later, Nebraska Republican Carl T. Curtis, who had led the push for a subpoena, still bristled at the party-line vote that spared Jenkins an appearance: "We could never get Walter Jenkins' testimony, contrary to the way that things went in the Watergate investigation."[34] If sympathy for Jenkins played a part, the larger reason was Johnson's dominance in 1965: Democrats had no interest in pursuing any inquiry that might embarrass the president at the height of his power.

By February, the Jenkinses had begun building a new life in Austin, renting an apartment and enrolling the twins in school there. Walter wrote to friends that he had "pretty well made up my mind what I am going to do in the future" and was "in reasonably good shape now and ready to get back to a productive career." As a step toward establishing a career as a business consultant, he opened an office in the Brown Building—constructed in 1938 by Johnson's patrons George R. and Herman Brown—and took short-term work with Texas firms in Johnson-friendly sectors such as aviation. Marjorie remained on the KTBC payroll, earning $4,800 in 1965. "They came in under the shelter of the Johnson family," recalled one Austin friend. George Bristol, who later joined Jenkins's consulting business, put it similarly: "I don't know whether they actively thought about it, but they drew up a protective cocoon around Walter and Marge and the family."[35]

Jenkins likely used Mary Lasker's gift to buy a new house, a large 1932 Tudor historic house in Austin's Old Enfield district, a prestigious, affluent, and secluded neighborhood just west of downtown. The family moved in on April 9, and he wrote a Dallas friend the same day: "We have a big house now, so come and see us." Ten days later, as his children's spring break ended, he wrote his brother Bill, "I bought a small boat Saturday morning, and we spent all afternoon Saturday and all day Sunday water skiing on Lake Austin. I think the Noxzema Co. is going to declare a dividend based on the amount everybody had to use last night before we could stop itching and burning from the sun." A month after that he wrote friends, "One of the great pleasures of the last few months has been getting to know my children."[36]

Yet Austin's welcome was tenuous. Days before the Jenkinses moved into their new house, Walter received a blunt reminder of how difficult rebuilding his life might be. The manager of the Austin Club, a downtown businessmen's club, sent him a curt note: "I am directed to inform you that it would be best that you not accept any invitations to this club. Your compliance will save great embarrassment to you, your prospective host and the club." Whatever prompted the message, the banishment proved short-lived; later that year he accepted at least one dinner invitation there. Still, the sting of exclusion must have been hard to shake.[37]

Out of sight, Lady Bird Johnson kept tending to the family. In July she invited Walter, Marjorie, and three of their children—John, Joe, and Lyndon—to dinner at the Haywood Ranch, a lakefront retreat the Johnsons had purchased in 1963. Located twenty-five miles north of the LBJ Ranch, the Haywood afforded greater privacy; the First Lady even arrived by helicopter. "Bird, it was good to see you and the children on Sunday," Marjorie wrote afterward. "I hope the day will come when we can see you both more often." As Julia Sweig has noted, Lady Bird "continued to feel responsible for their happiness," recording in her diary that she was pleased to hear they had found "acceptance" in Austin despite "some hold-backs, some little slurs." Walt Jr., who was sixteen in 1964 and attending a military school in Baltimore, recalls being bullied by a classmate: "Your dad's a queer, he's a fag."[38]

Early on, Jenkins pieced together work through small, opportunistic consulting assignments, mostly in Texas- and Johnson-linked fields where federal regulation mattered. For Struthers Wells, he contacted the incoming assistant secretary of the interior for mineral resources. For the Stephen-Leedom Carpet Company, he wrote oilman and rancher Perry Bass about carpeting a new office building; Bass declined but encouraged him to "keep swinging!" And at the request of his friend David Cunningham, the New York investment banker who had lent him office space, Jenkins approached KTBC station manager Jesse Kellam about a possible deal.[39]

By the standards of men dismissed after morals arrests, Jenkins was the exception, buffered by resources others lacked. He retained the loyalty of the First Lady, the discreet backing of Johnson's political network, and the modest but steady income Marjorie continued to draw from KTBC. Powerful friends lined up consulting work and even provided cash gifts—help unimaginable for most working- or middle-class men in his position. For them, a morals arrest might mean not only public exposure in the local paper but immediate job loss and no path back to respectable employment. Jenkins's notoriety and his exile from Washington were real, but his safety net was one most could only dream of.

Within a year, Jenkins reemerged not just as a consultant but as an employer, launching Walter Jenkins & Associates and hiring his first associate, George Bristol. Then in his twenties, Bristol had first met Jenkins while working for Congressman Homer Thornberry and, after Thornberry's 1963 appointment to the federal bench, his successor Jake Pickle. Back in Texas, Bristol received a call from Pickle urging him to consider working for Jenkins. He hesitated, mindful of the stigma of Jenkins's arrest and resignation, until, a few days later, the president and First Lady phoned to encourage him. "Based on my relationship with Jake and my respect for him, I probably would have gone to see Walter anyway," Bristol recalled, "but it damn sure didn't hurt when you hear from the president and the First Lady."[40]

In Austin, Jenkins occupied a place of civic esteem shadowed by lingering, sometimes pointed, slights. The "little slurs" Lady Bird Johnson had noted never entirely disappeared. George Bristol recalled that Jenkins once showed him the Austin Club's exclusion letter so he would be prepared if something similar happened. "I was frankly madder about it than I think Walter was," Bristol said, adding that he himself preferred the rival Headliners Club. On rare occasions the insults were open: "I forget where we were—at a nightclub or something—and the comedian made some really off-putting slur against Walter. He knew he was in the audience. . . . I just got up and walked out." Yet not every outing carried that risk. Bristol remembered dining with Jenkins at the Nighthawk, a restaurant on the Colorado River just south of the Congress Avenue Bridge, where owner and mayor Harry Aiken would "always come over to Walter's table and say hello." The prospect of a snub hovered, but Jenkins still commanded the respect of Austin's civic leaders—at once a pariah and a friend of the president.[41]

Visible proximity to the president remained off-limits, even as private ties persisted. Johnson never appeared publicly with Jenkins. Direct contact between the families was carefully limited: in 1964 there were only holiday phone calls; in June 1965, the lone public sighting came when Beth Jenkins, home for the summer from her first year at Marquette University, flew with the Johnsons on Air Force One to Washington and then by helicopter to the White House.[42]

The Jenkinses' friendship with Bob Waldron continued. Around the inauguration they saw each other at a gathering at the home of White House aides Jack and Mary Margaret Valenti. Living in different cities, they kept up a friendly, occasional exchange. Waldron enrolled in the New York School of Design to study interior decoration. He wrote Jenkins that he loved school and his new life, joking, "I realize now what little I knew about decorating," describing museum visits and a project building bookshelves for his apartment. In late 1966 he sent Marjorie Jenkins a fabric sample for a sofa. Like Jenkins, Waldron remained in the Johnsons' good graces; in the year before LBJ's death, they hired him to decorate a room at the

LBJ Ranch, a job he recalled with great pleasure. Waldron died of AIDS in 1995.[43]

By 1966, Jenkins pushed into cable television—a small but rapidly growing and highly profitable industry—with a new venture, Commco. He tapped his nephew Jay O'Neal to help run it, a job that meant courting local officials across Texas for permits to lay cable. O'Neal, a star quarterback on Oklahoma's 1955 and 1956 national championship teams and, by 1964, one of the program's top recruiters, fit the role. "Jay was a perfect one," Bristol recalled. "In that good old boy network of football in Texas, Jay O'Neal was welcomed, and he did a good job."[44]

Jenkins still did work for the Johnsons, but only at a remove. On a commercial flight to Dallas, Walter and Marjorie, startled to find Lady Bird aboard, waved and hurried on to coach. "Walter sadly did not attend" many public events, Bristol recalled. "He knew to keep his head down." Bristol also remembered Jenkins speaking with the president by phone "on a few occasions," always behind closed doors; he never knew what they discussed. Each spring, Jenkins and Mildred Stegall prepared the Johnsons' tax returns together in his Brown Building office, sandwiches on hand and papers everywhere. The families exchanged Christmas cards and birthday presents, but his name was effectively erased from the administration's public record. Even so, in 1967, publisher S. I. Newhouse approached Jenkins for help getting Lady Bird to speak at a *Vogue* event.[45]

Family milestones tested—and enforced—the distance between the Johnsons and the Jenkinses. In 1966, each man's daughter served as a bridesmaid in the other's wedding, but both fathers stayed away from the other's ceremony to avoid the spectacle of appearing together. Beth Jenkins's engagement that February was treated as White House news: Helen Thomas, writing on White House letterhead, apologized for publishing the story before reaching the family for comment. Walter's absence from Luci Baines Johnson's August 1966 wedding underscored the caution that still governed his public life. Watching the nationally televised ceremony from his office, Bristol recalled, "Walter knew the girls from the time they were born. He was very fond of 'em. And he couldn't even go to the wedding." In his view, "nobody in the crowd would have said anything if he were there, but some reporter could have." After Beth's wedding at year's end, Lady Bird wrote the Jenkinses that what she enjoyed "most of all" was that "every member of the Jenkins family looked healthy and just great."[46]

Late in 1966 he allowed himself a small loosening of discretion, leaving a paper record of his continuing ties to Johnson. Perhaps reassured that Luci's wedding had passed without adverse press, he wrote to Eisenhower's former ambassador to Mexico—an acquaintance from earlier years—on behalf of the LBJ Ranch: "The LBJ Ranch will be happy to sell you the animals you want. They will sell you three heifers for $275 each and a young bull for about $500." After a few more details, he noted, "These prices are on-the-hoof at the LBJ Ranch and you will have to make whatever arrangements you wish to make for transportation."[47]

Losing his government post made Jenkins a better breadwinner, thanks to his connections in the private sector: by 1966 he and Marjorie reported taxable income nearly triple their 1964 total and more than quadruple the 1963 amount. Among his new clients was Jim Novy, a leader in Austin's Jewish community and Johnson ally whose scrap-metal business faced complications from a congressional bill that Jenkins and George Bristol worked to explain to the Texas delegation. The couple soon organized an investment club, named for their street, Cromwell, which pooled funds from members including Luci and Pat Nugent, recently relocated from Washington, and Jay O'Neal. In 1968, as the Vietnam War escalated and the federal government requisitioned commercial passenger jets to fly men across the Pacific, they helped a Florida company, Modern Air, win bids on routes left vacant by the major carriers.[48]

The Vacuum at the White House

As Jenkins rebuilt a life in Austin, the West Wing had to cope with the hole he left. When Johnson asked Abe Fortas on October 14 to gauge the impact of Jenkins's resignation, Fortas cast it as a national loss: "In the first place it deprives the public of a great public servant."[49] How that loss altered the presidency's course is impossible to prove, since any one counterfactual cannot be disentangled from the many other forces shaping the administration. Even so, we can trace concrete ways his absence affected Johnson himself and those who worked around him.

Day-to-day operations showed the strain immediately. Mail was triaged, handoffs were messy, and several aides tried to cover the work of one. Staff who had already scrambled to keep the executive branch moving after November 22, 1963, were forced to improvise anew. Others took over answering Jenkins's office mail. "Walter had left instructions on who he wanted to handle this matter, and I have taken care of it," one claimed, though Jenkins had left no such instructions. Columnists Rowland Evans and Robert Novak observed that his departure "enlarged a vacuum that already existed" and that Johnson, "always loath to delegate power, has no ready reservoir of talent to fill it." Bill Moyers, then just thirty, moved into Jenkins's office and assumed some of his duties, but as Evans and Novak noted, Jenkins "was doing the jobs of two or three men."[50]

Johnson reassigned key functions. Marvin Watson, a Texas businessman whose politics were more conservative than most of the staff, assumed much of the managerial authority Jenkins had wielded. While Bill Moyers and Jack Valenti each took on pieces of Jenkins's portfolio, Watson's hiring in February 1965 as appointments secretary marked a turning point, launching "a process of reconsolidating management functions in a single aide." With between 250 and 275 staffers on hand at any given time, Watson became the White House's de facto "chief of management service," overseeing the president's calendar, travel, and "White House service operations." John Macy, chairman of the Civil Service Commission, assumed another of Jenkins's key roles after 1964, serving as "talent scout" for executive-branch personnel.[51] Beginning in 1965, Jenkins wrote Macy frequently to suggest potential appointees.

What no reassignment could replicate was Jenkins's decades-long knowledge of Johnson's personal networks and the access that sustained them. As historian Julian Zelizer has noted, "personal networks, contingency, and human agency" are central to state building. Those networks ultimately depend on staff who keep them running and help elected officials manage an ever-shifting web of relationships. In the White House, that work rests on intimacy with the president. "The only thing that counts where a White House assistant is concerned is his closeness to the president," George Reedy observed—and no one matched the closeness Jenkins provided. "He lost the most valuable man on his team," Bill Moyers recalled bluntly.[52]

The clearest early cost fell on a progressive tax policy: an ambitious revenue-sharing plan that unraveled without Jenkins's coordination. Walter Heller, chairman of the Council of Economic Advisers, said Jenkins's absence doomed an initiative to share surplus federal tax revenues with the states, which would have effectively boosted spending levels beyond what the House Budget Committee would approve. Heller had discussed the idea with Jenkins, who assured him Johnson supported it. But when Heller sought White House guidance before talking to a *New York Times* reporter, Jenkins was gone. The resulting lack of coordination, Heller later said, led him to disclose the plan prematurely in what became a front-page scoop. Labor leaders, blindsided and convinced their power was greater in Washington than in the fifty state capitals, quickly opposed it. "He never let me forget—either through third parties and occasionally in mild personal reproofs—my 'mishandling' of this," Heller recalled, quoting Johnson as calling it "a perfect example of how not to get a policy adopted." Heller concluded that consulting Jenkins would have prevented the fiasco.[53]

From the outside, veterans judged the operation wobbly, increasingly slow to answer and hard to reach. James Rowe wrote to Jenkins, "All of us who have had to deal with the White House these days feel it is a shambles since you left." He added, "I do not say this to flatter you, but because no one outside the White House seems to be able to get an answer on anything and we all feel it necessary to talk to everyone on the staff in the hope that someone may possibly get some kind of an answer."[54] Insiders who had once simply telephoned Jenkins now no longer knew how to convey their messages, or their needs, to President Johnson.

Inside the West Wing, the loss was acknowledged obliquely, in euphemism and silence. When staffers referred to Jenkins at all, they adopted the overwork or nervous exhaustion framing. Harry McPherson, who joined in 1965, recalled his doctor attributing Jenkins's behavior to stress and urging him to address health problems promptly lest he meet a similar fate.[55] Silence did not mean forgetting, however: many remained perplexed by Jenkins's disappearance. "The story had some rather peculiar aspects, it seemed to me," recalled George Reedy, who said that "to this day I'm not sure" whether he believed the charges.[56] Bill Moyers likewise noted, "I didn't hear anyone in the inner circle even mention the word 'homosexual,'" though he continued to wonder whether someone would come forward with more information about Jenkins.[57]

Outside the White House, his absence resurfaced in stray headlines.[58] By 1966, when Jenkins appeared in the mainstream press, his name evoked lost ease amid the administration's mounting troubles. After that year's midterm elections, syndicated columnist Ruth Montgomery noted that Democratic congressmen were having trouble "picking up the phone and getting the immediate ear of someone in authority at the White House," a "far cry from the days when Walter Jenkins, Johnson's longtime chief assistant, virtually lived with telephone-in-hand, providing instant access to the White House." The resulting "communications gap," she wrote, only deepened the "credibility gap" over Vietnam. Willie Day Taylor, the Johnsons' housekeeper, sent Jenkins the column; so did Congressman Jake Pickle.[59]

Even the White House's memory faltered: Jenkins's shorthand left key records effectively encrypted. Three years after his resignation, Johnson covertly asked him to recover the verbatim record of one of his presidency's most consequential meetings. On August 4, 1964, in the Cabinet Room, Johnson met congressional leaders about an alleged North Vietnamese attack on the USS *Maddox*. On the strength of that session, Congress passed the Gulf of Tonkin Resolution authorizing military force.[60]

Jenkins had been in the room, taking rapid shorthand only he could fully decipher. He later typed a summary and filed the verbatim transcript in his original shorthand. Mildred Stegall, his longtime secretary, knew some of his deviations from standard Gregg shorthand; in practice, his notes functioned like an informal private encryption system. Once he was gone, the White House had difficulty retrieving the exact words spoken.

The weakness surfaced in late summer 1967. As opposition to the Vietnam War mounted and legislators charged that Johnson had misled them about the Tonkin incident, Stegall tried to reconstruct Jenkins's notes but could not make out a crucial passage concerning Senate Majority Leader Mike Mansfield's views. Jenkins's 1964 summary said that "Mansfield read a paper expressing general opposition," without specifics, so staff arranged to show Jenkins the originals discreetly when he was next in Washington.[61]

Only he could unlock these notes—and what he restored mattered. Four days later, working with Stegall, he produced a fuller transcript. "There are a few places even my friend could not read," she wrote, "but we have done the best we could." Newly restored were Mansfield's warnings that a response could mean "getting involved in a third rate country" and that "The communists won't be faced down easily. . . . it will take a lot of lives to mow them down." Facing mounting congressional criticism, Johnson told Stegall, "Put that on my desk—I'll need it every day."[62]

By 1967, Johnson was battling Mansfield and other leaders who had once relied on Jenkins as their line into the White House. For three years he had lacked the full record of what they all said in that room. After a discreet consultation, he finally had it—but not the intermediary who had managed those relationships day to day. As Jenkins rebuilt a life in Austin, the costs of his absence in Washington kept accruing.

After the Presidency

As Johnson's term wound down, a theory took hold among some aides that the loss of Jenkins had set the presidency on a downward path. From the moment Jenkins resigned, contact between him and the president grew murky; of the White House staff, Mildred Stegall appears to be the one who stayed in close touch. "I don't know myself what relations the president had with him after that," said George Reedy in December 1968, adding that "it would be an extremely difficult thing for the President to be cut off from Walter Jenkins, because Walter was quite integral to his whole—almost integral to his life." Vicky McCammon, a White House secretary well placed to know, was likewise unsure: "Whether there were any personal conversations between the two of them, I don't know." Clark Clifford, who had advised Johnson during the crisis, could not recall ever speaking to the president again about it.[63]

Inside the West Wing, official silence still prevailed. After the 1968 election, as staff organized presidential records, the lid on discussing Jenkins stayed firmly in place. Joseph Califano asked White House counsel Larry Temple to "collect all background materials" on the 1964 Jenkins resignation and the failed 1968 nomination of Fortas as chief justice. Instead of a formal reply, Temple scrawled on the memo that there were "no papers in Central Files re Jenkins" and noted that he and Califano's aide had agreed to "forget this project." (In fact, thousands of pages in the White House Central Files concern Jenkins's departure.)[64]

Outside that guarded silence, the perception of Jenkins's departure as a turning point appeared in interviews and oral histories, as allies and critics alike traced Johnson's troubles to Jenkins's exit. Reedy, no longer on good terms with Johnson, told an oral history interviewer in December 1968, "I've often thought that a great deal of the president's difficulties in the White House can be traced to the fact that Walter had to leave," confessing to "an odd little feeling that all of history might have been different if it hadn't been for that episode." Hobart Taylor Jr. echoed the point: "The greatest loss to the Johnson administration was the loss of Walter Jenkins, who actually did the work of the president, you might say," adding, "I think his problems really date from that time."[65]

The theory spread far enough that the LBJ Library's first oral history director, Joe Frantz, began testing it directly in interviews. In mid-1969 he asked Mary Margaret Valenti whether the White House had "lost some effectiveness when Walter quit." "Yes," she replied, "I think the loss of Walter was a great blow to him and to the administration of his staff. . . . I think the staff lost a great deal of efficiency." In 1972 Frantz put a similar question to Texas journalist and sometime LBJ antagonist Sarah McClendon: did "part of Johnson's problems" begin when he no longer had Walter running the staff? McClendon cautioned that "that is a thing that is easy for a person to say," but still partly agreed: Johnson had problems before, "but Walter could surely iron out a lot of those problems."[66] Whether or not Jenkins's departure truly marked the decisive break, his absence was one of the few losses that Johnson's aides could name—years later—as having measurably diminished the presidency.

Once Johnson opted not to run again in 1968, he spoke openly with staff about reuniting with Jenkins. Vicky McKammon recalled, "The president used to say that the first thing that he was going to do and that he looked forward to whenever he left the White House was to go find Walter Jenkins and throw his arms around him and hug him, because he was the one man on earth that he loved." Joseph Califano likewise remembered Johnson saying there were "two things he was going to do" upon leaving office: "He was going to start smoking again, and he was going to throw his arms around Walter Jenkins and hug him." According to Califano, Johnson did both, lighting his first cigarette on the plane and greeting Jenkins at the airport in Texas.[67]

Out of office, Johnson could see Jenkins openly, and the old blend of friendship and business resumed. Free of White House optics, he socialized with the Jenkins family without fear of political fallout. Jenkins continued to handle the Johnsons' tax returns and accounting. In a 1971 letter to Mildred Stegall he wrote, "When I was out at the ranch the other night, I told Mr. Johnson about George Lusk's tax shelter project. He expressed interest in it and asked me to send him material on it. That material is enclosed. Perhaps you will want to get it out to him and let me know the reaction."[68]

Without the press glare, the Jenkins family could visit the LBJ Ranch without worry. "We always stayed in the first guest house down the way," Beth recalled. Walt Jr. remembered watching Johnson play with his grandson Lyn and being "pretty stern with that kid . . . that was the only time I saw the side of him that is often publicized." On another occasion, driving his first wife, Gail, to see flooding near the Pedernales River, he decided she should meet Johnson. With no notice, they stopped at the ranch gate; the Secret Service waved them through, and Johnson—though sick in bed—greeted them warmly, even remembering details he had heard about Gail's background despite never having met her.[69] Yet away from the ranch's easy hospitality, Walter and Marjorie's marriage was coming apart.

In the early 1970s, Jenkins reconfigured his private life: he and Marjorie separated, largely because of her alcoholism, even as he continued to support her. "He stayed by her, I am sure out of guilt," Beth recalled, "because she stood by him at a very tough time in his life, and I think he thought he owed it to her." They moved into a newer, smaller duplex property in Austin's Tarrytown neighborhood, living adjacent to one another but separately. Jenkins resigned from the Cromwell investment club, citing frequent travel and its couples-only norm, a small sign of how separation reshaped their social world. That same year, Beth—then on the board of Planned Parenthood in Austin—persuaded him to donate "a nice check" to the organization, even as Marjorie, a devout Catholic, gave to the right-to-life movement. "Nobody in the world would give to both sides!" he joked, adding that it might flag him for an audit.[70] Together, these choices show a man trying to honor marital obligations while redrawing the boundaries of a life no longer organized around a couple.

Jenkins followed his passion for duplicate bridge, competing in tournaments himself and launching a travel agency, Capital Bridge Tours, that specialized in taking large groups to them, such as a five-day 1974 trip to Mexico City for which the firm booked 100 hotel rooms. His daughters Beth and Anne became involved in the business.[71]

Jenkins stayed a loyal Democrat, though he was lukewarm about the party's 1972 standard-bearer. He disliked George McGovern's campaign, which repudiated LBJ's legacy, yet told his brother Charles—who was unhappily voting for McGovern—"just like a football team, if the quarterback makes a mistake, I don't go and play for the other side." He saved his sharper criticism for John Connally, who joined Nixon's cabinet in 1971 and later led "Democrats for Nixon." Connally "is my friend and always will be," he wrote, but "I have a tendency to agree with what Liz Carpenter said: It is a good thing he wasn't at the Alamo—he'd have been out recruiting for Santa Anna."[72]

Johnson's death in 1973 ended any lingering possibility that the two might appear together and stir controversy. During an all-night vigil, Jenkins stood watch with other members of Johnson's closest friends and staff at the LBJ Library. Not long afterward, he joined Lady Bird on a trip to Mexico, and he subsequently joined some of her annual winter trips to Acapulco.[73]

By 1975, as a more sympathetic view of Jenkins began to take shape, Bill Moyers wrote a *Newsweek* tribute that would be widely quoted in the years to come: "When they come to canonize political aides, he will be the first summoned, for no man ever negotiated the shark-infested waters of the Potomac with more decency and charity or came out on the other side with his integrity less shaken." By labeling Jenkins not as immoral but as a model of integrity, Moyers reprised on a grander scale the rhetorical move first made by William S. White in 1964. The political climate was shifting, too: that same month, twenty-four members of Congress publicly backed a proposed federal gay rights law. The American Psychiatric Association had recently removed homosexuality from its diagnostic manual.

And, after years of dragging its feet—and with security-clearance posts excluded—the Civil Service Commission was preparing to end its blanket ban on gay federal employees.[74]

"Now a Cable Television Executive"

In retrospect, Jenkins came to symbolize the most successful period of Johnson's leadership. After 1968, when he declined to run for reelection, the Democratic Party treated Johnson as a pariah over his escalation of the Vietnam War. Those crucial decisions to escalate came in early 1965—after Jenkins's departure and without his involvement.

By the 1970s, Jenkins was no longer just a casualty of Johnson's career; he was also treated as a knowledgeable witness to it. He helped edit Johnson's memoir *The Vantage Point* but received only the briefest mention in its pages. Before Johnson's death, he sat for two interviews for the LBJ Library's oral history project; he would go on to record a third in 1976 and another twelve between 1982 and 1984.[75] In 1976, Jenkins received and accepted an invitation to join John Macy in speaking to a class at the LBJ School for Public Affairs at the University of Texas at Austin.[76]

In 1977, in a remarkable turnabout, Jenkins was summoned to defend Lyndon Johnson in public against a new witness who claimed he had observed malfeasance on Johnson's part. That summer, a former election judge, Luis Salas, told the Associated Press that he had stolen the 1948 Democratic Senate runoff primary for Johnson. Salas claimed that, acting in Jim Wells County, he fabricated roughly 200 votes for Johnson from one of the boxes of paper ballots—and that Johnson himself was present when local political boss George Parr ordered him to find the extra votes.[77] The allegation received front-page coverage in Texas papers. In response, Johnson's last presidential press secretary, George Christian, arranged a press conference at the Texas state capitol where Jenkins, Mary Rather, and Charles Herring, three aides from the 1948 campaign, denied that the events could have happened as Salas described.[78]

In front of microphones and cameras, with Jenkins seated at the center, the trio offered themselves as character witnesses for the late president. Such an appearance would have been unthinkable while Johnson was alive. Christian made clear they were available only to discuss Salas's claim. The UPI identified Jenkins as "Johnson's administrative assistant at the time of the contested election" and "now an Austin radio executive"; the AP called him "his administrative assistant" in 1948 and "now a cable television executive."[79] Neither story mentioned his 1964 resignation. That, in itself, was remarkable: with a former election judge claiming to have fraudulently certified 200 votes for Johnson, the Associated Press was quoting Jenkins as a credible source in his defense.

In 1964, Jenkins's name was a problem to be kept out of the papers; in 1977, it was a credential worth printing. Once cast out of Washington, he now stood before microphones in Austin to defend his president, still doing what he had done for decades: protecting Lyndon Johnson.

CHAPTER 8

THE HOMOSEXUAL CITIZEN IN THE GREAT SOCIETY

Lyndon Johnson struggled to understand how restroom arrests worked. In his first conversation with Deke DeLoach about the Jenkins affair, he asked about the 1959 arrest, baffled that a plainclothes officer had detained Jenkins alone: "Why would they pick up a guy if he's just by himself?" DeLoach replied that Jenkins must have been fiddling with his zipper. Johnson was equally puzzled by the 1964 arrest: "How would these three policemen be peeping through the door and know he's there if they hadn't had some indication?" DeLoach explained that officers staked out places like Lafayette Park and the YMCA men's room, where "known homosexuals hang out."[1] Johnson's confusion underscored how far many straight Americans were from understanding the routines of cruising and police surveillance—even though Lafayette Park, a center of both, was only a two-minute walk from the West Wing.

The Jenkins affair forced into public view two intersecting systems: men who sought sex with one another in public places and the vice squads organized to catch them. It showed that same-sex behavior could not be reliably inferred from how a man looked, moved, or spoke, and it suggested that concealment was both common and often forced.

What the episode revealed depended on one's vantage point. For many gay people, very little about the arrest was surprising: men had sex in bathrooms, vice patrols watched, and the consequences of arrest could range from nuisance to catastrophe. For many straight people, by contrast, the fall of the president's most trusted aide was shocking: it was newly imaginable that seemingly conventional Catholic fathers might have sex in public bathrooms, and newly visible what the vice patrol was doing there. The affair thus alerted nongay Americans to the possible queerness of the family men around them and illuminated the reach—and intrusiveness—of postwar policing.

The publicness of this episode was without precedent. Never before had a public official's participation in same-sex acts been so openly revealed, or a man's career undone by homosexual charges so frankly discussed. Contemporaries registered its singularity. *Time*'s Hugh Sidey wrote that the episode "shocked this town and the White House like nothing since the assassination of John F. Kennedy," indeed that "all Washington has been possessed by this story." Theodore White observed that the 1964 campaign had revealed that "the President's closest personal assistant . . . was a sexual deviate," and he marveled that "perhaps the most amazing of all events of the campaign" was "that the nation faced the fact fully—and shrugged its shoulders."[2] The affair helped some straight Americans recognize that queer men lived among them and that the postwar architecture of conformity and the closet imposed costs they had not previously recognized.

As we have seen, elite reactions by two key Washington figures helped shape press responses to the exposure of same-sex acts. Lady Bird Johnson's warm public defense, praising Jenkins's character and noting the pain his family was enduring, modeled acknowledgment without disgust or condemnation. And even J. Edgar Hoover—whose name was synonymous with federal law enforcement—had, through society columnist Betty Beale and her unnamed source, signaled that Jenkins was "safe." The First Lady and the FBI director broadened the scope of what ostensibly nongay people in power might say and do when homosexuality surfaced in their social world. When I asked an interviewee for an unrelated queer oral history project in 2017 if he recalled the Jenkins affair, he volunteered that "The best thing about the Jenkins thing" was the way Lady Bird Johnson "helped to cover it over" by saying Jenkins had been "tired" and "that things like that happen. She made it okay."[3]

The Jenkins arrest pushed Americans to talk openly about gay life—especially in Washington, where official prohibitions on homosexuality had carried particular weight since the early Cold War—and the sympathetic response marked a break with the hostility pervading Lavender Scare rhetoric. "The disclosure of homosexuality in the White House via Jenkins is not without a silver lining," wrote the editor of a California homophile newsletter; it exposed to "the unknowing American" facets of gay life and occasioned a rapid shift in media discourse. Jenkins, he argued, "has shattered the stereotype of the homosexual," because "he is obviously not a homosexual, he is nothing more or less than sexual." He soon took delight in the pivot in "the volumes of print that was expended on the subject": what was "unmentionable and abhorrent" one day became a story of "overwork and intoxication."[4]

The episode did not put gay rights onto the policy agenda of the men crafting the Great Society. But it compelled the Metropolitan Police Department to explain and defend its surveillance of queer life. Frank Kameny's long-standing effort to challenge the practices of the Civil Service Commission—including a new case already set for argument the month after the election—drew new attention. As New York activist Dick Leitsch later wrote, a striking array of public figures "said point-blank" that homosexuality was "less immoral than other things." The Johnson administration, in his view, had more or less "staged a national teach-in against homophobia," surely an exaggeration but also a testament to how different things felt to him afterward.[5]

In the liberal Great Society moment, the Jenkins affair helped erode the governing consensus favoring harsh punishment of consensual same-sex acts. By altering the climate in which homophile activists operated, it helped set the stage for greater progay militancy in the second half of the 1960s. The repercussions unfolded along three fronts: law and state power; press and print culture; and activist repertoires.

"Homosexuality Replaced the World Series as the Major Topic of Conversation"

On the eve of the Jenkins affair, only small fissures had appeared in the Lavender Scare's legal and cultural framework. The 1952 immigration reform ended racial bars to naturalization but added a "psychopathic personality" exclusion aimed at homosexuals. As anticommunist purges waned, gay-related cases made up a growing share of security dismissals. In the realm of criminal law, there was movement toward liberalization. Nine states liberalized sodomy laws between 1951 and 1965. The American Law Institute recommended the decriminalization of consensual adult same-sex acts in 1955 and omitted such offenses from its 1962 Model Penal Code, though only Illinois enacted a repeal. In 1967, the American Civil Liberties Union adopted a policy statement acknowledging homosexuals' vulnerability and due-process claims while declining to challenge laws against "overt" or public acts.[6] Meanwhile, Supreme Court rulings—*One, Inc. v. Olesen* (1958) and *MANual Enterprises v. Day* (1962)—shielded gay publications and helped enable a commercial market in homoerotic imagery.

By now, gay activists had begun to pry open both national and local media. Major outlets—the *New York Times*, *Harper's*, and *Life*—ran pieces on gay life, including the tearoom scene. In New York, the young militant Randy Wicker secured interviews on local radio and even television to argue for homosexual rights. In Washington, the weekend before the Jenkins story broke, the *Washington Post*'s Jean White covered the conference of the East Coast Homophile Organizations at a local hotel. White noted that four venues had canceled the group's reservation before one allowed it to proceed. She devoted six paragraphs to the Civil Service Commission blanket ban on gay employees.[7]

In this moment, the Jenkins story landed with unusual force, inserting into the news cycle aspects of queer life that had previously been rarely talked about. A week after the election, a San Francisco gay man wrote to his birthday-party guests that "Walter Jenkins jokes are 'out'—dating the guest of honor is 'in'!" In Washington, another remembered "a scary moment"—"I think everybody I knew had been to that men's room," which friends dubbed the "Jenkins Memorial." One man heard the news on a car radio while riding with his college roommate; the report, he said, sharpened his awareness of "my still-hidden orientation." A young married lawyer and 1964 Republican convention delegate, who was accustomed to hiding both same-sex encounters and a stash of physique magazines, saved a copy of *Time* folded open to the Jenkins article.[8]

Queer Americans differed over what all this meant. One read the apparent lack of electoral effect as evidence of "social acceptance." Another argued that the episode revealed "the gigantic, great hatred" facing homosexuals, "so horribly similar to the anti-Semitism of Europe," and called for a national homophile organization to confront it. Either way, the affair became diagnostic.[9]

The universal praise of Jenkins's performance unsettled early Cold War assumptions about competence and risk. As the homophile writer put it, "We have heard that homosexuals do not have the ability to concentrate and hold down responsible jobs. Jenkins has shattered this."[10] Jenkins was the counterexample no one could ignore: a man who engaged in same-sex acts and had succeeded at the very center of power. In the months that followed, legal challenges to the federal employment ban gained a broader platform, and both harsh criminal penalties and blanket civil-service exclusions came under renewed scrutiny in the courts, the press, and American political culture.

Several activists began to sense an opening—"for three days in October," Leitsch recalled, "homosexuality replaced the World Series as the major topic of conversation in America." The editor of Los Angeles-based *ONE* magazine, taking J. Edgar Hoover's flowers as consequential, urged other pillars of "the opposition" to cooperate in dismantling antigay policies. In Washington, after the FBI said that Jenkins had not compromised national security, Frank Kameny wrote, as an individual, to all three daily papers that if anyone was "now totally invulnerable to threats of blackmail," it was Walter Jenkins; he urged President Johnson to restore Jenkins to his post, "the only proper course of action."[11]

On January 16, 1965—four days before Johnson's inauguration—members of the East Coast Homophile Organizations (ECHO) planning their fall conference chose a theme that echoed the president's domestic program: "The Homosexual Citizen in the Great Society." Frank Kameny alerted Jean White, the *Washington Post* reporter who had covered ECHO's October 1964 meeting. Aware that she was drafting a "forthcoming article" about homosexuality, Kameny suggested the theme might be a news scoop if she deemed it "worth while and important enough."[12]

White did not use Kameny's scoop, but she was at work on far more than a single article. Beginning January 31, the *Post* ran her five-part series on gay Washington—"Those Others" was its tagline—on consecutive days, with four installments on the front page. The opening piece declared that society "must decide how it is going to deal with the homosexual in its midst," observed that most gay people "try to pass in the 'straight' heterosexual world," estimated that "perhaps 85 percent go undetected," and asked whether the law should "reach into the bedroom and the area of private morals." Homophile publications hailed the series as "the most astute as well as most extensive coverage so far in U.S. papers."[13] Throughout the series, the *Post* foregrounded the everyday problems faced by gay Washingtonians, stressing jobs, policing, and stigma. Even White's science installment stressed uncertainty, setting the illness model of psychoanalysts Irving Bieber and Edmund Bergler alongside the more affirmative views of sex researchers Wardell Pomeroy and Evelyn Hooker and concluding that "adjustment" might be "preferable to a cure," given how often cures failed.[14]

White's reporting was a key early example of objections to vice-squad methods going mainstream. She cataloged criticisms of decoy tactics and clandestine surveillance, while a department spokesman defended the patrols and insisted officers spent minutes, not hours, at peepholes. White closed by situating Jenkins within this debate: "The public response to the Jenkins arrest has been encouraging of a more enlightened public attitude," she observed; Americans' comments "showed restraint, decency, and compassion." Yet she immediately stressed the disjunction between sympathy and the social structure: "But today society offers no place, no help, and no hope to the homosexual. Laws are harsh on him; his existence is precarious; exposure brings ruin and social ostracism."[15]

White's series marked an important step in Frank Kameny's public coming out. For years, he had struggled to obtain publicity for his legal and administrative campaign against antigay federal policies. Apart from letters to the editor, his name had appeared in the *Washington Post* chiefly in the context of Texas congressman John Dowdy's bid to revoke the Mattachine Society of Washington's charitable-solicitation license. A 1963 hearing about the issue had put the group's name in print, but also cast Kameny as a defender of a highly abstract right that few others wished to exercise—namely, to fundraise on behalf of a nonprofit homosexual rights organization. That limited publicity proved useful. The National Capital Area Civil Liberties Union, the local American Civil Liberties Union affiliate, opposed Dowdy's bill in the summer of 1964. The group's December statement on the Jenkins case, however, went further, urging an end to decoy operations in tearooms and declaring the Metropolitan Police Department's clandestine surveillance unconstitutional. Responding to the affiliate's stance, the *Post* weighed in strongly against both practices.[16]

Now, in the finale of her five-part series, White opened with Kameny's 1963 testimony against Congressman Dowdy's effort to revoke his group's charitable-solicitation license. But she gave it fuller treatment, highlighting Kameny's substantive critique of the Civil Service Commission's blanket ban on gay employees. The article ran on the front page under the headline "Homosexuals' Militancy Reflected in Attacks on Ouster from U.S. Jobs." White made the issue concrete by profiling two dismissed federal employees who sued. Without naming them, she sketched their cases. William Lyman Dew, a married father of three with no documented same-sex conduct since youth, had nonetheless seen his dismissal as a Federal Aviation Agency meteorologist upheld by the courts. Clifford Norton, a NASA budget analyst, was arrested in October 1963 after picking up a stranger near Lafayette Square; vice officers followed them to Norton's southwest Washington apartment building, arrested both in the parking lot, and summoned NASA security to assist in the interrogation. Although police issued only a traffic citation, NASA fired Norton. He filed suit on October 13, 1964—the day before the Jenkins story broke.[17]

Indeed, the courts soon began to narrow the government's latitude to punish. In December 1964, as Jenkins weighed his next steps, the DC Circuit heard Bruce Scott's appeal. Scott, a seventeen-year Department of Labor employee, had been removed after a long-ago morals arrest in Lafayette Park resurfaced and a district court upheld the dismissal. His challenge directly tested the federal exclusion of homosexuals from civil service. After six months, the court held in *Scott v. Macy*, 2–1, that the Civil Service Commission could not fire him without specifying the conduct on which the dismissal was based, an outcome neither side had anticipated. In a separate opinion, Judge David Bazelon emphasized that branding a man a homosexual "jeopardized his ability to find employment elsewhere," thus raising a constitutional issue.[18]

The homophile movement saw several media breakthroughs in the 1960s; White's series was Washington's. A 1995 study concluded that mainstream press coverage of queer life increasingly emphasized legal barriers over psychiatry, and that "to a large extent the shift was fueled" by the Jenkins affair. This same account called White's *Post* series distinctive in that she was "one of the first to try to describe everyday conflicts faced by homosexuals." Activists beyond Washington likewise noted a changing press climate. Dick Leitsch later observed that, in the wake of Jenkins, the media "discovered" Evelyn Hooker and other researchers whose studies found homosexuals indistinguishable from the general population. The most dramatic shift, he argued, came at the paper of record: the *New York Times* no longer defaulted to quoting Irving Bieber, promoter of homosexuality as a mental illness, "whenever homosexuality was mentioned." As strong Johnson backers, the editors were suddenly "no longer interested" in casting "all homosexuals, including the Number Two man in the White House, as dysfunctional people."[19]

Advice columns, too, became a mass forum in which readers narrated ordinary encounters with homosexuality and, by the mid-1960s, increasingly questioned the policing of consenting adults. In 1965 Ann Landers published letters about a boyfriend claiming to be gay to avoid the draft, a mother who found physique magazines under her son's mattress, and a woman whose daughter was dating a man who "told her about his homosexual tendencies." In 1967 a correspondent pressed Dr. Joyce Brothers on criminalization: after "the local florist in our town was arrested as a homosexual" along with his "long-time friend," the writer asked why the men had to be "humiliated like common criminals" and—amid "all this talk of civil rights"—when adults would be allowed to choose their companions without police interference.[20]

The Pickets of 1965

As civil rights marches made protest familiar, a few activists began to ask whether homosexuality, too, could become a cause for public protest. On September 19, 1964, without backing from the Mattachine Society of New York or the city's Daughters of Bilitis chapter, the young militant Randy Wicker had organized the nation's first gay picket—at the downtown army induction center—drawing eight participants and no press. Weeks later, Wicker sought to picket the FBI over Jenkins's arrest and dismissal. Perhaps sensing that such an action might draw negative coverage, the Mattachine Society of New York's president, Julian Hodges, consulted a relative in the administration, Commerce Secretary Luther Hodges, who warned that a demonstration would be impolitic and harmful. Armed with that advice, Hodges persuaded Wicker to stand down.[21]

By mid-1965, the climate had shifted: the protest tactic that had seemed risky in 1964 was being used in Washington, New York, and Philadelphia, aimed squarely at the policies that had ensnared Jenkins. On April 17, 1965, after Jean White's *Post* series ran and as a newly enlarged Democratic congressional majority prepared to enact Great Society programs, ten members of the Mattachine Society of Washington assembled on the sidewalk in front of the White House for the first ever gay rights picket in the capital. Aligning their message with a Cold War theme, they protested antigay policies in both the US and Cuba. One placard read "FIFTEEN MILLION U.S. HOMOSEXUALS PROTEST FEDERAL TREATMENT." Another group returned on May 29 and this time received more press attention, followed by a third White House picket on October 23 with some forty-five participants (see figure 8.1). In December 1964, the Philadelphia magazine *Drum* had wondered whether Jenkins would trigger a new "witch-hunt." By May 1965, the editors concluded that on the contrary, the Jenkins case and the response "probably set a backdrop that will, quietly, promote changes in official attitudes throughout the land."[22]

Early successes in Washington, and Frank Kameny's sustained promotion, established a pattern of respectable public protest. After the May White House action, the *Evening Star*'s "Federal Spotlight" column announced the Mattachine Society of Washington's plans to picket the Civil Service Commission. On June 26, the group did so, with eighteen men and seven women. On July 4, activists from Washington and New York gathered at Philadelphia's Independence Hall for the first in what became an annual series of pickets there. "We emphasized appearance," Kameny recalled. "The women all wore dresses, the men suits with white shirts." Similar pickets soon targeted the Pentagon and the State Department.[23]

In September, at the second East Coast Homophile Organizations conference in New York, attendees celebrated the small movement's turn toward visibility. One remarked that "two years ago it was

FIGURE 8.1 Gay and lesbian activists picket in front of the White House to protest federal employment policies, October 1965. Photo by Kay Tobin © Manuscripts and Archives Division, The New York Public Library.

enough just to talk about homosexuality," but "today that's no longer the case." A CBS crew filmed a lecture, cocktail party, and banquet for a forthcoming documentary. In his speech, the writer Paul Goodman invoked Jenkins and argued that in a "decent society" revulsion should attach to the peeping cops, not the arrested man. The audience was more vocal than in 1964. Some wore buttons—"LET'S

LOVE ONE ANOTHER" reportedly "stole the show." A Daughters of Bilitis member quipped that "half the impetus for the Great Society is in that little message."[24] In 1966 activists founded the National Conference of Homophile Organizations and held its first meeting in Kansas City, a tentative step toward nationalizing the movement and a precursor to the national gay organizations of the 1970s.

Even as the Jenkins case and the *Scott* decision brought federal exclusion practices into view, the Civil Service Commission resisted change. In May and June 1965—while activists picketed its offices—the commission stood firm in refusing to meet with representatives of the Mattachine Society of Washington. David K. Johnson has described the Jenkins affair as "a setback to the Mattachine Society," likely slowing Frank Kameny's campaign for a meeting. From chairman John Macy's perspective, agreeing might have drawn President Johnson's ire by calling fresh attention to homosexuality in government employment. By late August, however, the commission relented and agreed to meet.[25]

Parallel reform efforts gathered on the West Coast, led by Protestant clergy. In San Francisco, outrage over police mistreatment at a New Year's Eve 1964 queer ball—an event many clergy had attended—lent vitality to the Council on Religion and the Homosexual, which in June 1965 issued a "brief of injustices" documenting the scale and impact of antigay laws and policing. Its cover reproduced a close-up photo of an inscription on the Jefferson Memorial on the need for laws to keep pace with social change. The council soon became a clearinghouse for "homosexual law reform," invoking Jenkins as a case in point against clandestine surveillance.[26]

At the same time, vice-squad methods drew mounting criticism from legal thinkers and judges. By the late 1960s, courts, civil libertarians, and social scientists increasingly asked whether homosexual conduct in public places posed less danger to society than the police who surveilled it. A landmark UCLA Law School study, *The Consenting Adult Homosexual and the Law* (1966), documented the scope of antigay surveillance in California and fortified liberal arguments that tearoom arrests should not be a law-enforcement priority.[27]

Privacy doctrine was shifting at the Supreme Court as well. In *Katz v. United States* (1967), the court limited warrantless searches by protecting conversations in "temporarily private" spaces where a person can reasonably expect freedom from intrusion. The case involved a phone booth, but the logic resonated with controversies over clandestine observation in public toilets. As David Sklansky has noted, "stories like Walter Jenkins's were common" and may have influenced *Katz*. Justice William O. Douglas, appalled by antigay police tactics, repeatedly returned to the Jenkins case, asking his wife, "What do they tell their children when they ask, 'Daddy, what did you do today?' "[28]

At the DC Circuit, two decisions narrowed the government's authority to dismiss gay employees. *Scott v. Macy* (1965), as we have seen, required the Civil Service Commission to specify the conduct on which a dismissal rested. The more important case, *Norton v. Macy* (1969), arising from a NASA firing, barred discharge absent a demonstrable nexus to "the efficiency of the service." The court ruled that it was not "an appropriate function of the bureaucracy to enforce the majority's conventional view of conduct in the private lives of its employees." As in *Scott*, Judge David Bazelon emphasized the severe stigma of a gay-related firing—echoing a 1952 Supreme Court description of the "badge of infamy" attached to loyalty disqualifications—and required a "reasonably foreseeable, specific connection" between off-duty conduct and governmental efficiency.[29] Together, these rulings narrowed what the federal state could defend as a basis for exclusion and placed a new burden on agency officials to justify removals.

Popular culture reflected a similar turn. In 1968, the Washington correspondent Fletcher Knebel published *Vanished*, a bestseller loosely modeled on Jenkins. In this novel, the president's closest friend disappears during a reelection campaign. Rumors of homosexuality surface after revelations of weekly meetings with a man in a rented apartment. The president rejects the premise that his friend is either a "sexual deviate" or a "sordid security risk," noting the ordeal faced by the man's wife and daughter. The plot ultimately attributes the friend's disappearance to his participation in secret nuclear disarmament talks on a remote island, while the only leak of Oval Office secrets stems from a *heterosexual* affair, not a gay liaison.[30]

NBC's 1971 two-part adaptation of *Vanished* both amplified the Jenkins echoes and reflected the spread of mainstream skepticism toward Lavender Scare assumptions. In the film, the president's friend is recast as a White House adviser, while his alcoholic wife fumes that the president has not publicly cleared him of the charge of homosexuality. An elderly Southern senator, a stock figure of drawling old-guard reaction and illiberal scheming, declares, "I love that red, white, and blue, and I wouldn't want it to turn to lavender and lace," a line one reviewer singled out as risible. Placing this rhetoric in the mouth of a likely segregationist underscored the waning plausibility of the Cold War equation of queerness with subversion. A landlord, questioned about two men's weekly visits to an apartment, dryly replies that the police "ought to have something better to do," signaling popular unease with antigay surveillance.[31] As popular culture and the press showed increasing openness, queer activists became more assertive.

"Come Out"

At the end of the decade, gay activists began to defy the norm of concealment. In June 1969, a raid on New York's Stonewall Inn spiraled into several nights of clashes after patrons fought back and barricaded the police inside the bar. Tactical-riot reinforcements followed, and activists quickly cast the uprising as a watershed. Within a year, commemorative marches in multiple cities reframed the anniversary as an assertion of pride and liberation, an open claim to the streets that was meant for straight witnesses as well as queer participants.

While street confrontations with local police became the emblem of gay liberation, many movement activists still saw the federal state as their chief antagonist. In 1970, Ortez Alderson—former chairman of the Black Caucus of Chicago Gay Liberation, who was then facing eighteen years in prison in a high-profile federal trial for destroying draft records—opened a plea for gay resistance to the Vietnam War by declaring, "The United States Government has for the longest time taken an anti-homosexual stance." In the next sentence he pointed not to Stonewall but to "the Jenkins case," in which "we were supposedly a security threat," which showed "what this government thinks of us."[32] Alderson had little in common with Jenkins, but he treated Jenkins's exposure and security-risk label as wounds shared by gay people, folding him into gay liberation's "us."

Jenkins was not the last public figure to face the coercive disclosure of a bathroom arrest. Later examples included a former federal judge in Tallahassee in 1976, a congressman in Washington in 1981, a pop star in Beverly Hills in 1998, and a senator in Minneapolis in 2007. But as gay identity became less stigmatized, the meaning of being outed changed. During the AIDS crisis around 1990, and again in gay-marriage debates of the 2000s, activists exposed closeted politicians who opposed gay rights or hindered the AIDS fight. The offense lay not in being gay but in hiding it while backing antigay policies. That view made sense because coming out was more common. Openly gay elected officials—absent before the 1970s—numbered roughly fifty by 1990 and about 146 by 1998. Fewer than one in four Americans reported having a gay friend or close acquaintance in 1985; by 1996, a national majority did.[33]

The transition was uneven, and far from complete, but a key shift came at the turn of the 1970s, as activists turned disclosure into a political tactic and a part of movement strategy. Members of New York's Gay Liberation Front, asked to "pinpoint" the nature of oppression, replied that "the traditional homosexual has been forced to attempt to live two separate existences, which precludes his being able to live fully in either."[34] In the 1970s, gay liberationists promoted coming out as a way to bridge those separate existences, trusting that personal knowledge could change how straight acquaintances responded. The spread of "coming out" after the Stonewall riots—a brilliant and world-changing innovation—was possible because of changes not only in gay consciousness but also in the consciousness of straight Americans, as they confronted the extent of the closet.

Jenkins's 1964 arrest had left its mark on a presidency because of his high position. But the vulnerability it exposed was not exceptional: a double life could always be turned against the person living it. The decades after 1964 did not bring a simple victory for privacy. The logic of the "security risk" receded, but American politics became ever more saturated in scandal and exposure. Norms of discretion surrounding public figures began to weaken. Revelations about Thomas Eagleton's psychiatric history and Gary Hart's extramarital affair would reshape presidential politics more decisively than Jenkins's arrest had. Gay politicians, one Washington correspondent argued in 1989, might now be more vulnerable rather than less. Still, if most Americans in 1964 understood Jenkins's arrest primarily as a threat to Johnson's campaign and national security, by the early 1970s gay liberationists could see in it the cruelty of a political order that made homosexual life both necessary to hide and devastating to reveal. They answered by attacking the double life itself. In 1978, looking back over the previous decade, one gay journalist celebrated the coming out of respected public figures, and added parenthetically: "no more Walter Jenkins[es]."[35] The "homosexual citizen" may not have found a place in the Great Society, but by then they had begun to find one in American life that would outlast the Great Society's moment.

EPILOGUE

For some queer men, the fate of Walter Jenkins became a private touchstone they linked to their own intimate choices. One man, who had lived a relatively open gay life as a teenager in Philadelphia, wrote in 1979 that the scandal prompted him, at nineteen, to marry a woman "to appease my parents" and proceed more cautiously thereafter. Another man, newly separated from his wife at twenty-four and living in a new city, was inspired by reading about Jenkins to move into the YMCA, where he found community and work and within months accepted himself as gay.[1] For these men and others, the exposure of Johnson's most trusted aide was like a flare lighting up the night sky: some shielded their eyes, while others found their bearings.

As liberationist critiques of the double life recast concealment as a problem to be overcome, activists pressed to extend the antidiscrimination framework ushered in by the Civil Rights Act of 1964 to encompass queer people—and some invoked Jenkins to make the case. In 1971 New York City Council testimony on a gay rights bill, a progay evangelical minister pointed to Jenkins's private-sector success to rebut claims that being known as a homosexual was "necessarily bad for business." After all, "Perhaps no person's homosexuality was more widely publicized than his."[2]

Public recollection, however, differed across constituencies. As late as 1990, a straight political scientist wrote euphemistically that Jenkins's "exemplary" service "broke his health." In gay and lesbian circles, later discussions retrofitted postliberation norms onto 1964. In 1982, Laud Humphreys told the *Advocate* that some tearoom visitors were "superorthodox," naming Jenkins and claiming he "championed the institution of the family and personally issued an order to purge homosexuals from the State Department." That was incorrect: Jenkins neither issued—nor had the power to issue—such an order; Humphreys likely misremembered a 1964 memo instructing that appointments be announced only after FBI checks. While Jenkins was, as we have seen, eager for the FBI to record that he was a willing cog in the machinery that implemented Lavender Scare–era policies, he was no outspoken antigay crusader. Nor was being closeted unusual: even Clifford Norton, the plaintiff whose case narrowed the federal employment ban in 1969, remained closeted to relatives and feared that publicity would expose him.[3] Humphreys himself was closeted when *Tearoom Trade* was published in 1970.

The same impulse to read 1964 through post-Stonewall values extended to Andy Choka, though here the anachronism was avowedly fictional and thus less egregious. In 1977, John Mitzel's short story, "Highlights from My Imaginary Interview with the Trick in the Stall with Walter Jenkins Way Back When," recast the YMCA encounter as a tryst between two self-identified gay men and offered a supposed interview with Jenkins's sexual partner. The "trick" pointedly notes the Johnsons' behind-the-scenes loyalty: the couple "took care of Walter" by giving him a job at KTBC, and Jenkins in turn "helped me get started" as a hairdresser. Now he styles the "wives of the crème of San Antonio Society," spends weekends in New Orleans ("when you get away from home base you can feel a little gayer"), and hopes to escape the Texas heat by vacationing on Fire Island, where there is "*absolute* freedom, they say." Speaking to the Bostonian Mitzel, he adds, "One thing you fancy East Coast liberals with your Kennedy affiliations don't understand is that this

Johnson crowd . . . they, ah, know how to take care of their own." In Mitzel's reimagining, Lady Bird Johnson's generosity extends beyond Jenkins to a wider queer network.[4]

Mitzel's fanciful invention preceded the release of sources that would let listeners hear some of the principals themselves. In the late 1990s, as Johnson's presidential telephone recordings were released in batches amid a renewed congressional reexamination of the Kennedy assassination, listeners could hear what Johnson did and said at key moments. A September 1998 release included Johnson's calls about Jenkins's arrest and resignation, among them the early-morning October 15 conversation in which Lady Bird resolved to issue a statement of support and to find Jenkins work.[5]

Those recordings, in turn, shaped later portrayals and helped return Jenkins to the center of Johnson's first year in office. Drawing heavily on the tapes, Robert Schenkkan's *All the Way* presents Jenkins as indispensable during the year between Dallas and the 1964 landslide, with his departure depicted as the final crisis. The 2014 Tony Award–winning play restages several phone calls, including Lady Bird's insistence on a statement of support, as in-person scenes. While the dramatization takes reasonable liberties, one flourish misleads: Johnson's complaint that Jenkins "stabbed me in the back," a sentiment for which there is no evidence.[6]

At the same time, a shifting cultural climate—amplified by publicity around the tapes—made possible something that could not have occurred in 1964: Walter Jenkins's eldest child publicly said what she had long assumed, that her father was gay. A Texas journalist revisited the episode and interviewed several who had witnessed it up close, including Liz Carpenter and Mildred Stegall. "According to Beth Jenkins Bromberg," he noted, "there was never any kitchen-table discussion of the events of 1964." Later that year, a second account extended this reexamination for a queer readership when a gay journalist interviewed Beth for *Out* magazine. By then, Americans increasingly understood the episode as the outing of a closeted gay man, a shift Beth felt compelled to contextualize. "My dad never came out," she explained. "I assume he was gay, but it was a different time and a different place. It was nothing we ever discussed. He didn't bring it up and neither did I, in spite of the fact that we were exceedingly close."[7]

Luci Baines Johnson, who had grown up alongside Beth, read those sentences—"I assume my dad was gay"—with a jolt of protectiveness and recognition. "I wanted to put my arms around her," Luci told me, "to shield her from any pain." It brought back memories of "the chapter of her life when she is away at school and the world comes crashing down." Yet she also saw almost at once the nonchalance of Beth's assumption. "I thought to myself, the minute after I had that immediate instinctive reaction, *oh*, how *wonderful* it is that she assumes her father was gay, much as she might have assumed her father was"—and here she paused thoughtfully—"not as liberal as we thought, or Republican, or really a Buddhist." The state's regulation of sexuality had not vanished: sodomy statutes remained, vice stings continued, and federal and military rules still policed behavior. Luci, who had lost a close friend to AIDS, knew as much. At the same time, "gay" no longer functioned—for Luci and many of her contemporaries—as an automatic indictment. It could be named without presuming disgrace or disqualification. By the 1990s, she observed, many Americans had learned that "there was nothing about gay that was wrong."[8]

ACKNOWLEDGMENTS

Above all, I want to thank all the members of the Jenkins family who spoke with me. My deepest debt is to Beth Jenkins Bromberg, who met my earliest inquiries with uncommon warmth and candor and, over the next decade, kept saying yes. She gave freely of herself so that a difficult story of her father's life and times, a story that matters to gay people, could be told well. Beth shared memories, photo albums, and correspondence, and introduced me to relatives and friends. At her urging, the Lyndon B. Johnson Presidential Library opened Walter Jenkins's personal papers to me; without that access, there would be no book. She never tried to limit what I could ask, see, or write. She answered many follow-up emails, texts, and calls, including one eight days before her unexpected death in December 2024. Beth's beloved husband, John Bromberg, welcomed me into his home and shared his memories of Walter Jenkins, his father-in-law—the man who introduced him to Beth. I wish Beth could read these pages. I'm awed by the trust she placed in me and grateful beyond measure to have known her.

My thanks also go to Walt Jenkins Jr. and Anne Jenkins Mauel for their support, trust, and help over the last decade. Walt was initially more hesitant than Beth to revisit a painful time. When we first met, I told him I wanted to understand the cost to the country of his father's forced departure from government; I hope these pages honor that aim. Walt, who had himself worked as an air traffic controller until he was fired during the 1981 PATCO strike, helped with remaining details after Beth's death as I completed the manuscript. Anne, who was three years old in 1964, was the first family member I spoke with, in 2016, and she connected me with Beth. She had worked with her father at the travel agency he founded in Austin after leaving the White House. In 2022, Anne gathered additional materials and brought them to Beth's lake house for us to review. She said she thought her father would be pleased that his papers had proved useful to someone, even if he could not have anticipated how.

I am grateful to those who spoke with me about their memories of Walter Jenkins. Among them were Lloyd Hand, Kathleen Livingston, Sandy Silver, Michael Gillette, George Bristol, Laura Kalman, and others who wished not to be named. Luci Baines Johnson and the late Bill Moyers knew Walter well, saw the events of 1964 up close, and cared deeply that I get the story right. Luci welcomed me to her home and spoke with me at length about this era. Bill sat with me—first in his office for two formal interviews, later for a series of more casual discussions in a coffee shop on the Upper West Side, and finally around his dining room table—to share his memories of the man who first hired him to work in Lyndon Johnson's Washington office in 1954 as a summer employee in the correspondence section. Luci and Bill were uncommonly reflective about the cruelties of the world they grew up in and listened closely to the questions I brought to them. Their willingness to reckon with that world gives me hope at a moment when transgender and nonbinary Americans are being targeted and demonized by their own government.

I'm grateful to archivists and librarians at all the institutions where I conducted research, including Abigail Malangone at the JFK Library and Jane Parr at the Howard Gotlieb Archival Research Center at Boston University, who enabled me to view the Betty Beale Collection as soon as the library reopened after COVID-19 closures. The New York Public Library's Shoichi Noma Reading Room was a wonderful place to tie up last-minute research.

The extraordinary and devoted staff of the LBJ Library went above and beyond over a long period. I thank the archival staff who helped me—diligent public servants all. While this is not a complete list, I want to name Jenna de Graffenreid, Jennifer Cuddeback, Alexis Percle, and Claudia Anderson; Chris Banks, who located obscure photos; Sarah Cunningham, who digitized recordings of interviews with Walter Jenkins so I could listen to them; and particularly Brian McNerney, who worked closely with me on the complicated task of making the Jenkins personal papers accessible despite obstacles, including deterioration in parts of the collection. Brian helped with a steady stream of follow-up queries and has become a valued colleague and friend.

I am grateful for fellowship support from the Charles Warren Center for Studies in American History at Harvard, which afforded me time and space and the chance to work alongside co-conveners Elizabeth Hinton and Lisa McGirr; my fellow fellows Donna Murch, Stuart Schrader, Susan Reverby, and Heather Ann Thompson, among others; and Michael Bronski, whom I met that year and who alerted me to the short story by John Mitzel that I discuss in chapter 8. A Moody Research Grant from the LBJ Foundation made possible my first trip to Texas; on that visit Beth and John welcomed me with homemade barbecue at their table, a kindness I will not forget. A Rutgers Research Council grant supported a subsequent trip. I am lucky to work at Rutgers University–Newark and grateful for support from Nancy Cantor, Jacqueline Mattis, Mi Hyun Yoon, Karen Caplan, and the extraordinary Christina Strasburger. Jordan Baldridge and Molly Stevens provided skilled research assistance.

A conversation with Maggie Wittlin gave me one of my earliest inklings that the story of Walter Jenkins might be worth exploring further. David O. Stewart read an early version of the book proposal and offered terrific advice. Charles Kaiser made the all-important suggestion that Bill Moyers might be willing to speak with me. For help and hospitality during research trips to Washington, I'm grateful to Megan Chan, Jarrod Stuard, Payton Chung, and especially Atiba Pertilla and Steve Wamhoff. Michael Barnes, Ken Herman, and Glen Maxey helped orient me in Austin. Scott Larson photographed pages from Katie Louchheim's diary at the Library of Congress. I stand on the shoulders of Lee Edelman, who published the first scholarly study of the Jenkins affair in the Routledge *Lesbian and Gay Studies Reader*, where I encountered it as a college student in the late 1990s.

One of the pleasures and challenges of this book has been the way it touched on various fields that were relatively new to me. Julian Zelizer, Timothy Naftali, and Jeremi Suri introduced me to the sprawling field of presidential history. Catherine Osborne and Monica Mercado answered questions about mid-century Catholicism, and Donald Ritchie about the postwar Senate. Chris Geidner, James R. Jones, Jennifer Dominique Jones, Michael Mallon, Patrick Roberts, and BG Wright were insightful interlocutors about the intersection of public service and sexuality. Rabia Belt, Elizabeth Emens, Frank Pasquale, and Dan Johnson were helpful in thinking through the significance of the law.

I was lucky to have opportunities to present on this work and receive feedback from participants in the Workshop in Modern US History at Yale, the American Political History Seminar at Boston University, the Legal Histories of the Body and the State conference at Stanford, the Intimate State conference at Brown, the Ryland Lecture at the University of Richmond, and the Writing History Seminar in New York. Special thanks to Susan Lee Johnson for including me in her presidential plenary session on queer history at the Western History Association.

I want to thank the many other colleagues and friends who have discussed this project with me over the last decade. Among them are, besides those mentioned already, Brad Anderson, Adam Arenson, Kathleen Belew, Fred Bernstein, Barry Bienstock, Tim Burke, Thom Cantey, Julio Capó, Christopher Capozzola, Seth Carlson, Eric Cervini, Robert Chang, George Chauncey, Benson Cohen, Robert Cole, Nancy Cott, Serge Luc Desrayaud, Adrian Dimanlig, Brian Distelberg, Bruce Dorsey, Moon Duchin, David Dunlap, Adam Eli,

Gill Frank, Aston Gonzalez, Phillip Hales, Byron Harrison, Emily Hobson, Kwame Holmes, Edward Hui, David Isaak, Sasha Issenberg, Pieter Judson, Laura Kalman, Shon Keane, Tim Kirkman, Brian Klinksiek, Mark Krasovic, Patrick Kwan, Aaron Lecklider, Marc Levin, Patrick McKelvey, Pat McTiernan, Aaron Mertz, Joanne Meyerowitz, Chris Mitchell, Michael Moore, Davis Nguyen, Tavia Nyong'o, Matt O'Connor, Susan Pedersen, Anthony Petro, Joey Plaster, Elliott Powell, Lance Richardson, Kyle Riismandel, Mary Rizzo, Don Romesburg, Gabe Rosenberg, Dan Royles, Doris Morgan Rueda, Hugh Ryan, Bruce Schulman, Robert Self, Liam Stack, Jordan Stein, Dustin Stephens, Ben Steverman, Tom Sugrue, Stacie Taranto, Geoffrey Upton, Daniela Valdés, Rick Valelly, Stephen Vider, and the late Jan Ellen Lewis. For such conversations and for generously sending me primary sources, I thank David Greenberg, Lauren Gutterman, Regina Kunzel, Anna Lvovsky, Margot Canaday, David K. Johnson, Mary Dudziak, Marc Stein, and especially Beverly Gage. John Havard suggested the title. New friends Amos Toh, Tom Odell, and Jonathan Rakiec hung out while I wrote. Matthew Leifheit took a wonderful author photo. My thanks as well to those I've inadvertently omitted.

Kornel Chang, Joanna Curtis, Ruth Feldstein, Korey Garibaldi, Jim Goodman, Alison Lefkovitz, David Polk, Beryl Satter, and Whit Strub read portions of the manuscript and gave generous feedback, as did John Alexander Burton, who also helped me understand how Washington works. In the decade since I began this endeavor, no one has cheered me on more consistently than Justin Glasson, who talked through phrases, arguments, and ideas with me at every stage and never tired of discussing the meaning of Walter's life and times. All the mistakes are my own.

At the University of Chicago Press, I benefited from an extraordinary process of editorial guidance and review. Tim Mennel understood what I was trying to do from our first conversation, offered wise counsel at every step, and secured thoughtful and detailed anonymous reviews. I'm grateful to Lily Geismer, Brent Cebul, Geraldo Cadava, and N. D. B. Connolly for inviting me to publish this book in their series and for their high-quality comments. Lily and Brent offered especially generous written feedback and on short notice arranged a collective Zoom workshop on the manuscript with Margot Canaday and John D'Emilio, whose excellent, smart suggestions significantly shaped the final book. Andrea Blatz and Caterina MacLean expertly guided the manuscript across the finish line.

My brother, Nick Winter, shaped my understanding of politics and has always been a helpful sounding board. Thanks as well to Tucker Winter, Nate Winter, Maggie Winter, Beth Yarnelle Edwards, John Edwards, and Geoffrey Rothman. My father, David Winter, joined me in 2019 on a memorable research trip and accompanied me to archives in Wichita Falls and Austin. Both he and my mother, Abigail Stewart, read and offered comments on the entire manuscript and provided unflagging support and company.

To Greg, who once joked there should be a punch card for every time I "finish the book": thank you for your love, humor, and the steadiness you bring to every day.

ARCHIVES AND COLLECTIONS CONSULTED

Lyndon B. Johnson Library, Austin, Texas (LBJL)
- Personal Papers of Walter Jenkins (PPWJ)
- Presidential Papers
- Lyndon Baines Johnson Archives Collection
- United States Senate Papers, 1949–61
- Pre-Presidential Memo File
- House of Representatives Papers, 1937–1949
- National Security File—Intelligence File
- Recordings and Transcripts of Telephone Conversations and Meetings
- Office Files of Mildred Stegall
- Office Files of Paul M. Popple
- Office Files of Bill Moyers
- Office Files of Walter Jenkins
- White House Social Files
- Meeting Notes File
- Lady Bird Johnson's White House Diary Collection
- Oral Histories (OH)

John F. Kennedy Library, Boston, Massachusetts
- Theodore H. White Papers (THWP)
- Pre-Presidential Papers: Transition Files
- Oral Histories (OH)

National Archives, College Park, Maryland
- Records of the Bureau of Security and Consular Affairs, RG 59 (Department of State)

National Archives, Washington, DC
- Records of the US Senate Committee on Government Operations (RG 46)

District of Columbia Public Library
- The People's Archive, Washingtoniana Vertical File

University of Texas at Austin
- Benjamin C. Bradlee Papers, Harry Ransom Center
- Stephen Shadegg/Barry Goldwater Papers, Eugene C. Barker Texas History Center
- Vertical file, Dolph Briscoe Center for American History
- Frank Ikard Papers, Dolph Briscoe Center for American History

Library of Congress, Washington, DC
- Frank Kameny Papers
- Katie S. Louchheim Papers

Manuscripts and Archives Division, The New York Public Library
- Barbara Gittings/Kay Tobin Lahusen Papers
- Dick Leitsch Papers

Arizona State University Library, Tempe, Arizona
- Dean Burch Papers, Greater Arizona Collection

University of Delaware Library Special Collections, Newark, Delaware
- John J. Williams Papers

Yale University Library, New Haven, Connecticut
- Abe Fortas Papers

Stony Brook University, Stony Brook, New York, Special Collections and University Archives
- John Gagnon Papers

The George Washington University, Washington, DC, Special Collections Research Center
- University Hospital Records

Wesleyan University, Middletown, Connecticut, Special Collections and Archives

- William Manchester Papers

Columbia University Libraries, New York, New York

- Mary Lasker Papers

Cornell University Library, Ithaca, New York, Human Sexuality Collection

- Human Rights Campaign Records

Boston University Libraries, Boston, Massachusetts, Howard Gotlieb Archival Research Center

- Betty Beale Collection

Hoover Institution Archives, Stanford, California

- Walter H. Judd Papers (WHJP)
- Robert C. Hill Papers

GLBT Historical Society, San Francisco, California

- Ephemera Collection

ONE National Gay and Lesbian Archives at the USC Libraries, Los Angeles, California

- Manuel boyFrank Papers
- Vertical File

Rainbow History Archives

Special Collections and University Archives, Stony Brook University, Stony Brook, New York

- John Gagnon Papers

Beth Jenkins Bromberg Personal Papers, Bee Cave, Texas

Midwestern University Archives, Moffett Library, Midwestern University, Wichita Falls, Texas

Wichita County Archives, Wichita Falls, Texas

FBI files

NOTES

INTRODUCTION

1. Marie Fehmer Chiarodo oral history (hereafter "OH") II, August 16, 1972, by Joe B. Frantz, Lyndon B. Johnson Library, Austin, Texas (LBJL), 53.

2. Walter Jenkins OH II, August 24, 1971, by Joe B. Frantz, LBJL, 41. See also William Manchester, *The Death of a President: November 20–November 25, 1963* (Harper & Row, 1967), 369.

3. NBC archival television footage, https://www.youtube.com/watch?v=6XwscnjrMpY.

4. Robert A. Caro, *Master of the Senate*, vol. 3 of *The Years of Lyndon Johnson* (Vintage, 2002), 494, 498.

5. Luther Holcomb OH II, by T. H. Baker, July 8, 1969.

6. Tom Wicker, "Johnson Denies Jenkins Cover-Up; Sets F.B.I. Inquiry," *New York Times*, October 16, 1964; FBI, "For Immediate Release, October 22, 1964," in FBI file 161-HQ-2848. The Warren Commission gathered material from 552 individuals, including sworn testimony, depositions, and written statements submitted by FBI agents or others acting on the commission's behalf. See *Report of the President's Commission on the Assassination of President John F. Kennedy* (1964), appendix 5.

7. Unsigned letter to Walter Jenkins, October 15, 1964, Ohio folder, box 51, and "a friend indeed" to Marjorie Jenkins, October 24, 1964, Connecticut folder, box 39; both in Personal Papers of Walter Jenkins (PPWJ), LBJL. LBJ Library archivists are currently processing, reorganizing, and reboxing the collection; citations reflect pre-reorganization box numbers. Unless otherwise noted, the folder name for correspondence between Jenkins and others in PPWJ is the name of Jenkins's correspondent.

8. US Congress, Senate, Committee on Expenditures in the Executive Departments, *Employment of Homosexuals and Other Sex Perverts in Government*, Senate Doc. 241, 81st Cong., 2nd sess. (1950), 9. The estimate of 5,000–10,000 is that of David K. Johnson, the preeminent historian of the Lavender Scare. The precise toll is unknowable because of the distinctive dynamics of these purges: there was no centralized record of people

allowed to resign quietly, and often neither bosses nor workers had an incentive to record the true reason for a person's leaving the job. Suyin Haynes, "You've Probably Heard of the Red Scare, but the Lesser-Known, Anti-Gay 'Lavender Scare' Is Rarely Taught in Schools," *Time*, December 22, 2020, https://time.com/5922679/lavender-scare-history/; William N. Eskridge Jr., *Gaylaw: Challenging the Apartheid of the Closet* (Harvard University Press, 1999), 60.

9. Allen Drury, *Advise and Consent* (Doubleday & Company, 1959), 308.

10. J. Edgar Hoover, memo to Tolson et al., October 23, 1964, 10:34 a.m., in FBI file 161-HQ-2848; "Former LBJ Aide Jenkins Goes Home" (Herald-Tribune News Service), *Washington Post*, November 11, 1964; Telephone conversation no. 6335, sound recording, LBJ and ABE FORTAS, November 11, 1964, 10:30 p.m., LBJL.

11. Charles Roberts, *LBJ's Inner Circle* (Delacorte Press, 1965), 38; Brian McNerney, email to the author, December 22, 2020.

12. Interview with Luci Baines Johnson, Austin, Texas, April 5, 2018.

13. Vance Muse, "LBJ's Greatest Loss," *George* (May 1999), 92–104; Horace Busby memo, October 17, 1964, Pre-Election Material—Oct [1 of 2] folder, box 30, Office Files of Bill Moyers, LBJL. The first and still the only scholarly work devoted to Walter Jenkins is Lee Edelman's excellent "Tearooms and Sympathy, or, The Epistemology of the Water Closet," in *The Lesbian and Gay Studies Reader*, ed. Henry Abelove, Michèle Aina Barale, and David M. Halperin (Routledge, 1993), 553–74.

14. Interview with Beth Jenkins Bromberg and Walt Jenkins Jr., Bee Cave, Texas, June 4, 2016.

15. Handwritten notes [n.d. but October 1964], folder 7, box 97, Barbara Gittings/Kay Lahusen Papers, New York Public Library; on Kameny as the first, see Margot Canaday, *Queer Career: Sexuality and Work in Modern America* (Princeton University Press, 2023), 111.

16. David K. Johnson, *The Lavender Scare: The Cold War Persecution of Gays and Lesbians in the Federal Government* (University of Chicago Press, 2004).

17. This book thus builds on Lauren Gutterman's brilliant, parallel analysis of married women in the same period in *Her Neighbor's Wife: A History of Lesbian Desire Within Marriage* (University of Pennsylvania Press, 2019).

18. Laud Humphreys, *Tearoom Trade: Impersonal Sex in Public Places* (Aldine, 1970), 105.

19. Jean M. White, "Homosexuals' Militancy Reflected In Attacks on Ouster From U.S. Jobs," *Washington Post*, February 4, 1965.

20. *Scott v. Macy*, 349 F.2d 182 (DC Cir. 1965); *Norton v. Macy*, 417 F.2d 1161 (DC Cir. 1969); "Homosexuals Picket in Nation's Capital," *The Ladder* 9, nos. 10 and 11 (July/August 1965), 23–24.

21. Claire Bond Potter, "Paths to Political Citizenship: Gay Rights, Feminism, and the Carter Presidency," *Journal of Policy History* 24, no. 1 (2012): 95–114; Timothy Stewart-Winter, "The Gay Rights President," in *The Presidency of Barack Obama: A First Historical Assessment*, ed. Julian E. Zelizer (Princeton University Press, 2018), 95–110; Timothy Stewart-Winter, "Trans Rights and the Emerging Politics of Gender," in *The Presidency of Joseph R. Biden: A First Historical Assessment*, ed. Julian E. Zelizer (Princeton University Press, 2026), 159–72.

22. Alison Lefkovitz, "'The Peculiar Anomaly': Same-Sex Infidelity in Postwar Divorce Courts," *Law and History Review* 33, no. 3 (August 2015): 665–701.

23. Alfred Steinberg, *Sam Johnson's Boy: A Close-Up of the President from Texas* (Macmillan, 1968), 631; Robert A. Caro, *The Path to Power*, vol. 1 of *The Years of Lyndon Johnson* (Vintage, 1982), 495–96; Caro, *Master of the Senate*, 129 and 146 ("n***** slave"); elsewhere in the latter volume, Caro suggests that Johnson "broke Jenkins" (130) and, through verbal abuse, left him "stripped of any human dignity" (677). In *The Path to Power*, Caro calls Puls a friend of Jenkins when quoting him (631), but elsewhere identifies him as Johnson's classmate at Southwest Texas State Teachers College (160). I have located no references to Puls in the 306 boxes of Jenkins's personal papers or in LBJ Library oral histories. Caro does not provide a date for his interview with Puls, but since his Johnson research began long after 1964, Puls's recollections would have been informed by subsequent knowledge of Jenkins's fate. The influence of Caro's 1982 volume on subsequent scholarship is hard to overstate. Even Paul K. Conkin, though critical of that volume, echoed its distinction between Jenkins and certain other "near slaves," on the one hand, and male aides such as John Connally, Bill Moyers, and Jack Valenti, who are easy to portray as always self-possessed because their post-Johnson careers made them famous in their own right. Conkin, *Big Daddy from the Pedernales: Lyndon Baines Johnson* (Twayne, 1986), 181.

24. Interview with Luci Baines Johnson, Austin, Texas, April 5, 2018; "Victor in Texas House Race To Seek Full Term in '52" (AP), *Washington Evening Star*, September 10, 1951; Walter Jenkins to Paul Bolton, December 12, 1963, in Walter W. Jenkins/Messages—Rec'd folder, box 3, Office Files of Walter Jenkins, LBJL. In the winner-take-all 1951 special election, Jenkins placed second among eight candidates.

25. Interview with Bill Moyers, New York City, August 8, 2017. See also Walter Jenkins interview by Emmette S. Redford and Richard McCulley, November 12, 1980, LBJL, 21.

26. Walter Jenkins interview by Emmette S. Redford and Richard McCulley, November 12, 1980, LBJL; Randall B. Woods, *LBJ: Architect of American Ambition* (Harvard University Press, 2006), 734–35; Joseph Alsop, "President's Attitude Toward Facts Surfaces," *Los Angeles Times*, January 14, 1966.

27. Woods, *LBJ*, 666, 645, 720, 727–28; Frances FitzGerald, *Fire in the Lake: The Vietnamese and the Americans in Vietnam* (Vintage, 1972), 486–87. (Woods's *LBJ* is the only full-scale biography published since the release of Johnson's presidential recordings that covers the presidency.) On Johnson's paranoia and mishandling of the Fulbright hearings, including his use of DeLoach and the FBI to suggest Moscow's involvement, see William Conrad Gibbons, *The US Government and the Vietnam War: Executive and Legislative Roles and Relationships, Part IV: July 1965–January 1968* (Princeton University Press, 1995), 227–39.

CHAPTER 1

1. Roger H. Davidson, "The Advent of the Modern Congress: The Legislative Reorganization Act of 1946," *Legislative Studies Quarterly* 15, no. 3 (August 1990): 357–73, especially 367–69, quotation at 367.

2. "Walter was brought up in puritanical Baptist fashion," a high school classmate told a reporter in 1964. McCombs to Parker, October 16, 1964, Johnson, Lyndon (14 of

22) folder, box 31k, Theodore H. White Papers (THWP), John F. Kennedy Library, Boston, Massachusetts.

3. Katricia Cochran, "Lyndon Johnson Aide for 19 Years is Wichitan," *Wichita Falls Times*, December 1, 1963; "J.B. Jenkins Funeral to be Held Monday," *Wichita Daily Times*, January 2, 1944; "Wichita Falls," *The WPA Guide to Texas* (1940; rpt. ed., Texas Monthly Press, 1986), 363–70; Benjamin Heber Johnson, *Texas: An American History* (Yale University Press, 2025), 236; Charles C. Alexander, *The Ku Klux Klan in the Southwest* (University of Kentucky Press, 1965), 127.

4. *Wichita Falls City Directory 1927* (John F. Worley Directory Co., 1927), 280.

5. Houston to director, telegram, October 17, 1964, in FBI file 161-HQ-2848; "Sh——," *The Wichitan*, November 1, 1933; *The Wai-kun* (Wichita Falls Junior College yearbook, 1934); Walter Jenkins, "Blind Student Makes Unusually Fine Grades," *Wichita Daily Times*, May 20, 1934; "Staff Pays Tribute to Editor Jenkins," *The Wichitan*, May 22, 1935; "Walter Jenkins in Congress Race," *Wichita Falls Record News*, June 28, 1951; Walter W. Jenkins, application to Quartermaster Corps Officer Candidate School, April 8, 1942, in "Colonel Jenkins, Walter W.—A0 157 61 86" folder 2 of 2, box 29A, Office Files of Mildred Stegall, LBJL.

6. Walter Jenkins OH IV, May 13, 1982, by Michael L. Gillette, LBJL, 3; Walter Jenkins OH I, August 14, 1970, by Joe B. Frantz, LBJL, 6.

7. Kent Demaret to Parker, October 15, 1964, Johnson, Lyndon (16 of 22) folder, box 31k, THWP.

8. Allen Drury, *Advise and Consent* (Doubleday & Company, 1959), 21.

9. Walter Jenkins OH I, August 14, 1970, by Joe B. Frantz, LBJL.

10. Walter Jenkins OH IV, May 13, 1982, by Michael L. Gillette, LBJL, 9; John Connally with Mickey Herskowitz, *In History's Shadow: An American Odyssey* (Hyperion, 1993), 70.

11. Walter Jenkins OH I, August 14, 1970, by Joe B. Frantz, LBJL; "Call to Colors Strips Lyndon Johnson's Office Staff; Omar Burleson in New Post" (AP), *Abilene Reporter News*, March 8, 1942; Norman Powell Heine to Walter Jenkins, June 30, 1942, in Loose Correspondence Jun. 1942–Jan. 1943, box 45, PPWJ; see also Robert Dallek, *Lone Star Rising: Lyndon Johnson and His Times, 1908–1960* (Oxford University Press, 1991), 237–42.

12. Walter Jenkins to "Chick," August 12, 1942, in Loose Correspondence Jun. 1942–Jan. 1943, box 45, PPWJ; "Mother and Dad" to Walter Jenkins, October 24, 1942, in Loose Correspondence Jun. 1942–Jan. 1943, box 45, PPWJ; Jenkins military record in Historical Records folder, box 29A, Office Files of Mildred Stegall, LBJL; Rick Atkinson, *An Army at Dawn: The War in North Africa, 1942–1943* (Henry Holt, 2002), 413–15.

13. "Lib" to Walter Jenkins, n.d. but postmarked June 29, 1942, in Loose Correspondence Jun. 1942–Jan. 1943, box 45, PPWJ.

14. Mrs. Lyndon B. Johnson to Walter Jenkins, July 1, 1942, in Walter Jenkins folder, box 330, House of Representatives Papers, LBJL.

15. Walter Jenkins OH V, August 12, 1982, by Michael L. Gillette, LBJL, 4–5.

16. Art S. to Walter Jenkins, November 12, 1942, in Loose Correspondence, Jul.–Dec. 1942, box 44, PPWJ. See also George Stimpson, "Lyndon Johnson Is Man On Deck If US Gets New Secretary of Navy," *San Angelo Evening Standard*, October 20, 1942.

17. Jenkins military record; Richard E. Killblane, *Delivering Victory: The History of US Military Transportation* (Emerald, 2019), 57–95; Atkinson, *An Army at Dawn*, 413–15.

18. Richard T. Stout, "Senior Member of Johnson Staff Quiet Worker," *Philadelphia Inquirer*, December 6, 1963; "Engagement of Prominent Couple Announced During Morning Coffee," clipping [np], September 12, 1945, in Jenkins biographical file, Wichita County Archives, Wichita Falls, Texas; "Jenkins, Whitehill Marriage Vows Recited in Sheppard Field Chapel," *Wichita Daily Times*, October 4, 1945; Walter Jenkins OH V, August 12, 1982, by Michael L. Gillette, LBJL.

19. Walter Jenkins 1945 tax return, Walter Jenkins Personal folder, box 79, PPWJ; Lyndon B. Johnson to Harold D. Fangboner, February 12, 1948, 2022 addendum, PPWJ; interview with Beth Jenkins Bromberg, June 28, 2017, Dallas, Texas; Walter Jenkins to Paul Popple, April 4, 1947, copy in 2022 addendum, PPWJ.

20. Walter Jenkins to Norman Powell Heine, September 3, 1948, and Norman Powell Heine to Walter Jenkins, November 8, 1948, both in Walter Jenkins Personal folder, box 79, PPWJ.

21. Metropolitan Police Department report, March 26, 1949, exhibit G attached to "Report on Walter Wilson Jenkins," October 22, 1964 (hereafter "RWWJ"). All quotations from this report are either from the copy in box 29B, Office Files of Mildred Stegall, LBJL, or from a copy obtained by the author from the FBI via the Freedom of Information Act (request 1390108-000). The two versions contain different, partially overlapping sets of redactions.

22. RWWJ, 77–78. On the police accepting twenty-five-dollar collateral to dispose of arrests, see also US Congress, Senate, Committee on Expenditures in the Executive Departments, *Employment of Homosexuals and Other Sex Perverts in Government*, Senate Doc. 241, 81st Cong., 2nd sess. (1950), 18–19.

23. Norman Heine to Walter Jenkins, June 22, 1949, Walter Jenkins Personal folder, box 79, PPWJ. "That Saturday Morning at the end of April," Heine wrote, "I crawled on the PRR train for New York, and tritely, my head was bloody but unbowed." Here he invoked the second stanza of William Ernest Henley's 1875 Victorian poem "Invictus": "Under the bludgeonings of chance / My head is bloody, but unbowed."

24. David K. Johnson, *The Lavender Scare: The Cold War Persecution of Gays and Lesbians in the Federal Government* (University of Chicago Press, 2004), 59–63; Regina Kunzel, "Sex Panic, Psychiatry, and the Expansion of the Carceral State," in *The War on Sex*, ed. David M. Halperin and Trevor Hoppe (Duke University Press, 2017), 229–46; "Prosecutor Would Close Comfort Stations at Night," *Washington Evening Star*, October 17, 1950.

25. Norman Powell Heine to Walter Jenkins, July 24, 1950; Walter Jenkins to Norman Heine, July 28, 1950; Norman Heine to Walter Jenkins, September 25, 1951; "WDM," memorandum to Walter Jenkins, September 28, 1951; and Walter Jenkins to Norman Heine, October 2, 1951, all in Heine, Norman folder, box 60B, Lyndon Baines Johnson Archives Collection, LBJL. This collection is a file created in 1958 by Johnson Senate staff. See also Sam Zagoria, "Services Speed Up Recruiting To Reach Authorized Strength," *Washington Post*, July 9, 1950; Paul P. Kennedy, "Call for Reserves Will Come at Once," *New York Times*, July 20, 1950.

26. In 1960 he legally changed his name to Norman Heine Powell (RWWJ, 77). At his death in 1972, aged fifty-four, he was a vice president at an advertising agency and survived by two married sisters living in Texas. His obituary noted his service on Johnson's staff "in 1941–42 and again in 1949." "Norman Powell, 54, Ad Executive, Dies," *New York Times*, February 2, 1972.

27. *The WPA Guide to Washington, D.C.* (Hastings House, 1942), 250; Henry Gerber to "my dear Saint Francis," June 20, 1945, folder 2, box 1, Manuel boyFrank Papers, ONE National Gay and Lesbian Archives, Los Angeles.

28. Johnson, *Lavender Scare*, 163–65; Genny Beemyn, *A Queer Capital: A History of Gay Life in Washington, DC* (Routledge, 2015), 101–6; Kwame Holmes, "Beyond the Flames: Queering the History of the 1968 D.C. Riot," in *No Tea, No Shade: New Writings in Black Queer Studies*, ed. E. Patrick Johnson (Duke University Press, 2016), 304–22, at 315; District of Columbia Office of Planning, "Historic Context Statement for Washington's LGBTQ Resources," September 2019, https://planning.dc.gov/publication/dc-lgbtq-resources, 2–59; Allen Young interview, April 24, 2012, by Peter Jeffs, Rainbow History Project, https://archives.rainbowhistory.org/files/original/02eabb5b2116e3e23df7e61dd08bb1a5.pdf.

29. Ed Wallace OH, by Genny Beemyn, May 25, 1994, Queer Capital Oral History Collection, Rainbow History Project, https://archives.rainbowhistory.org/files/original/51d325ba2af871c6ad6a76708094020b.pdf.

30. Jerry Kluttz, "The Federal Diary," *Washington Post*, July 16, 1950; F. D. Flanagan, memo, "Perversion Probe—Metropolitan Police Department," June 16, 1950, and James F. Sheridan to Francis D. Flanagan, July 26, 1950 (incorrectly giving Heine's first name as Herman), 40-21-17, Numbered Case Files, Permanent Subcommittee on Investigations, Records of the US Senate Committee on Government Operations (RG 46), National Archives, Washington, DC.

31. Johnson, *Lavender Scare*, 43–46; James Gilbert, *Men in the Middle: Searching for Masculinity in the 1950s* (University of Chicago Press, 2005); Rebecca L. Davis, *Fierce Desires: A New History of Sex and Sexuality in America* (W. W. Norton, 2024), 209–26; Robert D. Dean, *Imperial Brotherhood: Gender and the Making of Cold War Foreign Policy* (University of Massachusetts Press, 2001).

32. Clayton Howard, "Building a 'Family-Friendly' Metropolis: Sexuality, the State, and Postwar Housing Policy," *Journal of Urban History* 39, no. 5 (September 2013), 933–55; J. R. Ylitalo to D. L. Nicholson, August 27, 1951, "Checks on Security Risks (Including Moral + Sex Deviates) I-E/2" folder, box 12, Decimal Files, 1953–60, Records of the Bureau of Security and Consular Affairs, RG 59 (Department of State), National Archives, College Park, Maryland; C. P. Russell, "Senators Ask U.S. Dismiss 'Bad Risks,'" *New York Times*, July 21, 1950; "Summary Dismissal Of U.S. Employees," in *CQ Almanac 1950*, 6th ed., 398–400 (Congressional Quarterly, 1951), http://library.cqpress.com/cqalmanac/cqal50-1378092. All Armed Services Committee members except Wayne Morse of Oregon (then a Republican) voted for the measure. Within the committee, Styles Bridges, a right-wing New Hampshire Republican, successfully argued for removing a House provision that would have allowed some dismissed employees to remain in other jobs. An amendment

by Lester Hunt, a liberal Wyoming Democrat, to soften the bill's emphasis on "security" was rejected.

33. *Employment of Homosexuals and Other Sex Perverts in Government*, 9, 18.

34. Margot Canaday, *The Straight State: Sexuality and Citizenship in Twentieth-Century America* (Princeton University Press, 2009), 142.

35. See William N. Eskridge Jr., *Gaylaw: Challenging the Apartheid of the Closet* (Harvard University Press, 1999); Johnson, *Lavender Scare*; Anna Lvovsky, *Vice Patrol: Cops, Courts, and the Struggle over Urban Gay Life before Stonewall* (University of Chicago Press, 2021); and Timothy Stewart-Winter, *Queer Clout: Chicago and the Rise of Gay Politics* (University of Pennsylvania Press, 2016).

36. Margot Canaday, "Heterosexuality as a Legal Regime," in *The Cambridge History of Law in America*, vol. 3, ed. Michael Grossberg and Christopher Tomlins (Cambridge University Press, 2008), 442–71, here 445.

37. Timothy Stewart-Winter, "Queer Law and Order: Sex, Criminality, and Policing in the Late Twentieth Century United States," *Journal of American History* 102, no. 1 (June 2015), 61–72; John Howard, "The Library, the Park, and the Pervert: Public Space and Homosexual Encounter in Post–World War II Atlanta," *Radical History Review* 62 (1995), 166–87; Fred Fejes, "Murder, Perversion, and Moral Panic: The 1954 Media Campaign against Miami's Homosexuals and the Discourse of Civic Betterment," *Journal of the History of Sexuality* 9, no. 3 (2000): 305–47; John G. Gerassi, *The Boys of Boise: Furor, Vice, and Folly in an American City* (Macmillan, 1966); Neil Miller, *Sex-Crime Panic: A Journey to the Paranoid Heart of the 1950s* (Alyson Books, 2002); "One Officer Called Morals Trials," *Greensboro News & Record*, August 17, 2006, http://www.greensboro.com/news/general_assignment/one-officer-called-morals-trials/article_70dfd5b9-d675-5c80-a98f-274fc5f0c0fe.html.

38. Anna Lvovsky, "Cruising in Plain View: Clandestine Surveillance and the Unique Insights of Antihomosexual Policing," *Journal of Urban History* 46, no. 5 (2020), 980–1001, here 983.

39. Among the few newspapers to carry Drew Pearson's column were the *Rapid City Journal* ("Pearson Says Sen. Hunt Feared Political Blackmail Involving Son," June 23, 1954), the *Detroit Free Press* ("Who Killed Senator Hunt? The Untold, Tragic Story," June 22, 1954), and the *Capital Times* [Madison, WI] ("Says Senator Hunt Was Blackmailed On Son's Morals," June 22, 1954). Marquis Childs later confirmed parts of Pearson's account ("Smears and Tears Plague the Senate," *Washington Post*, July 6, 1954). See Rodger McDaniel, *Dying for Joe McCarthy's Sins: The Suicide of Wyoming Senator Lester Hunt* (Cody, Wyoming: WordsWorth, 2013); Rick Ewig, "McCarthy Era Politics: The Ordeal of Senator Lester Hunt," *Annals of Wyoming* 55 (Spring 1983), 9–21; Donald A. Ritchie, *The Columnist: Leaks, Lies, and Libel in Drew Pearson's Washington* (Oxford University Press, 2021).

40. Mike Manatos's recollection in 1964 is described in McDaniel, *Dying for Joe McCarthy's Sins*, Kindle edition, 276.

41. Marquis Childs, "Smears and Tears Plague the Senate," quoted in Ewig, "McCarthy Era Politics," 15; US Congress, *Memorial Services Held in the Senate and House of Representatives of the United States: Together with Remarks Presented in Eulogy of Lester Callaway*

Hunt, Late a Senator from Wyoming, 83d Cong., 2d sess., 1954 (Government Printing Office, 1955), 14; Walter Jenkins to Senator Johnson, June 21, 1954, in Memos: Walter Jenkins to the Senator, 1954 folder, box 1, Pre-Presidential Memo File, LBJL. Hunt and Johnson were elected together in 1948 and served together on the Armed Services Committee.

42. Drury, *Advise and Consent*, 292, 410.

43. Susan M. Hartmann, "Prescriptions for Penelope: Literature on Women's Obligations to Returning World War II Veterans," *Women's Studies* 5 (1978), 223–39; Rickie Solinger, *Wake Up Little Susie: Single Pregnancy and Race Before Roe v. Wade* (Routledge, 2000).

44. Jeff Shesol, *Mercury Rising: John Glenn, John Kennedy, and the New Battleground of the Cold War* (W. W. Norton, 2022), 91.

45. Max Lerner, "The Washington Sex Story: No. 1—Panic on the Potomac," *New York Post*, July 10, 1950.

46. William H. Whyte Jr., *The Organization Man* (Simon and Schuster, 1956), 3.

47. Lyndon B. Johnson to Harold D. Fangboner, February 12, 1948, in PPWJ, 2022 addendum; Lyndon B. Johnson to Leo Corrigan, December 2, 1949, Walter Jenkins—Personal—1950 folder, box 93, PPWJ; "Housing Unit Sale Reported," *Arlington Daily*, January 2, 1947.

48. Walter Jenkins OH VI, September 16, 1982, by Michael L. Gillette, LBJL; Abigail McCarthy, "Political Wife" (1972), in *Katharine Graham's Washington* (Vintage, 2002), 640–45, here 643; Dallek, *Lone Star Rising*, 362; interview with Beth Jenkins Bromberg and Walt Jenkins, Jr., Bee Cave, Texas, June 4, 2016.

49. Walter Jenkins to Lyndon B. Johnson, April 10, 1947, in Memos: Walter Jenkins to the Senator, 1946–1951 folder, box 1, Pre-Presidential Memo File, LBJL; Jacob R. Straus, "Enforcement of Congressional Rules of Conduct: A Historical Overview," Congressional Research Service, February 23, 2015.

50. Walter Jenkins OH VIII, July 22, 1983, by Michael L. Gillette, LBJL; Walter Jenkins OH I, August 14, 1970, by Joe B. Frantz, LBJL; Glynn Stegall to Walter Jenkins, November 17, 1946, Memos: Inter-Office, prior to 1952 [1939–1946] folder, box 1, Pre-Presidential Memo File, LBJL; Walter Jenkins to J. C. Kellam, October 20, 1949, Walter Jenkins Personal folder, box 79, PPWJ. On Johnson hiring the wives of employees in response to the wives' complaints about their husbands' hours, see Alfred Steinberg, *Sam Johnson's Boy: A Close-Up of the President from Texas* (Macmillan, 1968), 279.

51. Marj to Walter Jenkins, "Friday" [Nov. 1950], and Marjorie Jenkins to Walter Jenkins, n.d., "Thursday" [Thanksgiving Day, 1950], both in Walter Jenkins—Personal—1950 folder, box 93, PPWJ.

52. Lyndon B. Johnson to Leo Corrigan, December 2, 1949, Walter Jenkins—Personal—1950 folder, box 93, PPWJ; "Housing Unit Sale Reported," *Arlington Daily*, January 2, 1947.

53. Jessica Weiss, *To Have and To Hold: Marriage, the Baby Boom, and Social Change* (University of Chicago Press, 2000), 121, 124; Constance Casey, "Memoirs of a Congressman's Daughter" (first published 1992), in *Katharine Graham's Washington*, 229–40, here 236, 240; Marvella Bayh, "Life Intertwines Along the Potomac" (1979), in *Katharine Graham's Washington*, 90–99, here 95.

54. Hans Kraus, MD, in Jenkins medical record, January 10, 1964, exhibit I, attached to RWWJ; Ellen Proxmire, *One Foot in Washington: The Perilous Life of a Senator's Wife* (Robert B. Luce, Inc., 1963), 32–33; interview with Luci Baines Johnson, Austin, Texas, April 5, 2018.

55. Walter Jenkins to Helen Grace Gould, May 6, 1955, Walter Jenkins Personal May–December 1955 folder, box 187, PPWJ.

56. Envelope accompanying letter to Walter Jenkins from Committee on Arrangements to "B.B.A. Exes," January 12, 1952, in Walter Jenkins Personal folder, box 79, PPWJ; Douglass Cater, "Lyndon Johnson, Rising Democratic Star," *The Reporter*, January 20, 1953, 37; Walter Jenkins to Lela Belle O'Neal, October 20, 1952, in Walter Jenkins Personal folder, box 79, PPWJ. On a federal-state dispute over offshore oil that contributed to Eisenhower's victory that year in normally Democratic Texas, see Edward A. Fitzgerald, "The Tidelands Controversy Revisited," *Environmental Law* 19, no. 2 (Winter 1989): 209–56.

57. Lyndon B. Johnson to Walter Jenkins, June 27, 1951, in Correspondence—Jenkins, Walter folder, box 439, Senate Papers, LBJL; "Opening Speech, Wichita Falls, July 23," in speeches notebook, box 250, PPWJ; Walter Jenkins OH X, October 6, 1983, by Michael L. Gillette, LBJL, 23; Walter Jenkins to George R. Brown, October 26, 1951, in Walter Jenkins Personal folder, box 79, PPWJ.

58. Walter Jenkins to Paul Popple, April 4, 1947, copy in PPWJ, 2022 addendum; "The Communists—There is No Peace in Their Hearts," "I'll Have Tens of Thousands of Bosses—Speech No. 3," and "Henrietta Rally, August 18, 1951," all in speeches notebook, box 250, PPWJ.

59. C. P. Masters to Lyndon Baines Johnson, August 25, 1951, in Correspondence—Jenkins, Walter folder, box 439, Senate Papers, LBJL; Walter Jenkins OH I, August 14, 1970, by Joe B. Frantz, LBJL; Walter Jenkins OH X, October 6, 1983, by Michael L. Gillette, LBJL; W. T. Knight to Walter Jenkins, November 7, 1951, in Walter Jenkins Personal folder, box 79, PPWJ. On the 1928 election in Texas, see John Gunther, *Inside U.S.A.* (Harper & Brothers, 1947), 847.

60. Walter Jenkins OH X, October 6, 1983, by Michael L. Gillette, LBJL, 26; conversations with Beth Jenkins Bromberg, Bee Cave, Texas, October 7–9, 2022.

61. Donald R. Matthews, *US Senators and Their World* (Vintage, 1960), 135–36; Dallek, *Lone Star Rising*, 470–75; Walter Jenkins OH XII, April 25, 1984, by Michael L. Gillette, LBJL.

62. "Men Behind Senators," *Newsweek*, January 28, 1957, 33–35, here 33.

63. Walter Jenkins to Lyndon B. Johnson, June 16, 1953, in Walter Jenkins to the Senator 1953 folder, box 2, Pre-Presidential Memo File, LBJL; Walter Jenkins memo, June 26, 1959, in "Master File Index, 1959: Jenkins, Walter [1 of 2]," Master File Index, box 96, Senate Papers, LBJL; Walter Jenkins, memo, July 2, 1954, in "Master File Index, 1955: Jenkins, Walter," Master File Index, box 96, Senate Papers, LBJL.

64. Walter Jenkins OH II, August 24, 1971, by Joe B. Frantz, LBJL; Walter Jenkins interview by Emmette S. Redford and Richard McCulley, November 12, 1980, LBJL; George Reedy, *Lyndon B. Johnson: A Memoir* (Andrews and McMeel, 1982), 37; Walter Jenkins to Lyndon B. Johnson, October 26, 1954, Pre-Presidential Memo File, LBJL.

65. Walter Jenkins to Lyndon B. Johnson, August 29, 1957, in box 5, Pre-Presidential Memo File, LBJL; Dallek, *Lone Star Rising*, 526; Walter Jenkins to Lyndon B. Johnson, undated [ca. March 30, 1953], box 2, Pre-Presidential Memo File, LBJL; Walter Jenkins OH I, August 14, 1970, by Joe B. Frantz, LBJL.

66. Walter Jenkins OH IX, September 22, 1983, by Michael L. Gillette, LBJL; "Texas Scientists Play Major Role in Oil Research," *Odessa American*, October 11, 1953; "UT's Off-Campus Science Laboratories Renamed 'Balcones Research Center,'" *Austin American-Statesman*, May 14, 1953; "University Prime Asset in R & D Growth Here," *Austin American-Statesman*, September 6, 1962, "Balcones Lab Draws Industry in Southwest," *Austin American-Statesman*, February 17, 1964.

67. Dallek, *Lone Star Rising*, 486; Booth Mooney, *The Politicians: 1945–1960* (Lippincott, 1970), 230; Walter Jenkins to W. R. Langston, August 18, 1955, Walter Jenkins Personal May–December 1955 folder, box 187, PPWJ; *Letters from the Hill Country: The Correspondence Between Rebekah and Lyndon Baines Johnson*, ed. Philip R. Rulon (Thorp Springs Press, 1982), 51–54; telephone conversation no. 2384, sound recording, LBJ and WALTER JENKINS, March 7, 1964, 11:55 a.m., LBJL. Writing checks and paying bills "wasn't considered personal work in those days," Jenkins explained. Walter Jenkins OH VI, September 16, 1982, by Michael L. Gillette, LBJL, 13.

68. Walter Jenkins to Lyndon B. Johnson, May 25, 1954, box 2, Pre-Presidential Memo File, LBJL; interview with Bill Moyers, New York City, August 8, 2017.

69. Russell Baker, "Senate Approves Filibuster Curb Asked by Johnson," *New York Times*, January 13, 1959; Allen Drury, "Senate Increases Committee Posts," *New York Times*, January 15, 1959; *Congressional Record—Senate*, January 14, 1959, 671.

70. "Officer's Bad Discharge Upheld," *Washington Post*, December 19, 1961; "Four Fined $50 in Morals Case," *Washington Post*, April 22, 1961.

71. J. R. Wiggins, "The Famous Have Less Protection," *Bulletin of the American Society of Newspaper Editors* 481 (December 1, 1964), 1, 15, folder 87, box 155, Abe Fortas Papers, Yale University Library.

72. Louis A. Fochett to Scott E. Moyer, October 15, 1964, attached to RWWJ, enclosure E; "3 Detectives Promoted," *Washington Post*, August 4, 1962; "Police Lt. Louis Fochett, Served in Morals Unit," *Washington Post*, April 16, 1968.

CHAPTER 2

1. Sidey to Parker, October 15, 1964, in Johnson, Lyndon (16 of 22) folder, box 31k, THWP; interview with Bill Moyers, New York City, August 8, 2017; Walter Jenkins interview by Emmette S. Redford and Richard McCulley, November 12, 1980, LBJL, 21.

2. Walter Jenkins OH II, August 24, 1971, by Joe B. Frantz, LBJL, 16; Walter Jenkins to Lyndon Baines Johnson, November 16, 1959, Walter Jenkins [Administrative] Memoranda folder 1 of 2, box 633, Senate Papers, LBJL; Walter Jenkins OH II, August 24, 1971, by Joe B. Frantz, LBJL, 20–22.

3. Walter Jenkins OH II, August 24, 1971, by Joe B. Frantz, LBJL, 20–22; Rowland Evans and Robert Novak, *Lyndon B. Johnson: The Exercise of Power* (New American Library, 1966), 276.

4. Doris Whitehill to Walter Jenkins, September 23, 1960, in 2022 addendum, PPWJ; Walter Jenkins OH II, August 24, 1971, by Joe B. Frantz, LBJL, 24.

5. Walter Jenkins OH II, August 24, 1971, by Joe B. Frantz, LBJL.

6. Walter Jenkins OH II, August 24, 1971, by Joe B. Frantz, LBJL, 28–29.

7. Sheldon M. Stern, *The Cuban Missile Crisis in American Memory: Myths Versus Reality* (Stanford University Press, 2012), 148–53; David G. Winter, *Roots of War: Wanting Power, Seeing Threat, Justifying Force* (Oxford University Press, 2017), 179.

8. Walter Jenkins OH II, August 24, 1971, by Joe B. Frantz, LBJL, 28; Walter Jenkins interview by Emmette S. Redford and Richard McCulley, November 12, 1980, LBJL, 11.

9. Walter Jenkins interview by Emmette S. Redford and Richard McCulley, November 12, 1980, LBJL, 11; Mitchell Lerner, "'A Big Tree of Peace and Justice': The Vice Presidential Travels of Lyndon Johnson," *Diplomatic History* 34, no. 2 (2010): 357–93.

10. Sally Bedell Smith, *Grace and Power: The Private World of the Kennedy White House* (Random House, 2004), 144–66, quotation at 155.

11. Walter Jenkins OH II, August 24, 1971, by Joe B. Frantz, LBJL, 43; Beverly Gage, *G-Man: J. Edgar Hoover and the Making of the American Century* (Viking, 2022), 564; "White House Telephone Line Security" (on FBI director's letterhead), December 27, 1963, "Ex FG 11-8-1/Jenkins, Walter" folder, box 86, Presidential Papers, LBJL.

12. Elizabeth Brenner Drew, "The Health Syndicate," *Atlantic* (December 1967), 75–82; Mary Lasker OH I, November 10, 1969, by Joe B. Frantz, LBJL (in this interview, Lasker recalls Johnson saying on the evening of November 24, "I've already heard 962 things he was going to do"); Mary Lasker OH I, April 18, 1966, by Charles T. Morrissey, JFK Library.

13. Walter Jenkins to Lyndon B. Johnson, November 24, 1963, in Memoranda to the President, "November 23, 1963–Nov. 1964" folder, box 53, Office Files of Mildred Stegall and Walter Jenkins, LBJL; Walter Jenkins to Lyndon B. Johnson, December 4, 1963, "Johnson, Lyndon B.—Memos to [3 of 3] [1963]" folder, box 27, Office Files of Mildred Stegall and Walter Jenkins, LBJL. Lasker later cited the nationwide spread of intensive-care units as one of the most important long-term effects of the 1965 law (Mary Lasker OH II, July 19, 1978, by Michael L. Gillette, LBJL).

14. Lee C. White OH I, September 28, 1970, by Joe B. Frantz, LBJL; Ralph Dungan OH I, April 18, 1969, by Paige E. Mulhollan, LBJL.

15. George Reedy, *Lyndon B. Johnson: A Memoir* (Andrews and McMeel, 1982), 45. He added, "In most cases it worked alright. Some of them were kind of prima donnas like Arthur Schlesinger." Walter Jenkins interview by Emmette S. Redford and Richard McCulley, November 12, 1980, LBJL, 23.

16. Walter Jenkins OH II, August 24, 1971, by Joe B. Frantz, LBJL.

17. President's Daily Diary, December 7, 1963, LBJL; Lorraine Barnes, "Loosely, It's Luci," *Austin American-Statesman*, February 26, 1964; interview with Luci Baines Johnson, Austin, Texas, April 5, 2018; "Today in Washington" (AP), *Lebanon Daily News*, December 23, 1963; SAC, WFO to Director, October 18, 1964, in FBI file 161-HQ-2848.

18. Carol Foley, "Johnson Aides Fill Key Roles," *Fort Worth Star-Telegram*, November 24, 1963; Howard M. Ziff, "Johnson's Men: Practical Texas Politicians," *Chicago Daily*

News, November 25, 1963; Tom Wicker, "Johnson's Men: 'Valuable Hunks of Humanity,'" *New York Times Magazine*, May 3, 1964.

19. William S. White, "Walter-Jenkins: New Man Closest to the President," *Houston Chronicle*, December 13, 1963. Erwin Knoll and Laurence Stern described White as Johnson's "journalistic Boswell": "Closing the Books on Baker," *The Reporter*, April 9, 1964, 20.

20. Walter Jenkins interview by Emmette S. Redford and Richard McCulley, November 12, 1980, LBJL; "Jenkins, Johnson's Aide for 19 Years, is Key Man on White House Staff," *Washington Evening Star*, December 8, 1963.

21. Betty Beale, "Convention Plan; Jenkins Party," *Washington Evening Star*, January 24, 1964; Karen Klinefelter, "Potomac Patter," *Dallas News*, July 5, 1964, in Jenkins, Walter vertical file, Dolph Briscoe Center for American History, University of Texas at Austin. On Dale Miller—the Texas lobbyist and a former University of Texas classmate of Mrs. Johnson, whose clients included the Dallas Chamber of Commerce and various Texas firms—see David S. Broder, "The President's Favorite Lobbyist," *Look*, April 4, 1965, 66–68.

22. Jack Valenti OH, February 19, 1971, by Joe B. Frantz, LBJL; Walter Jenkins interview by Emmette S. Redford and Richard McCulley, November 12, 1980, LBJL, 9.

23. Cabell Phillips, "Johnson Weighs Make-Up of Staff but Asks Kennedy Aides and Cabinet to Stay," *New York Times*, October 24, 1963; Walter Jenkins interview by Emmette S. Redford and Richard McCulley, November 12, 1980, LBJL, 17; Charles Roberts, *LBJ's Inner Circle* (Delacorte Press, 1965), 44.

24. Walter Jenkins interview by Emmette S. Redford and Richard McCulley, November 12, 1980, LBJL, 22; Betty Beale, "Newsmaking Names Long for a Change," *Washington Evening Star*, December 29, 1963.

25. Alfred Steinberg, *Sam Johnson's Boy: A Close-Up of the President from Texas* (Macmillan, 1968), 280; telephone conversation no. 1530, sound recording, LBJ and WALTER JENKINS, January 24, 1964, 6:40 p.m., LBJL; "NASA Official Cancels Speech," *Jackson Daily News*, January 28, 1964; telephone conversation no. 1828, sound recording, LBJ and JOE KILGORE, February 3, 1964, 1:20 p.m., LBJL. In November Yarborough easily defeated Republican George Bush, whose father Prescott had recently retired as a US senator from Connecticut and who later rose to the presidency.

26. Carl M. Brauer, "Kennedy, Johnson, and the War on Poverty," *Journal of American History* 69, no. 1 (June 1982): 98–119, here 115; John C. Donovan, *The Politics of Poverty* (Pegasus, 1967), 36–37, quotation at 36; telephone conversation no. 4795, sound recording, LBJ and LARRY O'BRIEN, August 7, 1964, 12:50 p.m., LBJL.

27. Telephone conversation no. 4821, sound recording, LBJ and WALTER JENKINS, August 8, 1964, 10:52 a.m., LBJL.

28. Jack Landau, "Senate Official is Named in Influence Split," *Washington Post*, September 12, 1963; Robert A. Caro, *The Passage of Power*, vol. 4 of *The Years of Lyndon Johnson* (Knopf, 2012), 275; Horace Busby, *The Thirty-First of March: An Intimate Portrait of Lyndon Johnson's Final Days in Office* (Farrar, Straus and Giroux, 2005), 129. See also Laurence Stern and Jack Landau, "FBI Probes Vending Machine Firm Linked to Senate Aide," *Wash-*

ington Post, October 3, 1963, Jack Landau and Laurence Stern, "Baker Resigns as Probe Widens," *Washington Post*, October 8, 1963; Laurence Stern, "Senate Votes Full Baker Case Probe," *Washington Post*, October 11, 1963.

29. Bobby Baker with Larry L. King, *Wheeling and Dealing: Confessions of a Capitol Hill Operator* (W. W. Norton, 1978), 170–76; Caro, *Passage of Power*, 279; Sarah McClendon with Jules Minton, *Mr. President, Mr. President: My Fifty Years of Covering the White House* (General Publishing Group, 1996), 116. McClendon recalled that she tried to scandalize Jenkins, a Catholic, by noting that abortions were a minor, rumored element of the story, apparently thinking this might change his view of the matter, though she acknowledges omitting any mention of abortion from her published stories.

30. Robert Dallek, *Lone Star Rising: Lyndon Johnson and His Times, 1908–1960* (Oxford University Press, 1991), 477.

31. Dallek, *Lone Star Rising*, 499; Ted Lewis, "Johnson Dodging Baker, Korth Barbs," *Philadelphia Inquirer*, October 31, 1963; "Baker and Korth" (editorial), *New York Times*, November 10, 1963; Jack Raymond, "TFX Case Typifies Conflict-of-Interest Problem," *New York Times*, August 3, 1963.

32. Laurence Stern and Erwin Knoll, "Washington: Outsiders' Exposé," *Columbia Journalism Review* (Spring 1964), 18–23; "That High-Living Baker Boy Scandalizes the Capital," *Life*, November 8, 1963, 32; Keith Wheeler, "Scandal Grows and Grows in Washington," *Life*, November 22, 1963, 40.

33. Robert A. Caro, *Master of the Senate*, vol. 3 of *The Years of Lyndon Johnson* (Vintage, 2002), 404–9.

34. George E. Reedy to Walter Jenkins, November 25, 1963, in "Memoranda inner office [1957–1961]" folder, box 8, Office Files of Mildred Stegall and Walter Jenkins, LBJL; Clark Mollenhoff, "Baker Owned $1 Million in Serv-U Stock," *Des Moines Register*, January 1, 1964.

35. Cabell Phillips, "Kickback Linked to Johnson Aide," *New York Times*, January 22, 1964; Cabell Phillips, "Major Political Scandal Looming in the Bobby Baker Case," *New York Times*, January 26, 1964; Cabell Phillips, "TV Data Received by Baker Inquiry," *New York Times*, January 28, 1964; "GOP Plugs Jenkins Quiz" (AP), *Dallas Times Herald*, January 29, 1964; Lawrence Stern, "Jenkins Story Upheld on Details of TV Deal," *Washington Post*, February 1, 1964; Baker, *Wheeling and Dealing*, 196.

36. Telephone conversation no. 1410, sound recording, LBJ and ABE FORTAS, January 17, 1964, 7:40 p.m., LBJL; telephone conversation no. 1612, sound recording, LBJ and RICHARD RUSSELL, January 29, 1964, 10:30 a.m., LBJL; telephone conversation no. 1664, sound recording, LBJ and ABE FORTAS, January 30, 1964, 5:55 p.m., LBJL; telephone conversation no. 1499, sound recording, LBJ and WALTER JENKINS, January 23, 1964, 4:33 p.m., LBJL.

37. Charles B. Seib and Alan L. Otten, "Abe, Help!—LBJ," *Esquire*, June 1965, 86–88, 147–49, at 88; Paul Hope and John Barron, "Baker Probers Study 1959 Gift to Johnson," *Washington Evening Star*, January 19, 1964; Cabell Phillips, "White House Aides Seek to Impugn Baker Witness," *New York Times*, February 8, 1964; Stern and Knoll, "Washington: Outsiders' Exposé," 21.

38. Telephone conversation no. 2381, sound recording, LBJ and WALTER JENKINS, March 7, 1964, 11:41 a.m., LBJL; telephone conversation no. 2384, sound recording, LBJ and WALTER JENKINS, March 7, 1964, 11:55 a.m., LBJL.

39. Louis M. Kohlmeier, "The Johnson Wealth: How President's Wife Built $17,500 Into Big Fortune in Television," *Wall Street Journal*, March 23, 1964; Louis M. Kohlmeier, "Johnson & the FCC: Agency Curb on Rival of Wife's TV Station Spotlights Touchy Issue," *Wall Street Journal*, March 24, 1964.

40. Erwin Knoll and Laurence Stern, "Closing the Books on Baker," *The Reporter*, April 9, 1964, 19; Patrick Munroe, "Washington News Correspondents," in *The Press in Washington*, ed. Ray Eldon Hiebert (Dodd, Mead, 1966), 15–16 ("increasing emphasis"). The Baker scandal came early in a gradual and uneven shift in the Washington press corps' approach to misconduct by the powerful, as reporters began actively seeking records and documents. The investigation of Baker foreshadowed not only later inquiries into Adam Clayton Powell and Thomas Dodd but also the still greater prominence that scandal would assume in US politics in the 1970s. Julian E. Zelizer, *On Capitol Hill: The Struggle to Reform Congress and Its Consequences, 1948–2000* (Cambridge University Press, 2004), 84.

41. James Reston, "Washington: Who Will Dare Investigate the Investigators?" *New York Times*, November 1, 1963; Ben H. Bagdikian and Don Oberdorfer, "Bobby Was the Boy to See," *Saturday Evening Post*, December 7, 1963, 26–29, here 26. For a similar comparison in the British press see Karl E. Meyer, "Washington's Profumo Scandal," *New Statesman* 66 (November 1, 1963), 601. On Profumo, see Colin Frost, "Profumo Quits, Admits Affair with Model," *Washington Post*, June 6, 1963; "Macmillan Faces Crisis on Profumo," *New York Times*, June 10, 1963.

42. The Advance newspaper chain reported on Carole Tyler, a young Baker employee whom he falsely listed as a "cousin" on an application for an FHA-underwritten mortgage for a Capitol Hill townhouse and with whom he was having an affair. Erwin Knoll and Theodor Schuchat, "Democratic Ex-Aid Baker Revealed As Owner of House Occupied By Girls," *St. Louis Globe-Democrat*, October 21, 1963. Soon after, Clark Mollenhoff of the *Des Moines Register* and the Cowles newspaper chain reported on a "German beauty" named Ellen Rometsch, part of Baker's circle, who Mollenhoff alleged had been linked romantically with "some White House figures" before being abruptly deported to West Germany in the summer of 1962; see "Mystery Surrounds Party Girl Story" (AP), *Tucson Daily Citizen*, October 28, 1963. See also Clark Mollenhoff, "House Hears About Baker and 'Beauties,'" *Minneapolis Star and Tribune*, October 29, 1963.

43. "Agent Who Wrote Johnson Insurance Says He Was Asked to Buy Ads on Family Station," *Wall Street Journal*, January 22, 1964; Baker, *Wheeling and Dealing*, 80 ("guilt"), 201 ("refused").

44. Gage, *G-Man*, 553, 582–83; Jenkins, handwritten draft responses to inquiry from Senate Select Committee to Study Governmental Operations with Respect to Intelligence Activities, n.d. [1976], Senate Intelligence Committee folder, box 305, PPWJ. In these drafts Jenkins denied that he knew in 1964 that the FBI was electronically surveilling Martin Luther King Jr. and other civil rights activists during the Democratic convention in Atlantic City, although later-released phone recordings show he did know.

45. Kenneth O'Reilly, *Racial Matters: The FBI's Secret File on Black America* (Free Press, 1989), 154; David J. Garrow, *The FBI and Martin Luther King Jr.: From "Solo" to Memphis* (W. W. Norton, 1981), 117–18; J. Edgar Hoover to Walter W. Jenkins, July 17, 1964, in Martin Luther King folder 1 of 2, box 32, Office Files of Mildred Stegall, LBJL.

46. Taylor Branch, *Pillar of Fire: America in the King Years, 1963–65* (Simon & Schuster, 1998), 456–73; Gage, *G-Man*, 594–603.

47. Telephone conversation no. 5156, sound recording, LBJ and WALTER JENKINS, August 24, 1964, 4:31 p.m.?, LBJL; Chalmers M. Roberts, "Atlantic City Dispute Solution Work of Many," *Washington Post*, September 5, 1964. Many accounts of the convention give short shrift to the risk that other Southern delegations would walk out; see, among others, James Reston Jr., *The Lone Star: The Life of John Connally* (Harper & Row, 1989), 354–55.

48. Telephone conversation no. 5177, sound recording, LBJ and WALTER JENKINS, August 25, 1964, 11:23 a.m., LBJL; Julia Sweig, *Lady Bird Johnson: Hiding in Plain Sight* (Random House, 2021), 103–5.

49. Gage, *G-Man*, 597–99; Branch, *Pillar of Fire*, 460–75; telephone conversation no. 5210, sound recording, LBJ and WALTER JENKINS, August 25, 1964, 9:33 p.m., LBJL. DeLoach later boasted that he had sent Jenkins forty-four pages of raw intelligence and kept "Jenkins and Moyers constantly advised by telephone of minute to minute developments. This enabled them to make spot decisions to adjust Convention plans to meet potential problems before serious trouble developed." C. D. DeLoach to J. Mohr, August 29, 1964, in FBI JFK file 62-116395-1134 (https://www.archives.gov/files/research/jfk/releases/docid-32989549.pdf).

50. J. Edgar Hoover to Walter W. Jenkins, August 14, 1964, in Kennedy, Robert F. folder, box 31A, Office Files of Mildred Stegall, LBJL.

51. Mike Mosettig, "LBJ: Producer-Writer-Director," *Variety*, September 2, 1964, 31.

52. Nicole Hemmer, *Messengers of the Right: Conservative Media and the Transformation of American Politics* (University of Pennsylvania Press, 2016), 166–68, 172. The three books were *None Dare Call It Treason* by John Stormer, *A Choice Not an Echo* by Phyllis Schlafly, and *A Texan Looks at Lyndon* by J. Evetts Haley.

53. See, e.g., "Barry Says LBJ Ordered New Baker Probe Delay" (AP), *New York Post*, October 14, 1964.

54. RWWJ, appended medical records, July 25, 1962; "Easter Parade 'Better Deal' Style," *Washington Evening Star*, March 29, 1964.

CHAPTER 3

1. RWWJ, 3, exhibit A-2.

2. Max Lerner, "'Scandal in the State Dept.: VIII—Blick of the Vice Squad," *New York Post*, July 18, 1950; US Congress, Senate, Committee on Expenditures in the Executive Departments, *Employment of Homosexuals and Other Sex Perverts in Government*, Senate Doc. 241, 81st Cong., 2nd sess., 1950, 19; on judges, see Anna Lvovsky, *Vice Patrol: Cops, Courts, and the Struggle over Urban Gay Life before Stonewall* (University of Chicago Press, 2021).

3. "Morals Arrests Here, in Washington Compared," *Los Angeles Times*, October 18, 1964.

4. RWWJ, exhibit A; Scott E. Moyer memo, October 16, 1964, in RWWJ, exhibit E. Responding to the FBI report, Moyer pledged to close the gap that "compassion" had opened in enforcement by ensuring that reports of morals arrests would henceforth "include accurate descriptions of suspects' occupations." Whether or not this was implemented, the division nonetheless scaled back morals arrests in public places, which fell by half from 1964 to 1965. Alfred E. Lewis and Willard Clopton, "Changes in Police Rules Follow Jenkins Arrest," *Washington Post*, October 24, 1964; "Morals in the Parks," *Washington Post*, January 1, 1966.

5. Report of interview with [Scott E. Moyer; originally redacted], October 16, 1964, in FBI file 161-HQ-2848.

6. Douglas Dillon to Nicholas Katzenbach, October 16, 1964, Walter Jenkins folder, box 10, National Security File—Intelligence File, Presidential Papers, LBJL; "The Charge: Washington Police Reporters Failed," *Bulletin of the American Society of Newspaper Editors* 481 (December 1, 1964), 2.

7. "The Charge: Washington Police Reporters Failed."

8. Saul Bellow, *Herzog* (Viking, 1964), 227. On liberal criticism, see Lvovsky, *Vice Patrol*.

9. Lvovsky, *Vice Patrol*, 21.

10. Anne Gray Fischer, "'Land of the White Hunter': Legal Liberalism and the Racial Politics of Morals Enforcement in Midcentury Los Angeles," *Journal of American History* 105 (March 2019), 868–84; Wayne R. LaFave, *Arrest: The Decision to Take a Suspect Into Custody* (Little Brown, 1965), 143n69 ("often"), 143n68 ("learned").

11. Loudon Wainwright, "What Road Back From Ruin?" *Life*, October 30, 1964, 31.

12. 1964 appointment book, box 250, PPWJ; Harry Jaffe, "Who Killed Newsweek?" *The Washingtonian*, January 27, 2011, https://www.washingtonian.com/2011/01/27/who-killed-newsweek/; summary of October 17 interview with Benjamin C. Bradlee, in "Investigation Re Activities of Walter Jenkins Following Newsweek Party 10/7/1964," in FBI file 161-HQ-2848.

13. Walter Jenkins interview by Emmette S. Redford and Richard McCulley, November 12, 1980, LBJL, 22; Stanlee Miller, "They Didn't Laugh Much—They Were Listening," *Washington Daily News*, March 27, 1964. Jenkins's calendar listed the screening on March 26, 1964: "Motion Picture Assn—The Best Man—Invited by Les C.—8PM" (1964 appointment book).

14. Andrew J. Glass, "Jenkins' Fall: Gala Before the Disgrace," *New York Herald-Tribune*, October 17, 1964; Katharine Graham, *Personal History* (Vintage, 1998).

15. Osborn Elliott, *The World of Oz* (Viking Press, 1980), 47–48.

16. William Walton, *The Evidence of Washington* (Harper & Row, 1966), 114; James Kirchick, *Secret City: The Hidden History of Gay Washington* (Henry Holt, 2022), 253–55.

17. Sidey to Parker, October 21, 1964, in Johnson, Lyndon (17 of 22) folder, box 31k, THWP; Glass, "Jenkins' Fall"; summary of October 17 interview with Benjamin C. Bradlee. Tom Wicker had cited "conflicting reports from those who attended the party as to whether Mr. Jenkins had had too much to drink." Tom Wicker, "Secret Service Had Jenkins File," *New York Times*, October 17, 1964.

18. Sidey to Parker, October 15, 1964, in Johnson, Lyndon (16 of 22) folder, box 31k, THWP.

19. RWWJ, 33–34; Chalmers M. Roberts, "Atlantic City Dispute Solution Work of Many," *Washington Post*, September 5, 1964.

20. David Wise, "'I'm in Terrible Trouble'—Jenkins' Tragedy," *New York Herald-Tribune*, October 18, 1964; RWWJ, 11. Wise's article, written with the cooperation of Abe Fortas, is the most detailed contemporaneous account of Jenkins's actions on October 7 and 14. Wise concluded that Jenkins probably did not leave through the back door of 1750 Pennsylvania Avenue, "which would have been simpler, because the rear entrance is normally locked at 6 p.m., and was that night."

21. Report of interview with Lieutenant [Fochett; originally redacted], October 15, 1964, in FBI file 161-HQ-2848.

22. Report of interview with [Drouillard; originally redacted], October 15, 1964, in FBI file 161-HQ-2848.

23. Wise, "'I'm in Terrible Trouble.'"

24. Report of interview with Lieutenant [Fochett; originally redacted], October 15, 1964, in FBI file 161-HQ-2848.

25. Editorial cartoon by Paul Conrad, *Los Angeles Times*, October 16, 1964; Charles Denton, "Anti-Social Notes From All Over," *San Francisco Examiner*, October 20, 1964.

26. Genny Beemyn, *A Queer Capital: A History of Gay Life in Washington, D.C.* (Routledge, 2015), 37–38; Russell Baker, "It's Middletown-on-the-Potomac," *New York Times Magazine*, February 14, 1965; Laud Humphreys, *Tearoom Trade: Impersonal Sex in Public Places* (Aldine, 1970), 3.

27. Alfred E. Lewis, "Police Move to Tighten Morals Setup," *Washington Post*, June 19, 1952; "Blick Assumes Lutz's Command As Plaudits Fly," *Washington Post*, April 2, 1958; Anna Lvovsky, "Cruising in Plain View: Clandestine Surveillance and the Unique Insights of Antihomosexual Policing," *Journal of Urban History* 46, no. 5 (2020), 980–1001.

28. Spencer E. Cahill with William Distler, Cynthia Lachowetz, Andrea Meaney, Robyn Tarallo, and Teena Willard, "Meanwhile Backstage: Public Bathrooms and the Interaction Order," *Urban Life* 14 (April 1985), 33–58; Simon Toner, "'The Paradise of the Latrine': American Toilet-Building and the Continuities of Colonial and Postcolonial Development," *Modern American History* 2 (2019), 299–320; Susan L. Carruthers, "Latrines as the Measure of Men: American Soldiers and the Politics of Disgust in Occupied Europe and Asia," *Diplomatic History* 42, no. 1 (2018), 109–37; Elizabeth Abel, "Bathroom Doors and Drinking Fountains: Jim Crow's Racial Symbolic," *Critical Inquiry* 25, no. 3 (1999), 435–81; Ruth Barcan, "Dirty Spaces: Separation, Concealment, and Shame in the Public Toilet," in *Toilet: Public Restrooms and the Politics of Sharing* (NYU Press, 2010), 25–46.

29. Sally Bedell Smith, *Grace and Power: The Private World of the Kennedy White House* (Random House, 2004), 372.

30. Douglas M. Charles, *Hoover's War on Gays: Exposing the FBI's "Sex Deviates" Program* (University Press of Kansas, 2015), 147; Donald Webster Cory, *The Homosexual in America: A Subjective Approach* (Greenberg, 1952), 56; Berry Werth, *The Scarlet Professor: Newton Arvin: A Literary Life Shattered by Scandal* (Anchor, 2001). See also Regina Kunzel,

"Sex Panic, Psychiatry, and the Expansion of the Carceral State," in *The War on Sex*, ed. David M. Halperin and Trevor Hoppe (Duke University Press, 2017), 229–46.

31. Jon J. Gallo et al., "The Consenting Adult Homosexual and the Law: An Empirical Study of Enforcement and Administration in Los Angeles County," *UCLA Law Review* 13, no. 3 (March 1966): 643–832, esp. 707n138; Paul Welch, "The 'Gay' World Takes to the City Streets," *Life*, June 24, 1964, 68–80, quotation at 71; "ISR H Study Code Book," 142–43, box 186, John Gagnon Papers, Special Collections and University Archives, Stony Brook University, Stony Brook, NY.

32. Lvovsky, *Vice Patrol*; Clare W. Kyler, "Camera Surveillance of Sex Deviates," *Law and Order* 11 (November 1963), 16–18, 20; "Boys Beware" (1955), produced by Unified School District and Police Department of Inglewood, California, https://www.pbs.org/video/american-experience-boys-beware/; "T-Room Traps," *Citizens News* 3, no. 8 (January 27, 1964), 5; Margot Canaday, *The Straight State: Sexuality and Citizenship in Twentieth-Century America* (Princeton University Press, 2009), 227.

33. Theodore H. White, *The Making of the President 1964* (Signet/New American Library, 1965), 436.

34. *Report of the President's Commission on Crime in the District of Columbia* (US Government Printing Office, 1966), 18, 7; Chris Myers Asch and George Derek Musgrove, *Chocolate City: A History of Race and Democracy in the Nation's Capital* (University of North Carolina Press, 2017), 352. The police ledger records all arrests citywide between 12:10 a.m. on Thursday, January 15, 1959, and 1:00 a.m. on Friday, January 16, 1959. It was reproduced in the Jenkins case report because of questions over whether the word "pervert" had been added to Jenkins's arrest record. RWWJ, exhibit F. Like most US urban departments, DC's Metropolitan Police Department did not retain mid-twentieth-century arrest records; the surviving Jenkins investigation materials are therefore especially significant.

35. Holmes, "Beyond the Flames," 308.

36. Humphreys, *Tearoom Trade*, 105; "ISR H Study Code Book," 57.

37. Gore Vidal, "The Race into Grace, or the Civilization Gap," *Esquire*, August 1961, 120, 123 (here 123); Downing to Parker, October 16, 1964, in Johnson, Lyndon (13 of 22) folder, box 31k, THWP.

38. Steele and Hannifin to Parker, October 15, 1964, in Johnson, Lyndon (16 of 22) folder, box 31k, THWP. This unpublished teletype dispatch by *Time* reporters John L. Steele (former White House correspondent and then Washington bureau chief) and Jerry Hannifin (defense and aerospace reporter), written for their editors in New York, is the most detailed account of newsroom deliberations that day. Steele and Hannifin identify the *Washington Daily News* police-beat reporter John Burch (no relation to Republican National Committee chairman Dean Burch) as the one who received a tip on Friday. *Time*'s article noted a Friday telephone tip but not the reporter's name, while the *New York Times* instead reported that a *Daily News* police reporter, presumably Burch, was "told of the arrests on Monday by a member of the Washington Metropolitan Police Department." "Nation: The Senior Staff Man," *Time*, October 23, 1964, 21; John D. Morris, "Johnson Friends Called on Press," *New York Times*, October 16, 1964.

39. Untitled memo, October 13, 1964, folder 112, box 32, John J. Williams Papers, University of Delaware Library, Newark, Delaware.

40. Wise, "'I'm in Terrible Trouble'"; telephone conversation no. 5877, sound recording, LBJ and ABE FORTAS, October 14, 1964, 3:56 p.m., LBJL; Wicker, "Johnson Denies Jenkins Cover-Up, Sets F.B.I. Inquiry," *New York Times*, October 16, 1964.

41. Wise, "'I'm in Terrible Trouble.'"

42. Chalmers M. Roberts, "Abe Fortas Withdraws As Lawyer for Baker," *Washington Post*, December 3, 1963.

43. "Attempts to Soft Pedal Jenkins Story Revealed," *Los Angeles Times*, October 17, 1964; telephone conversation no. 5876, sound recording, LBJ and ABE FORTAS, October 14, 1964, 3:56 p.m., LBJL. I have not located the mug shot.

44. "Arrest LBJ Aid as 'Disorderly'" (UPI), *New York Daily News*, October 15, 1964; "Arrest Disclosures Bring Resignation of a Top LBJ Aide" (AP), *Buffalo Evening News*, October 15, 1964. The formulation "tipsters, who were anonymous" also appears in Morton Mintz, "Jenkins, Aide to LBJ, Resigns After Arrest," *Washington Post*, October 15, 1964.

45. John D. Morris, "Johnson Friends Called on Press," *New York Times*, October 16, 1964 ("acted"); Wicker, "Johnson Denies Jenkins Cover-Up" ("responsibility").

46. Steele and Hannifin to Parker, October 15, 1964; Ted Lewis, "Capitol Stuff," *New York Daily News*, October 16, 1964.

47. James McCartney, "Phone Call Opened Pandora's Box," *Philadelphia Inquirer*, October 18, 1964 ("took"); John Barron, "Top Johnson Aide Quits After Arrest," *Washington Evening Star*, October 15, 1964 ("report"); Julius Frandsen, "Wire Services in Washington," in *The Press in Washington*, ed. Ray Eldon Hiebert (Dodd, Mead, 1966), 41–49, at 46 ("extraordinarily").

48. Steele and Hannifin to Parker, October 15, 1964, in Johnson, Lyndon (16 of 22) folder, box 31k, THWP; Wise, "'I'm in Terrible Trouble.'"

49. Steele and Hannifin to Parker, October 15, 1964, in Johnson, Lyndon (16 of 22) folder, box 31k, THWP.

50. "Was There a Winking Protection?" *Bulletin of the American Society of Newspaper Editors* 481 (December 1, 1964), 1–2, 15–16, in folder 87, box 155, Abe Fortas Papers, Yale University Library.

51. "Was There a Winking Protection?"

52. Memo no. 28, from Benjamin C. Bradlee to "Nation, Elliott, Manning, Bernstein," n.d. (likely October 20, 1964, given the reference to "Betty Beale's column tonight" about flowers), folder 4, box 6, Benjamin C. Bradlee Papers, Harry Ransom Center, University of Texas at Austin. See also Lewis and Clopton, "Changes in Police Rules Follow Jenkins Arrest."

53. RWWJ, 55–57. Hoover reportedly believed that, given the number of people in Washington with access to top-secret information, government agencies should focus on restricting access to their most sensitive materials rather than attempting to trace the sources of leaks. Donald A. Ritchie, *The Columnist: Leaks, Lies, and Libel in Drew Pearson's Washington* (Oxford University Press, 2021), 125. This was precisely what Blick had done by creating a sanitized version of Morals Division arrest reports.

54. Wise, "'I'm in Terrible Trouble'"; James McCartney, "Phone Call Opened Pandora's Box," *Philadelphia Inquirer*, October 18, 1964; "Attempts to Soft Pedal Jenkins Story Revealed," *Los Angeles Times*, October 17, 1964.

55. Carl Bernstein, *Chasing History: A Kid in the Newsroom* (Henry Holt, 2022), 295–96. Bernstein's account contains three minor errors: the arrest book did not list Jenkins's name as "John W. Jenkins"; UPI broke the story not "by early afternoon" but in the early evening; and Jenkins officially resigned not "by seven o'clock" but at about 9 p.m. (296). Nonetheless, the account includes many accurate details that lend credibility to his description of the conversation with Welch.

56. "Johnson Aide Goes on Trial," *Washington Post*, December 21, 1950 (involving an aide to Edwin C. Johnson, Democrat of Colorado); "Usefulness of Sex Squad Questioned by Kronheim," *Washington Post*, June 5, 1954; *Guarro v. United States*, 237 F.2d 578 (DC Cir. 1956), at 582; Morrey Dunie, "Court Warns Police on Methods of Getting Evidence in Morals Cases," *Washington Post*, September 28, 1956. See also Lvovsky, *Vice Patrol*, 135.

57. David K. Johnson, *The Lavender Scare: The Cold War Persecution of Gays and Lesbians in the Federal Government* (University of Chicago Press, 2004), 183; RWWJ, 62–63. See also "Lafayette, Here We Come," *Washington Post*, November 16, 1960 (suggesting that Thomas had arrested Fochett's colleague "on a suspicion of homosexuality" when Fochett intervened). After a *Post* editorial complained that the Morals Division plainclothesmen's "ugly errand . . . borders on provocation and entrapment," Fochett and others sued the *Post* for libel. "Lafayette, Here We Come," *Washington Post*, November 16, 1960; "Three Policemen File Libel Suit," *Washington Post*, April 5, 1961. On Thomas, see also Risa L. Goluboff, *Vagrant Nation: Police Power, Constitutional Change, and the Making of the 1960s* (Oxford University Press, 2016), 224. In his study of plainclothes policing, Gary T. Marx recounts a similar episode: "An undercover New York City policeman in a homosexual bar struck up a conversation with an effeminate man wearing mascara. The men decided to go for a walk, and, after several blocks and a series of suggestive comments, the undercover policeman said, 'You're under arrest.' The other man said, 'You can't arrest me. I was about to arrest you.' He was also a New York City policeman." *Undercover: Police Surveillance in America* (University of California Press, 1988), 173.

58. RWWJ, 62–63. The report notes that the official Thomas contacted had previously "assisted Mr. Thomas who had a discrimination problem" (62).

59. Report of interview with Lieutenant [Fochett; originally redacted], October 15, 1964, in FBI file 161-HQ-2848.

60. Lewis and Clopton, "Changes in Police Rules Follow Jenkins Arrest." At the time of Jenkins's arrest, "only his thumb print was taken Oct. 7 and it was not forwarded to the FBI," since "it has been the Morals Division's practice to take only thumb prints of persons with prior records." Moyer announced that henceforth "a full set will be taken from all suspects, including repeat offenders."

61. "Washington arrests for immoral behavior in public places were cut in half during 1965 as compared with 1964," the *Post* reported, noting that decoys were no longer

used in parks—a change the editorial board praised as a "diminution of pointless punishment of individuals who intended no harm." "Morals in the Parks"; see also Lvovsky, "Cruising in Plain View"; "Roy Blick to Retire, Recommends Moyer," *Washington Post*, June 10, 1964.

CHAPTER 4

1. David Wise, "'I'm in Terrible Trouble'—Jenkins' Tragedy," *New York Herald-Tribune*, October 18, 1964; telephone conversation no. 5877, sound recording, LBJ and ABE FORTAS, October 14, 1964, 3:56 p.m., LBJL.

2. Telephone conversation no. 5876, sound recording, LBJ and ABE FORTAS, October 14, 1964, 3:56 p.m., LBJL.

3. Max Frankel, "President's Aide Quits on Report of Morals Case," *New York Times*, October 15, 1964.

4. On the West Wing and East Wing in the Johnson White House, see Liz Carpenter, *Ruffles and Flourishes* (Texas A&M University Press, 1993 [1970]), 7–13.

5. Sidey to Parker, "Walter Jenkins Take X (Nation)," October 16, 1964, in Johnson, Lyndon (14 of 22) folder, box 31k, THWP, emphasis mine.

6. Wise, "'I'm in Terrible Trouble'"; telephone conversation no. 5902, sound recording, LBJ and DON COOK, October 17, 1964, 2:35 p.m., LBJL.

7. Telephone conversation no. 5876, sound recording, LBJ and ABE FORTAS, October 14, 1964, 3:56 p.m., LBJL; telephone conversation no. 5877, sound recording, LBJ and ABE FORTAS, October 14, 1964, 3:56 p.m., LBJL; Wise, "'I'm in Terrible Trouble.'"

8. Russell Baker, "Sherman Adams Resigns; Sees 'Vilification' Drive; President Voices Sadness," *New York Times*, September 23, 1958; Sherman Adams, *Firsthand Report: Eisenhower Administration* (Greenwood Press, 1961); Michael J. Birkner, "Sherman Adams's Fall, and the Scandal Behind the Scandal," in *Scandal! An Interdisciplinary Approach to the Consequences, Outcomes, and Significance of Political Scandals*, ed. Alison Dagnes and Mark Eachleben (Bloomsbury, 2014), 127–54.

9. Telephone conversation nos. 5876 and 5877, sound recording, LBJ and ABE FORTAS, October 14, 1964, 3:56 p.m., LBJL. Robert David Johnson, *All the Way with LBJ: The 1964 Presidential Election* (Cambridge University Press, 2009), contends that Johnson wanted the safe emptied to conceal a campaign finance scandal involving Mary Lasker. While it is highly likely the safe contained material Johnson regarded as potentially damaging and that it included documents relating to Lasker, in my view the available evidence does not permit firm conclusions about the nature of the material Fortas removed.

10. Jenkins medical record, January 3, 1964, RWWJ, exhibit I; telephone conversation no. 5876, sound recording, LBJ and ABE FORTAS, October 14, 1964, 3:56 p.m., LBJL.

11. "Senator Bridges Enters Hospital," *Washington Post*, January 31, 1961; "Justice Frankfurter Taken to Hospital," *New York Times*, April 6, 1962; "Sen. Wherry Dies; GOP Floor Leader," *Washington Post*, November 30, 1951; "Eugene Meyer Dies; Publisher, Banker," *New York Times*, July 18, 1959; "F. [sic] Franklin Frazier, Sociologist and Teacher at Howard U., Dead," *Washington Post*, May 18, 1962; "GWU Takes Formal Possession of 5-Million-Dollar Hospital," *Washington Post*, March 24, 1948; Jenkins medical record,

January 31, 1960, exhibit I, RWWJ; Beverly Gage, *G-Man: J. Edgar Hoover and the Making of the American Century* (Viking, 2022), 533; James A. Hamilton Associates, Inc., "A Program of Development: The George Washington University Hospital, Washington, D.C.," May 1972, table I, 3, folder 8, box 1, series 3, University Hospital records, RG0061, Special Collections Research Center, George Washington University, Washington, DC; Statement in "Accounts—Jan 1965 expenses" folder, and "Walter Jenkins—Check book, 1/13/1964-," both in box 61, PPWJ. The bill totaled $1,234.15, with $789.50 covered by insurance, and included $21.50 for "guard service." Jenkins paid $346.65 on November 9, 1964, and the remaining $98.00 on January 29, 1965.

12. "Nixon Recovered, Leaves Hospital," *New York Times*, September 10, 1960; John A. Farrell, *Richard Nixon: The Life* (Vintage, 2017), 278, 284; Fredrik Logevall, *JFK: Coming of Age in the American Century, 1917–1956* (Random House, 2020), 374, 516. Robert Dallek argues that Kennedy believed disclosures about his health would prove more damaging than revelations about his private life; the official White House physician was kept unaware of many ailments and treatments, perhaps so he could credibly attest to Kennedy's fitness during the 1964 campaign. Robert Dallek, *An Unfinished Life: John F. Kennedy, 1917–1963* (Little, Brown, 2003), 212, 581–82.

13. Robert A. Caro, *The Path to Power*, vol. 1 of *The Years of Lyndon Johnson* (Vintage, 1982), 444; Robert A. Caro, *Means of Ascent*, vol. 2 of *The Years of Lyndon Johnson* (Knopf, 1990), 202–3; Robert A. Caro, *Master of the Senate*, vol. 3 of *The Years of Lyndon Johnson* (Vintage, 2002), 436; Katharine Graham, *Personal History* (Vintage, 1998), 311–12.

14. "Doctor 50 Years Puts Stethoscope to 1954 World, Finds It Nervous," *New York Times*, May 31, 1954; Dr. Peter J. Steincrohn, "Ask the Doctor: 'My Husband Overworks'" (syndicated column), in *Detroit Free Press*, June 26, 1964; "Pope Gives Talk Despite Fatigue," *New York Times*, June 3, 1956; "Rita Hayworth Enters Hospital" (AP), *Washington Evening Star*, August 22, 1962; "Doctor Prescribes More Rest for Mays" (AP), *New York Times*, September 4, 1963; Thomas F. Brady, "Indian Prime Minister, 59, Must Cancel Appointments for the Next Few Days," *New York Times*, June 28, 1964; John S. Monagan, "Campaign for Short Campaigns," *New York Times Magazine*, May 8, 1960; Richard Fryklund, "Air Force Charges TFX Probe 'Abuse,'" *Washington Evening Star*, March 21, 1963.

15. Caro, *Means of Ascent*, 140; Drew Pearson, "Goldwater's Nervous Breakdowns," *Santa Barbara News-Press*, May 20, 1964; Drew Pearson, "Delegates Know Little About Barry Goldwater's Background," *Salisbury [MD] Daily Times*, July 14, 1964; "Walter Scott's Personality Parade," *Independent Star-News* (Pasadena), August 23, 1964; Drew Pearson, "Goldwater's Misfit Crack Raises Questions of Generals," *Jackson Clarion-Ledger*, September 15, 1964.

16. Barbara Ehrenreich, *The Hearts of Men: American Dreams and the Flight from Commitment* (Anchor/Doubleday, 1983), 70, 78.

17. Ashbrook P. Bryant to Walter Jenkins, October 15, 1964, box 65, PPWJ.

18. Notes in Telephone Calls folder, box 70, PPWJ.

19. President's Daily Diary, October 15, 1964, LBJL; Mike McManus to Parker, October 16, 1964, in Johnson, Lyndon (13 of 22) folder, box 31k, THWP.

20. Evelyn E. Brown, RN, to Walter Jenkins, October 28, 1964, and reply dated February 4, 1965, box 42, PPWJ. Jenkins wrote her in reply, "Thanks too for taking such good care of me. I don't think I ever saw a more cooperative, more helpful or nicer person. I hope I will never be sick again, but if I ever am, I am going to hunt you up."

21. James Reston, "Setback for Johnson," *New York Times*, October 15, 1964; telephone conversation no. 5877, sound recording, LBJ and ABE FORTAS, October 14, 1964, 3:56 p.m., LBJL.

22. "LBJ Visits Jackie in New York" (AP), *Miami Herald*, October 15, 1964 (calling the visit "unscheduled"); "LBJ Visits Jackie in NY Home" (UPI), *Sacramento Bee*, October 15, 1964 (labeling it "a surprise"); R. W. Apple Jr., "President Takes Unnoticed Trip," *New York Times*, October 15, 1964. AP photos of LBJ with Mrs. Kennedy appeared, for example, in the October 15 issues of the *Minneapolis Star*, *Sacramento Bee*, *Atlanta Constitution*, and—on the front page—the *Boston Globe* and *Cincinnati Enquirer*. Months later, Johnson reminisced about the moment in a phone conversation with Mrs. Kennedy: "I was sitting there with one of the sweet, beautiful creatures of my life and all the time my mind was down here about who was going to jail that night." Telephone conversation no. 7158, sound recording, LBJ and JACQUELINE KENNEDY, March 25, 1965, 4:56 p.m., LBJL.

23. Telephone conversation no. 5886, sound recording, LBJ and CLARK CLIFFORD, October 14, 1964, 9:36 p.m., LBJL; Jerome S. Cahill, "Johnson Aide Quits in Morals Scandal; GOP Raises Furor," *Philadelphia Inquirer*, October 15, 1964; telephone conversation no. 5901, sound recording, LBJ and GEORGE REEDY, October 17, 1964, 2:20 p.m., LBJL; Wise, " 'I'm in Terrible Trouble.' "

24. Telephone conversation no. 5880, sound recording, LBJ and ABE FORTAS, October 14, 1964, 8:02 p.m., LBJL. Fortas had firmly instructed the hospital not to put any calls through to Jenkins's room, and thus required him to return in person to request Jenkins's resignation. Jenkins immediately agreed. This reportedly occurred at about 9:15 p.m., when Jenkins was still sharing a room with "an elderly Negro man, a curtain divider between them." Wise, " 'I'm in Terrible Trouble.' " Fortas may have obtained Jenkins's written signature on a resignation letter, but I have not been able to locate it.

25. Telephone conversation no. 5885, sound recording, LBJ and MILDRED STEGALL, October 14, 1964, 9:36 p.m., LBJL.

26. Telephone conversation no. 5888, sound recording, LBJ and ABE FORTAS, October 15, 1964, 1:13 a.m., LBJL.

27. Thomas W. Ottenad, "Goldwater Says Jenkins Report Is Not Enough," *St. Louis Post-Dispatch*, October 22, 1964; "Jenkins Memo Warned of Undesirables" (UPI), *Philadelphia Evening Bulletin*, October 16, 1964; telephone conversation no. 5888, sound recording, LBJ and ABE FORTAS, October 15, 1964, 1:13 a.m., LBJL. Jenkins had written that "security name checks, particularly from files of the Federal Bureau of Investigation," had to be completed before any job offer, warning that "irreparable harm can be done to a person's reputation" if publicity preceded a check that later halted the appointment. Walter Jenkins, "Memorandum to the Heads of Executive Departments and Agencies," September 10, 1964, copy in Walter Jenkins folder 2, box 10, Intelligence File, National Security File, Presidential Papers, LBJL.

28. Telephone conversation no. 5888, sound recording, LBJ and ABE FORTAS, October 15, 1964, 1:13 a.m., LBJL; James Kirchick, *Secret City: The Hidden History of Gay Washington* (Henry Holt, 2022), 149–54.

29. Telephone conversation no. 5889, sound recording, LBJ and ABE FORTAS, October 15, 1964, 1:13 a.m., LBJL.

30. Fischer to Parker, October 15, 1964, in Lyndon Johnson (16 of 22) folder, box 31k, THWP.

31. "Text of President Johnson's Speech to the Alfred E. Smith Dinner at the Waldorf," *New York Times*, October 15, 1964; Fischer to Parker, October 14, 1964, in Lyndon Johnson (16 of 22) folder, box 31k, THWP.

32. Telephone conversation no. 5880, sound recording, LBJ and ABE FORTAS, October 14, 1964, 8:02 p.m., LBJL; telephone conversation no. 5886, sound recording, LBJ and CLARK CLIFFORD, October 14, 1964, 9:36 p.m., LBJL.

33. "Johnson: Democratic Father," *Time*, November 24, 1958, 19; telephone conversation no. 5876, sound recording, LBJ and ABE FORTAS, October 14, 1964, 3:56 p.m., LBJL; telephone conversation no. 5886, sound recording, LBJ and CLARK CLIFFORD, October 14, 1964, 9:36 p.m., LBJL. Caro quotes the 1958 *Time* interview, which he incorrectly identifies as off-the-record, from a manuscript in Steele's papers. *Master of the Senate*, 1020.

34. Telephone conversation no. 5891, sound recording, LBJ and NICHOLAS KATZENBACH, October 15, 1964, 7:26 a.m., LBJL; Sidey to Parker, October 16, 1964, Johnson, Lyndon (14 of 22) folder, box 31k, THWP.

35. "Johnson on Jenkins, Baker . . . New GOP Charges," *New York Herald-Tribune*, October 25, 1964.

36. Telephone conversation no. 5884, sound recording, LBJ and CARTHA "DEKE" DELOACH, October 14, 1964, 9:00 p.m., LBJL.

37. October 15 newspapers with Jenkins banner headlines all the way across the front page in at least one edition: *Honolulu Advertiser* ("Assistant to Johnson Resigns After Arrest on Morals Charge"), *Muncie Star* ("LBJ Aide in Morals Case Quits"), *Central New Jersey Home News* ("Morals Cover-Up Blamed on LBJ"), *Des Moines Register* ("Top Johnson Aide Arrested"), *Arizona Republic* ("LBJ Aide in Scandal"), *Baltimore Sun* ("Jenkins Resigns As Special Aide to President After Report of Arrests By D.C. Morals Squad"), *Los Angeles Times* ("Aide to Johnson Resigns Top Job"), *Newsday* ("LBJ Aide Quits After Arrest"), and *Nashville Banner* ("Sex Pervert in White House Spreads Shock Across Nation").

38. "Blow from a Friend," *Economist*, October 17, 1964, 241; Philippe Ben, "Un Proche Conseiller de M. Johnson Compromis Dans des Affaires de Moeurs est Obligé de Donner sa Démission" ["Close Advisor to Mr. Johnson Compromised in Moral Matters Forced to Resign"], *Le Monde*, October 16, 1964; "Jenkins Linked to Both U.S. Candidates" (Havana Domestic Television Service in Spanish 1800 GMT 17 October 1964), October 19, 1964 (FBIS-FRB-64-204), HHHH-4, and "Stages of U.S. Presidential Campaign Reviewed" (Cairo Domestic Service in Arabic 1230 GMT 30 October 1964), November 2, 1964 (FBIS-FRB-64-214), B-1, both in Foreign Broadcast Information Service, *Daily Reports, 1956–1996* (Readex).

39. Lady Bird Johnson, audio diary and annotated transcript, January 27, 1964, LBJL. In the published version of the diary, the sentence ended "and I hope the party provided an hour's respite from the long hours of work he's struggling with now." Lady Bird Johnson, *A White House Diary* (Holt, Rinehart, and Winston, 1970), 62.

40. Telephone conversation no. 5895, sound recording, LBJ and LADY BIRD JOHNSON, October 15, 1964, 9:12 a.m., LBJL. On Acheson's statement "I do not intend to turn my back on Alger Hiss," see Allen Weinstein, *Perjury: The Hiss-Chambers Case*, 3rd ed. (Hoover Institution Press, 2013 [1978]), 529; Rick Perlstein, *Nixonland: The Rise of a President and the Fracturing of America* (Scribner, 2008), 32–33.

41. Statement of Mrs. Lyndon B. Johnson, October 15, 1964, "EX FG 11-8-1/Jenkins, Walter" folder, box 86, White House Central Files, LBJL.

42. J. B. West with Mary Lynn Kotz, *Upstairs at the White House: My Life With the First Ladies* (Coward, McGann and Geoghegan, 1973), 285; Julia Sweig, *Lady Bird Johnson: Hiding in Plain Sight* (Random House, 2021), 48.

43. Merle Miller, *Lyndon: An Oral Biography* (G. P. Putnam's Sons, 1980), 487. Wiggins erroneously believed that the First Lady had issued the statement without speaking with her husband.

44. The AP story ran in many Friday, October 16, papers: "'My Heart Aching,' Says Lady Bird" (*Boston Globe*); "'My Heart Is Aching,' Mrs. Johnson Says" (*Honolulu Star-Bulletin*); "Lady Bird's Heart 'Aches for Jenkins'" (*San Angelo Standard-Times*); "Mrs. Johnson Lauds Jenkins' Service to the Nation" (*Buffalo News*); "First Lady Praying for Jenkins" (*Louisville Courier-Journal*). I have found only one evening paper—that of Jenkins's hometown—whose Thursday edition included Mrs. Johnson's statement: "First Lady In Praise of Jenkins," *Wichita Falls Times*, October 15, 1964 (front page). The UPI does not appear to have published its own story about Mrs. Johnson's statement but included, in a broader piece about Jenkins developments, the fact that although "Johnson himself has said nothing," nonetheless "Mrs. Johnson issued a statement." "Burch, Nixon Demand LBJ Discuss Jenkins in Public" (UPI), *Tyler Morning Telegraph*, October 16, 1964.

45. Elizabeth D. Tihany to Lady Bird Johnson, October 15, 1964, and Mrs. J. Wiencek to Lady Bird Johnson, October 26, 1964, both in "Jenkins, Mr. & Mrs. Walter (only)" folder 2 of 2, box 1022, White House Social Files, LBJL.

46. Statement of the President, October 15, 1964, "Statement of the President following Jenkins' Resignation, October 15, 1964" folder, box 8, Office Files of Walter Jenkins, LBJL.

47. The two versions of Laurence Stern's article ran with the headlines "LBJ Orders FBI Probe on Jenkins" and "No Reports On Jenkins Sent to LBJ," *Washington Post*, October 16, 1964.

48. Tom Wicker, "Johnson Denies Jenkins Cover-Up, Sets F.B.I. Inquiry," *New York Times*, October 16, 1964; John Barron, "Didn't Know Jenkins' Past, Johnson Says," *Washington Evening Star*, October 16, 1964; Julian Morrison, "LBJ Denies Any Cover-Up In Jenkins Case; Orders FBI Probe," *Washington Daily News*, October 16, 1964. Many papers ran versions of the wire service stories.

49. Mrs. K. M. Kirby to Lady Bird Johnson, October 22, 1964; Mrs. A. J. Lesousky to Lady Bird Johnson, October 18, 1964; M. Jeannette Mackenzie to Lady Bird Johnson, October 18, 1964; and Jean Jackley to Lady Bird Johnson, October 18, 1964, all in "Jenkins, Mr. & Mrs. Walter (only)" folder 1 of 2, box 1022, White House Social Files, LBJL.

50. "Goldwater: 'I Don't Intend to Comment on It,'" *Boston Globe*, October 16, 1964; Kathleen Hall Jamieson, *Dirty Politics: Deception, Distraction, and Democracy* (Oxford University Press, 1992), 83.

51. Richard Dudman, "Two-Part Goldwater Strategy in Morals Arrest of President's Aid," *St. Louis Post-Dispatch*, October 18, 1964, and Ruth Montgomery, "Goldwater Continues to Hit on Morality Issue," *New York Journal-American*, October 21, 1964 (signs); Shirley Uhl (stringer) to Robert Parker, October 16, 1964, in Johnson, Lyndon (14 of 22) folder, box 31k, THWP (pink cards); Ben H. Bagdikian, "The Columnist as Prophet," *Columbia Journalism Review* 5, no. 2 (Summer 1966), 35–39, at 38 (Buckley); McWhirter to Parker, "Jenkins, Take Two," October 16, 1964, in Johnson, Lyndon (13 of 22) folder, box 31k, THWP (bishop).

52. Zim to Parker, October 16, 1964, in Johnson, Lyndon (14 of 22) folder, box 31k, THWP ("person"); Gart and the Chicago Bureau to Parker, October 16, 1964, Johnson, Lyndon (13 of 22) folder, box 31k, THWP ("break"); John C. O'Brien, "Had No Previous Reports on Jenkins, Johnson Says," *Philadelphia Inquirer*, October 16, 1964 ("come"); "Goldwater Releases Letter to J. Edgar Hoover," quoted in Dean Burch, Victory Bulletin for October 20, 1964, box 3H510, Stephen Shadegg/Barry Goldwater Collection, Eugene C. Barker Texas History Center, University of Texas at Austin ("opinion").

53. "Goldwater is Jenkins' 'CO'" (UPI), *Waco Times-Herald*, October 15, 1964; Carl Bernstein, *Chasing History: A Kid in the Newsroom* (Henry Holt, 2022), 297; Marquis Childs, "Goldwater Finds a Bull Market," *Washington Post*, March 14, 1961; Albon B. Bailey, "Congressmen Meet for Briefings As Members of Newest AF Unit," *Washington Post*, April 16, 1961; Drew Pearson, "Goldwater Sets Up Hill Junkets," *Washington Post*, October 10, 1961.

54. Loye Miller to Parker, October 15, 1964, Johnson, Lyndon (14 of 22) folder, box 31k, THWP; RWWJ, 94.

55. David Lawrence, "Jenkins' Part in the Baker Case," *New York Herald-Tribune*, October 16, 1964; Scott W. Dean to Dean Burch, October 27, 1964, folder 15; William A. Richmond to Dean Burch, October 17, 1964, folder 17; W. T. Robinson to Dean Burch, October 18, 1964, folder 17 (skinny-dipping); Ted L. G. Calvo telegram to Dean Burch, October 21, 1964, folder 15 ("instigator"); Ellen F. Boyce to Burch, October 18, 1964, folder 15; Raymond G. Barnett to Dean Burch, October 15, 1964, folder 15 (spies); Norman L. Arenander telegram to Dean Burch, October 15, 1964, folder 15 ("pursue"); all in box 7, Dean Burch Collection, FM MSS 142, Arizona Historical Foundation, Arizona State University, Tempe, AZ. See Walter Trohan, "Skinny-Dippin' With LBJ Is Latest in Status Symbols," *Omaha World-Herald*, January 22, 1964; "Manipulating the News LBJ Style," *Human Events*, July 11, 1964, 16.

56. C. A. Graft to Dean Burch, October 15, 1964 ("will pick up"); J. B. Anderson to Dean Burch, October 18, 1964 ("so many"); Glenn A. Green to Dean Burch, October 15,

1964 ("tried out"); John A. Earl to Dean Burch, October 15, 1964 ("get rid of"); Peter N. Crossland to Dean Burch (n.d. but postmarked October 21, 1964) ("ugly"), all in folder 15, box 7, Burch Collection. Burch's standard reply letter stated that there were "a large number of letters and telegrams on this issue" and thanked the letter writer "Without going into the pros and cons of the matter." Dean Burch to Mrs. C. A. Graft, October 29, 1964, folder 15, box 7, Burch Collection.

57. Barry M. Goldwater with Jack Casserly, *Goldwater* (Doubleday, 1988), Kindle edition, locations 3861–901. Goldwater also falsely asserted that Johnson "was told of the arrest but remained silent" prior to October 14, which was disproved by the subsequently released audio recordings showing LBJ's genuine shock. As we have seen, Johnson did not "hav[e] his pals" Fortas and Clifford suppress the story; rather, they undertook that effort without his knowledge.

58. James Reston, "Washington: Barry Goldwater Examples of Morality," *New York Times*, October 23, 1964; "Clerics Hit Morality as Issue in Campaign" (UPI), *Los Angeles Times*, October 30, 1964; cartoon by Tom Engelhardt, *St. Louis Post-Dispatch*, October 25, 1964. An example of liberal praise for Goldwater, citing the Arizonan's memoir and an interview with him, is Mark Shields, "A Measure of Character That's Rarely Seen Today," *Star-Democrat* (Easton, MD), June 28, 2017.

59. Steele to Parker, October 16, 1964, in Johnson, Lyndon (13 of 22) folder, box 31k, THWP.

60. Alfred Steinberg, *Sam Johnson's Boy: A Close-Up of the President from Texas* (Macmillan, 1968), 689; Theodore H. White, *The Making of the President 1964* (Signet/New American Library, 1965), 369–70.

61. Mrs. Marjorie Ramey to Dean Burch, October 22, 1964, folder 17, box 7, Burch Collection; Berger to Parker, "Jenkins—Take Three," in Johnson, Lyndon (13 of 22) folder, box 31k, THWP. See Martin Meeker, *Contacts Desired: Gay and Lesbian Contacts and Community, 1940s-1970s* (University of Chicago Press, 2006), chapter 4; Anna Lvovsky, *Vice Patrol: Cops, Courts, and the Struggle over Urban Gay Life before Stonewall* (University of Chicago Press, 2021), chapter 6; and Neil J. Young, *Coming Out Republican: A History of the Gay Right* (University of Chicago Press, 2024).

CHAPTER 5

1. D. B. Hardeman OH III, April 22, 1969, by T. H. Baker, LBJL, 31; Katie Louchheim, October 15, 1964 diary entry, folder 2, box 79, Katie S. Louchheim Papers, Library of Congress; Richard W. Budd, Malcolm S. MacLean Jr., and Arthur M. Barnes, "Regularities in the Diffusion of Two Major News Events," *Journalism Quarterly* 43, no. 2 (1966), 221–30, quote at 222. Word spread faster the next day of the ouster of Nikita Khrushchev, which the researchers attributed to the time of day and the story's greater importance (223). They also suggested that the World Series "tended to focus public attention on the media during the study period" (222). See also Harold Mendelsohn, "Broadcast vs. Personal Sources of Information in Emergent Public Crises: The Presidential Assassination," *Journal of Broadcasting* 8, no. 2 (Spring 1964): 147–56.

2. Drew Pearson, *Washington Merry-Go-Round: The Drew Pearson Diaries, 1960–1969*, ed. Peter Hannaford (Potomac Books/University of Nebraska Press, 2015), 256; "Jenkins Scandal May Prove Decisive," *Dallas News*, October 22, 1964.

3. Betty Beale, "Friends Console the Jenkinses," *Washington Evening Star*, October 21, 1964; redacted to Hoover, October 23, 1964, in FBI file 161-HQ-2848.

4. Dean Burch, interview by Stephen Shadegg, 16, n.d. but ca. December 1964, folder of "conversation with and notes from individuals involved in the campaign," box 3J9, Stephen Shadegg/Barry Goldwater Collection, Dolph Briscoe Center for American History, University of Texas at Austin; Betty Beale, *Power at Play: A Memoir of Parties, Politicians and the President in My Bedroom* (Regnery Gateway, 1993), 105. Beale also claimed to have later conversed with Hoover about the matter "when Hoover made a rare appearance at a party given by hostess Gwen Cafritz" (105). The National Press Club lifted the ban on women in 1971. See Kathryn J. McGarr, *City of Newsmen: Public Lies and Professional Secrets in Cold War Washington* (University of Chicago Press, 2022), 15–40; Maurine H. Beasley, *Women of the Washington Press: Politics, Prejudice, and Persistence* (Northwestern University Press, 2012), 126–30.

5. "Cronkite News insert with Dan Rather 10-15-64 take 2," CBS News archival video.

6. Steele to Parker, October 16, 1964, Johnson, Lyndon (13 of 22) folder, box 31k, THWP; Edward W. O'Brien, "Jenkins Case," *Harrisburg Patriot*, October 17, 1964. Shortly after Grover Cleveland secured the Democratic presidential nomination in 1884, allegations arose that he had fathered a ten-year-old illegitimate child, a claim he did not deny even though the mother's relations with several of his friends left the paternity uncertain. Jeffrey D. Schultz, *Presidential Scandals* (CQ Press, 2000), 180–82.

7. "Top LBJ Aide Quits Following Arrest," *Washington Daily News*, October 15, 1964; Elsie Carper, "Shipley, Rauh Clash in Debate Over Walter Jenkins Case," *Washington Post*, October 21, 1964; "Leedom, Clark Views on Jenkins Case Differ," *Dallas Morning News*, October 16, 1964; "Why Secret Service Cleared Jenkins" (UPI), *New York Journal-American*, October 18, 1964; "Secrecy Role of Jenkins Suspended" (UPI), *Washington Post*, October 25, 1964; Earl Ubell, "Sexual Deviation—Many Theories, No Cure," *New York Herald-Tribune*, October 18, 1964; cartoon by Burris Jenkins Jr., *New York Journal-American*, October 16, 1964.

8. Kenneth Gross, "A Family in Queens Caught in the Scandal," *New York Post*, October 16, 1964; Norman and Charlotte Teifeld to Walter Jenkins, October 16, 1964, box 216, PPWJ (the article was in the *Ventura County Star*, October 15, 1964).

9. Mab Ashforth Goldman to the Jenkinses, November 3, 1964, New York folder, box 51, PPWJ; Gart and the Chicago Bureau to Parker October 16, 1964, in Johnson, Lyndon (13 of 22) folder, box 31k, THWP.

10. McWhirter to Parker, October 16, 1964, in Johnson, Lyndon (13 of 22) folder, box 31k, THWP; Rowland Evans and Robert Novak, "Inside Report: Reaction to Jenkins—Small," *New York Herald-Tribune*, October 19, 1964.

11. Samuel Lubell, "Jenkins Case to Cut Shift of GOP Voters," *Los Angeles Times*, October 17, 1964; "Jenkins Case Makes D.C. Negroes 'Worry,'" *Chicago Defender*, October 26,

1964; Kenneth Crotty, "Report on Rhode Island—Oct. 20, 1964," FG 11-8-1/Jenkins, Walter folder, box 88, Presidential Papers, LBJL.

12. Larry Still, "Sex, Khrushchev's Fall Dominate News in Washington," *Jet*, October 19, 1964, 6–7; Jennifer Dominique Jones, *Ambivalent Affinities: A Political History of Blackness and Homosexuality after World War II* (University of North Carolina Press, 2023), 83–84. On Aaron Henry, see John Howard, *Men Like That: A Southern Queer History* (University of Chicago Press, 1999), 165.

13. Holmes Alexander, "Does the Great Society Mirror Itself In Capital?" *Indianapolis Star*, October 20, 1964; James J. Kilpatrick, "Jenkins Scandal May Prove Decisive," *Dallas News*, October 22, 1964; Raymond Moley, "Perspective: An Amoral Climate," *Newsweek*, November 2, 1964, 112.

14. Murray Kempton, "Our Boy Leader," *New York World Telegram*, October 30, 1964; Walter Lippmann, "His Last Ploy," *New York Herald-Tribune*, October 28, 1964; Drew Pearson, "Homosexuality in the Capital," *San Francisco Chronicle*, October 19, 1964. On campaign use of Kennedy's war record, see Fredrik Logevall, *JFK: Coming of Age in the American Century, 1917–1956* (Random House, 2020), 373, 421–22. On Guylay, see telephone conversation no. 5971, sound recording, LBJ and CARTHA "DEKE" DELOACH, October 27, 1964, 1:45 p.m., LBJL; Pearson, *Washington Merry-Go-Round*, 266; and Kathleen Hall Jamieson, *Packaging the Presidency: A History and Criticism of Presidential Campaign Advertising*, 3rd ed. (Oxford University Press, 1996), 208. On the questionable basis of Pearson's belief about Jenkins's legal situation, see Anna Lvovsky, *Vice Patrol: Cops, Courts, and the Struggle over Urban Gay Life before Stonewall* (University of Chicago Press, 2021). Joseph Alsop had recently taken a leave of absence for health reasons. See note in *Washington Post*, September 30, 1964, and labels on October substitute columns, e.g., Edward T. Folliard, "Politics: Wind of Change Touches Vermont," *Washington Post*, October 16, 1964.

15. William S. White, *The Making of a Journalist* (University Press of Kentucky, 1986), 97–102 (Churchill), 106 (D-Day), 123 (Hemingway); William S. White, "GI of Mexican Origin, Denied Rites in Texas, to Be Buried in Arlington," *New York Times*, January 13, 1949; William S. White, "Emergence of Johnson," *New York Times*, September 2, 1957.

16. See, among many examples, *The Taft Story* (Harper & Brothers, 1954), which won the Pulitzer Prize for biography; *Citadel: The Story of the United States Senate* (Harper, 1957); "Medicine Man from Alabama," *Harper's* (November 1959), 91–92; "The Invisible Gentleman from Kansas City," *Harper's* (May 1961), 83–87.

17. White, *Making of a Journalist*, 232 ("clear"), 233 ("enforce"), 14 ("midnight"); William S. White, "Acheson's Uncomplaining Testament," *New York Times Book Review*, November 20, 1955 (review); White, *Making of a Journalist*, 235–36 (friendship with Acheson); "William White, 88, Reporter and Author" (AP), *New York Times*, May 2, 1994.

18. William S. White, "'Consensus American'—A Portrait," *New York Times Magazine*, November 25, 1956 (views in general); White, *Citadel*, 55–66 (filibuster); William S. White, "The U.S. and All-or-Nothing Groups," *Washington Evening Star*, July 24, 1963 (Kennedy); William S. White, "Negro March on Washington," *Washington Evening Star*, September 2, 1963 (Rustin); William S. White, "The White Protest," *Washington Evening Star*, May 22,

1964 (Civil Rights Act); William S. White, "Public Women," *Harper's Magazine* (January 1960), 86–88 (women officeholders). Johnson knew, White wrote, that "I believed that at times he went too far too fast" on civil rights (*Making of a Journalist*, 223). In 1969, he expressed dismay that it took "the beach episode" to put an end to talk of a Ted Kennedy presidential campaign, since, to White, "if his capacity for the presidency is in question now, it was also in question yesterday" ("Unfortunate Solution," *Abilene Reporter-News*, August 1, 1969).

19. White, *Making of a Journalist*, caption on photo in the middle of the book; Karl E. Meyer, "The Washington Press Establishment," *Esquire* (April 1964), 73–75, at 74; Charles Roberts, *LBJ's Inner Circle* (Delacorte Press, 1965), 169. See also William L. Rivers, *The Opinionmakers* (Beacon, 1965), 168–69.

20. White, "Johnson's Right-Hand Man," *Washington Evening Star*, December 9, 1963; Walter Jenkins to Miss Ethel E. Goddard, February 3, 1964, in Ohio folder, box 51, PPWJ; White, "New Voice at the White House," *Washington Evening Star*, March 25, 1964.

21. This and the next five paragraphs refer to White, "A Graveyard Marked Despair," *Washington Evening Star*, October 16, 1964. The column appeared under headlines including "Jenkins: His Dedicated Service Outweighs His Alleged Lapses" (*Los Angeles Times*, October 20), "Jenkins' Human Tragedy" (*Honolulu Advertiser*, October 21), "Jenkins Is Now a Broken Man" (*Charlotte Observer*, October 21), "'I Stand As a Human Being With Walter Jenkins'" (*Burlington Free Press*, October 19), and "Better Side of Walter Jenkins" (*Greenville [SC] News*, October 21).

22. White had once previously written that as majority leader, Johnson was "a good deal like a respected, if cantankerous, captain of an infantry company." White, "Who Is Lyndon Johnson?" *Harper's Magazine*, March 1958, 57.

23. Barbara Ehrenreich, *The Hearts of Men: American Dreams and the Flight from Commitment* (Anchor/Doubleday, 1983), 70.

24. Fred Korth to William S. White, October 20, 1964, in William S. White folder, box 306, PPWJ. On loyalty, see White, "A Political Weighing of the Vaughan Case," *New York Times*, September 4, 1949; William S. White, "Never Condoned Disloyalty, Says Acheson of Hiss Stand," *New York Times*, March 1, 1950. In his 1986 memoir, White compressed the episode into a single line: he filed the column and only afterward visited Jenkins in the hospital (*Making of a Journalist*, 211). If that sequence is accurate, the hospital visit described in the column would have been fictional. More likely, he misremembered the details; as he later summarized it, the column's "substance" was that even if Jenkins was guilty as charged, his behavior was "not unlike the atypical acts of a soldier in a state of combat fatigue" (210–11).

25. James A. McCurdy to William S. White, October 21, 1964, and Mrs. Miriam F. Jonas to William S. White, October 21, 1964, both in William S. White folder, box 306, PPWJ.

26. Richard E. Berlin to Lyndon B. Johnson and Lady Bird Johnson, in "Ex FG 11-8-1/Jenkins, Walter" folder, EX FG 11-8-1/Holborn, box 86, Presidential Papers, LBJL (enclosing "Columnist Visits Walter Jenkins: Report on Tragedy's Handiwork," *New York Journal-American*, October 16, 1964); J. C. Kellam to William S. White, October 20, 1964,

in William S. White folder, box 306, PPWJ; Sim Gideon to Walter Jenkins, October 26, 1964, box 42, PPWJ.

27. Anonymous letter to William S. White, October 19, 1964, William S. White folder, box 306, PPWJ.

28. M. Irene Ruskin to William S. White, October 16, 1964, and anonymous letter to William S. White, October 20, 1964, both in William S. White folder, box 306, PPWJ.

29. William S. White, "Walter Jenkins: Battle Casualty?" *Tampa Times*, October 17, 1964; William W. Eaton, letter in "White's Jenkins Case Views Draw Comment," *Los Angeles Times*, October 24, 1964; Phyllis Moreland, letter in "White's Jenkins Case Views Draw Comment"; White, *Making of a Journalist*, 211–12; Mrs. Pearl M. Campbell, letter in "White's Jenkins Case Views Draw Comment."

30. President's Daily Diary entry, October 20, 1964, LBJL; Marquis W. Childs, "FBI's Report on Jenkins Is Said to Show No Security Leak," *St. Louis Post-Dispatch*, October 22, 1964.

31. Telephone conversation no. 5912, sound recording, LBJ and WILLIAM S. WHITE, October 17, 1964, 8:55 p.m., LBJL; Mary Rather to Lyndon and Lady Bird Johnson, October 22, 1964, in Jenkins, Walter—Investigation [1 of 3] folder, box 29B, Office Files of Mildred Stegall, LBJL.

32. Beasley, *Women of the Washington Press*, 134. Vera Glaser and Malvina Stephenson's Knight-Ridder–syndicated "Offbeat Washington" column did not begin until 1968. Kimberly Wilmot Voss, "Gossip in the Women's Pages: Legitimizing the Work of Female Journalists in the 1950s and 1960s," in *When Private Talk Goes Public: Gossip in American History* (Palgrave Macmillan, 2014), 183–202, at 195.

33. Betty Beale, "Exclusively Yours: Innovation Observed at White House Reception Tuesday Draws Pleased and Surprised Comments from Diplomats," *Washington Evening Star*, January 30, 1953; "Highballs and Old Fashioned at White House Delight Diplomats," *Fort Worth Star-Telegram*, January 31, 1953; "Diplomats Sip 'Liquids' at White House," *Washington Post*, January 31, 1953; "Ambassadors 'Surprised' at Being Served Highballs at White House" (AP), *Abilene Reporter-News*, January 31, 1953; "Did White House Spike an Ancient Policy? Drinks at Reception Said to 'Delight' Envoys," *New York Times*, January 31, 1953; Ann Cottrell Free, "On Drinking at Capitol," *Washington Evening Star*, February 1, 1953. According to Beale, the Eisenhower White House never again served alcohol at a function covered by reporters (*Power at Play*, 48).

34. The communications scholar Kimberly Wilmot Voss has described as "quilted news" the mixing by women's-page reporters of news that might be considered "soft" and "hard." Voss, "Gossip in the Women's Pages," 184. See also Linda J. Lumsden, "The Essentialist Agenda of the 'Woman's Angle' in Cold War Washington: The Case of Associated Press Reporter Ruth Cowan," *Journalism History* 33, no. 1 (Spring 2007), 2–13.

35. Beale, *Power at Play*, 47–48; Winzola McLendon and Scottie Smith, *Don't Quote Me: Washington Newswomen and the Power Society* (E. P. Dutton, 1970), 108; Beale, *Power at Play*, footnote at 95; Betty Beale, "Exclusively Yours: Will Other Great Americans Receive White House Bid?," *Washington Evening Star*, January 19, 1958.

36. Betty Beale, "Exclusively Yours: Enquiry Prompts Discussion On New Era in Official Life," *Washington Evening Star*, May 28, 1961; Betty Beale, "Convention Party; Jenkins Party," *Washington Evening Star*, January 24, 1964; Betty Beale, "Johnson Charms Senators," *Washington Evening Star*, January 31, 1964. By March 1967, with norms shifting, a profile in *The Washingtonian* mentioned her use of the antiquated phrase "colored butler" (Tom Kelly and Judy Hennessee, "The Remarkable Betty Beale," March 1967, 33–35, 61, quote at 35). The limits to Beale's racial progressivism are suggested by the account in her memoir about the 1968 riots following the assassination of Martin Luther King Jr.: "The shaken city watched in shame, horror, and pity while blacks devastated their own most-frequented areas" (Beale, *Power at Play*, 125).

37. McLendon and Smith, *Don't Quote Me*, 113; Betty Beale, "Exclusively Yours: Poolmanship at Hickory Hill Party," *Washington Evening Star*, June 20, 1962; "Ethel and 2 Guests Made a Big Splash" (AP), *Charlotte Observer*, June 21, 1962; Betty Beale, "Packed Galleries A Somber Scene," *Washington Evening Star*, November 27, 1963; Betty Beale, "Capital's Political Experts See Convention Movie," *Washington Evening Star*, March 27, 1964; Betty Beale, "Luci to Work as MD's Aide," *Washington Evening Star*, May 22, 1964.

38. Beale, *Power at Play*, 95, 99–100.

39. Beale, *Power at Play*, 95 (press secretary); Robert A. Caro, *Means of Ascent*, vol. 2 of *The Years of Lyndon Johnson* (Knopf, 1990), 270–71 (1948 primary); program for Women's National Press Club Annual Dinner and Stunt Party, May 19, 1955, Hotel Statler, Washington DC, in Betty Beale Collection, Howard Gotlieb Archival Research Center, Boston University; "Lady Bird Picks Press Aide," *Washington Post*, August 16, 1960. See also "Elizabeth Carpenter Feted By Dale Millers Last Night," *Washington Evening Star*, July 9, 1954; Maxine Cheshire, "Their Sad Tale Had Suite Ending," *Washington Post*, April 12, 1961; Jan Jarboe Russell, *Lady Bird: A Biography of Mrs. Johnson* (Simon and Schuster, 1999), 191–95; Betty Boyd Caroli, *Lady Bird and Lyndon: The Hidden Story of a Marriage That Made a President* (Simon and Schuster, 2015), 130; Julia Sweig, *Lady Bird Johnson: Hiding in Plain Sight* (Random House, 2021), 10–12.

40. November 1964 calendar, in Beale, Betty: Calendars (2) folder, box 27, and Betty Beale to Liz Carpenter, November 29, 1963, copy in Johnsons folder, box 15, both in Beale Collection. See also "LBJ Aides Breathe Efficiency, If At All," *Washington Post*, December 27, 1963; Betty Beale, "The Lyndon Johnsons Will Lend New Flavor to White House Society," *Washington Evening Star*, December 1, 1963.

41. McLendon and Smith, *Don't Quote Me*, 73; Beale, *Power at Play*, 96; Liz Carpenter to Edward E. Rice, February 3, 1965, copy, box 15, Beale Collection; "White House Reporter: Betty Beale's Capital Beat," *Miami Herald*, March 22, 1964. In her 1970 memoir, Carpenter praised Beale—"She covers a social event as though it were a summit meeting, knowing that in this company town (U.S. Government, Inc.) it frequently is"—but, in keeping with the norms of the White House she had recently left, made no mention of Jenkins. Liz Carpenter, *Ruffles and Flourishes* (Texas A&M University Press, 1993 [1970]), 196. On Carpenter, see also Nan Robertson, "First Lady's Lady Boswell," *New York Times Magazine*, April 11, 1965. The Johnson administration's new rule did require that the escort

be a newsman. On LBJ's good relationship with women of the press, see Vera Glaser, "LBJ Love Story," *Parade*, October 24, 1965, 11.

42. "Note to Editors" attached by the Hall Syndicate to Beale's October 20, 1964 column typescript, box 10, Hall Syndicate 6/1/1964–8/3/1965 carton, Beale Collection.

43. Beale's October 20, 1964 column typescript, box 10, Hall Syndicate 6/1/1964–8/3/1965 carton, Beale Collection; Betty Beale, "Friends Console the Jenkinses," *Washington Evening Star*, October 21, 1964.

44. "Friends—Even FBI Chief—Back Jenkins," *Battle Creek Enquirer and News*, October 21, 1964; "Jenkins Cheered by Support of Well-Wishers," *Chicago Daily News*, October 22, 1964; "Messages Aiding Jenkins," *Greensboro Daily News*, October 22, 1964; "Friends Ease Jenkins Family's Tragedy," *Charlotte Observer*, October 22, 1964; "Jenkins' Wife Stands By Him," *Durham Morning Herald*, October 22, 1964; "FBI Chief Sends Flowers to Jenkins," *Miami Herald*, October 22, 1964; "Friends Rally to Jenkins' Defense," *Winston-Salem Journal*, October 22, 1964; "Compassion Shown," *Evansville Courier and Press*, October 25, 1964; "J. Edgar Hoover Among Walter Jenkins Well-Wishers," *Raleigh News and Observer*, October 25, 1964; "Top Officials Wish Jenkins Well," *Arizona Republic*, October 25, 1964; "From Inside Washington," *The State and the Columbia Record* [SC], October 25, 1964; "A Journey Into the Past" [with column rearranged], *San Francisco Examiner*, October 25, 1964; "Wife's Hopes Brighten for Stricken Walter Jenkins," *Fresno Bee*, October 22, 1964 [with "which" instead of "that"]. Slightly different wordings ran in "FBI Boss Sends Jenkins Flowers," *Pittsburgh Press*, October 21, 1964, and "Wife Feels Friends' Quick Help Will Aid Jenkins In Recovery," *Indianapolis Star*, October 25, 1964.

45. Redacted to Hoover, October 23, 1964, in FBI file 161-HQ-2848.

46. "Get Well, Harry!" editorial in *The Daily Times* [Mamaroneck, NY], October 16, 1964.

47. C. D. DeLoach to Mr. Mohr, October 16, 1964, describing October 16 meeting at 11 a.m. with Fortas at the White House, in 161-HQ-2848 FBI file.

48. Beale, draft labeled "Chapter 7, 2/27/90," 7-41 to 7-42, box 17, Beale Collection; Betty Beale, *Power at Play*, 104.

49. Notes in Telephone Calls folder, box 70, PPWJ; Beasley, *Women of the Washington Press*, 143; "Sympathy Told for Jenkins" (AP), in *Austin Statesman*, October 22, 1964; "Expressions of Sympathy Hearten Jenkins Family" (UPI), *Dallas News*, October 23, 1964; "Jenkins Kin Heartened by Signs of Sympathy" (UPI), *Washington Post*, October 23, 1964 (in another edition, the headline was "Jenkins Kin Consoled By Notes of Sympathy"); "Jenkins Case: FBI Chief Did Send Flowers" (headline on inside page), *New York Post*, October 22, 1964; "Neighbors Offer Services, Gifts To Assist Walter Jenkins Family," *Washington Post*, October 25, 1964. McLendon and Smith characterize Lewine and Thomas as unique among White House correspondents in covering both "hard" news and "women's" stories (*Don't Quote Me*, 20).

50. Beverly Gage, *G-Man: J. Edgar Hoover and the Making of the American Century* (Viking, 2022), 398 ("often"), 407 ("upon"); Pearson, *Washington Merry-Go-Round*, 262. See also Claire Bond Potter, "Queer Hoover: Sex, Lies, and Political History," *Journal of the History of Sexuality* 15, no. 3 (July 2006), 355–81.

51. Dean Burch to Robert P. Cushman, October 27, 1964, folder 15, box 7, Burch Collection; David McReynolds, "The Case for November 3," *Village Voice*, October 29, 1964; R. F. B. to J. Edgar Hoover, October 28, 1964, and [redacted] to Hoover, October 29, 1964, in FBI file 161-HQ-2848.

52. Henry Gemmill, "The Jenkins Affair: Arrest of Johnson Aide Could Bolster GOP's Election Day Chances," *Wall Street Journal*, October 16, 1964; "Secrecy Role of Jenkins Suspended" (UPI), *Washington Post*, October 25, 1964 (Loeb); Ted Lewis, "Capitol Stuff," *New York Daily News*, October 27, 1964; Bill Baggs, "Strange Rock," *Miami News*, October 30, 1964.

53. "Secrecy Role of Jenkins Suspended"; "Hoover Sent Flowers to Jenkins" (UPI), *Pensacola News Journal*, October 26, 1964. For identical language, see, for example, J. Edgar Hoover to [redacted, Seabrook, TX], October 29, 1964, in FBI file 161-HQ-2848.

54. M. S. W. to J. Edgar Hoover, n.d.; [redacted] to "Mr. Hoover and 'staff,'" October 27, 1964; and [redacted] to Hoover, October 26, 1964, all in FBI file 161-HQ-2848.

55. [Redacted] to Hoover, n.d., and [redacted] to Hoover, October 28, 1964, both in FBI file 161-HQ-2848.

56. [Redacted] to Hoover, n.d. (received ca. October 27, 1964), and [redacted] to Hoover, October 26, 1964, both in FBI file 161-HQ-2848.

57. M. J. S. to Hoover, November 2, 1964, in FBI file 161-HQ-2848.

58. Ben A. Franklin, "Hoover Assailed on Jenkins Case," *New York Times*, October 28, 1964; Mary Norris to Walter H. Judd, October 29, 1964, and Gladys T. McGarry to Walter H. Judd, November 13, 1964, both in folder 2, box 97, Walter H. Judd Papers (WHJP), Hoover Institution, Stanford, California.

59. "Kup's Column," *Chicago Sun-Times*, October 29, 1964; Clyde Tolson to Walter H. Judd, October 30, 1964, folder 2, box 97, WHJP.

60. William G. Lais to Walter H. Judd, November 2, 1964 ("challenge"); James R. Healy to Walter H. Judd, October 30, 1964 ("admired"), John Mohr to Walter H. Judd, October 29, 1964 ("completely"); Carl Freyman to Walter H. Judd, November 3, 1964 ("even one"); Walter H. Judd to Cartha D. DeLoach, November 3, 1964, copy; all in folder 2, box 97, WHJP.

61. [Redacted] to Hoover, October 28, 1964, in FBI file 161-HQ-2848; Matthew Cecil, *Hoover's FBI and the Fourth Estate: The Campaign to Control the Press and the Bureau's Image* (University Press of Kansas, 2014), 214.

62. For an example of a Checkers speech suggestion, see Ralph M. Goldman to Bill Moyers, October 15, 1964, FG 11-8-1/Jenkins, Walter 9/1/1964–10/19/1964 folder, box 88, GEN FG 11-8-1/Jenkins 9/1/1964, Presidential Papers, LBJL. Beale declared in a 1967 radio interview, "I don't belong to the keyhole school"; "I just don't believe in this snooping business"; "I don't write a keyhole column." "Interview with Betty Beale," transcript of "Betty Groebli Show," WRC Radio, March 13, 1967, 6, Johnsons folder, box 15, Beale Collection.

63. Dean Burch, interview by Stephen Shadegg, 16, n.d. (but likely ca. December 1964), in "Publications: Shadegg book" folder, box 3J9, Stephen Shadegg/Barry Goldwater Collection, Eugene C. Barker Texas History Center, University of Texas at Austin.

64. Katie Louchheim, November 4, 1964, diary entry, folder 2, box 79, Katie S. Louchheim Papers, Library of Congress; Walter Jenkins to J. Edgar Hoover, December 16, 1964, copy, Washington DC folder, box 85, PPWJ.

CHAPTER 6

1. "A friend indeed" to Marjorie Jenkins (postmarked Naugatuck, CT), October 24, 1964, Connecticut folder, box 39, PPWJ. In 1968, *Good Housekeeping* published an anonymously submitted article by a woman whose story has enough similarities to the one in this letter that I wonder if they might share an author. See Anonymous, "The Story of a Tragic Marriage," *Good Housekeeping*, July 1968, 36–46.

2. Ari Adut, *On Scandal: Moral Disturbances in Society, Politics, and Art* (Cambridge University Press, 2008), 34. This major theoretical intervention in the study of scandal offers many insights; his description of the Jenkins coverage as "sparse and circumspect" (200) perhaps fits the comparative frame of political scandals, but it reads differently against the period's near-total mainstream-press silence about same-sex acts.

3. Mrs. F. J. Miltner to Walter Jenkins, n.d. but February 9, 1965, Ohio folder, box 51, PPWJ; emphasis in original.

4. Robert O. Self, *All in the Family: The Realignment of American Democracy Since the 1960s* (Hill and Wang, 2012), 75.

5. B. V. to Walter Jenkins, October 18, 1964, New York folder, box 51, PPWJ (ellipsis in original); Kristin Celello, *Making Marriage Work : A History of Marriage and Divorce in the Twentieth-Century United States* (University of North Carolina Press, 2009), 75; "R.N. Nurse" to Walter Jenkins, n.d. (postmarked October 30, 1964, from New York City), in Mean Letters folder, box 70, PPWJ, emphasis in original. The author claimed to be a registered nurse and to have "discussed your husband's case with M.D.s and conclusion—your husband was a pervert when he married you."

6. Minnie Lee Wire to Marjorie Jenkins, October 18, 1964, Virginia folder, box 70, PPWJ; J. M. L. to Lady Bird Johnson, October 17, 1964, in "Jenkins, Mr. & Mrs. Walter (only)" folder 2 of 2, box 1022, White House Social Files, LBJL; and Earl E. Markey to Walter Jenkins and Marjorie Jenkins, October 28, 1964, New York folder, box 70, PPWJ. In the early 1960s, when birth control pills were new, "many journalists gave the impression that 'science' was working to improve oral contraceptives and therefore current shortcomings would soon be remedied." Elizabeth Siegel Watkins, *On the Pill: A Social History of Oral Contraceptives, 1950–1970* (Johns Hopkins University Press, 1988), 41.

7. Frances Forbes to Walter Jenkins, November 8, 1964, Misc. Texas Cities folder, box 70, PPWJ ("slow"); Mrs. Judd D. Baker and Mrs. John M. Schwartz to Walter Jenkins, n.d., DC folder, box 39, PPWJ ("soon"); Mr. and Mrs. Leo E. Harless to Walter Jenkins, n.d., DC folder, box 39, PPWJ ("fine"). In twentieth-century America, women were the primary buyers and senders of greeting cards; the industry expanded steadily in the two decades after World War II. Barry Shank, *A Token of My Affection: Greeting Cards and American Business Culture* (Columbia University Press, 2004), 6, 252.

8. Katie Louchheim, October 15, 1964, diary entry, folder 2, box 79, Katie Louchheim Papers, Library of Congress, Washington, DC.

9. Mildred Stegall to Doris Whitehill, October 26, 1964 ("improving"), in 2022 addendum, PPWJ; Vera Glaser, "His Wife Stands by Jenkins," *New York Post*, October 16, 1964 (quoting Nichols); Barbara Kendall to Marjorie Jenkins, October 16, 1964, DC folder, box 39, PPWJ; Bette Runge to Marjorie Jenkins, n.d., box 41, PPWJ.

10. Charles Luckman to Walter Jenkins, October 27, 1964, box 215, PPWJ; Gloria Marx to Marjorie Jenkins, October 23, 1964, South Carolina folder, box 51, PPWJ. In late 1964, in the immediate aftermath of the Jenkins scandal, a Civil Service Commission official allowed that a homosexual might, in theory, offer persuasive "evidence of rehabilitation." John W. Steele to O. Glenn Stahl, November 17, 1964, https://mattachinesocietywashingtondc.files.wordpress.com/2020/05/32-the-legal-advisory-files-1-of-3.pdf.

11. Tim F. Moriarty to Marjorie Jenkins, October 26, 1964, Pennsylvania folder, box 39, PPWJ; Sargent Shriver to Walter Jenkins, n.d., box 41, PPWJ; Ben Bradlee to Marjorie Jenkins, October 17, 1964, box 42, PPWJ.

12. Connie Kazen to Marjorie Jenkins, October 26, 1964, Misc. Texas Cities folder, box 70, PPWJ; Jack Bush to Marjorie Jenkins, October 16, 1964, box 42, PPWJ; James Rowe to Marjorie Jenkins, March 1, 1965, box 305, PPWJ; Carolyn Kellam Curtis to Walter Jenkins, October 16, 1964, box 42, PPWJ; Dwight H. Oglesby to Walter Jenkins and Marjorie Jenkins, November 27, 1964, box 42, PPWJ.

13. Nicholas Fremont-Smith to Walter Jenkins, November 8, 1964, New York folder, box 51, PPWJ; Helen R. Dyar to Walter Jenkins, October 29, 1964, Connecticut folder, box 39, PPWJ.

14. Hank J. Wrigley Jr. to Walter Jenkins, February 1, 1965, California folder, box 71, PPWJ; Peter and Betty Gillespie to Walter Jenkins, October 21, 1964, Massachusetts folder, box 39, PPWJ; Emil Homick to Walter Jenkins, November 2, 1964, Indiana folder, box 39, PPWJ.

15. Ole Lilleland to Walter Jenkins, October 27, 1964, California folder, box 71, PPWJ.

16. The Reverend Carl York Smith to Walter Jenkins, December 12, 1964, Hawaii folder, box 39, PPWJ.

17. Mab Ashforth Goldman to Walter Jenkins, November 3, 1964, and reply dated March 2, 1965, New York folder, box 51, PPWJ.

18. James Rowe to Marjorie Jenkins, October 14, 1964, box 305, PPWJ.

19. Myer Feldman to Walter Jenkins, October 15, 1964, box 41, PPWJ; Frank X. Dooley to Marjorie Jenkins, n.d. but fall 1964, box 67, PPWJ; Betty and Jim Burke to Marjorie Jenkins and Walter Jenkins, San Antonio folder, box 70, PPWJ; Thomas D. Finney, Jr., to Marjorie Jenkins, October 15, 1964, box 41, PPWJ; Bruce Thomas to Walter Jenkins, box 42, PPWJ.

20. "A citizen of St. Paul Minnesota" to Walter Jenkins, November 1, 1964, Minnesota folder, box 51, PPWJ; Theodore H. von Laue to Walter Jenkins, October 25, 1964, in Missouri folder, box 51, PPWJ; George Nokes to Walter Jenkins, November 5, 1964, box 156, PPWJ.

21. Fred F. Smith MD to Walter Jenkins, October 16, 1964, box 216, PPWJ; Louis Harris to Walter Jenkins, n.d. but Christmas card, box 70, PPWJ; Sargent Shriver to Walter Jenkins, n.d., box 41, PPWJ; Horace Busby to Walter Jenkins, n.d., box 42, PPWJ; Mary

Busby to Marjorie Jenkins, box 42, PPWJ; Fr. Donald Brice to Walter Jenkins, n.d., Washington DC folder, box 39, PPWJ; Dottie Bebb to Walter Jenkins, n.d., Wichita Falls folder, box 70, PPWJ.

22. Liz Carpenter to Walter Jenkins, n.d., box 42, PPWJ; James W. Wilson to Walter Jenkins, November 20, 1964, box 42, PPWJ; Richard L. Callaghan to Walter Jenkins, October 15, 1964, box 42, PPWJ.

23. Mr. and Mrs. Steve Palmer to Walter Jenkins, n.d., Ohio folder, box 51, PPWJ; Lee White to Walter Jenkins, October 17, 1964, box 43, PPWJ.

24. Samuel C. Brightman to Walter Jenkins, October 16, 1964, box 42, PPWJ (Jenkins replied to Brightman on February 4, 1965: "I am about ready for that golf game you suggested and will meet you at Kenwood whenever the cold weather subsides"); William D. Little Jr. to Walter Jenkins, November 6, 1964, box 70, PPWJ; Richard L. Callaghan to Walter Jenkins, October 15, 1964, box 42, PPWJ (Jenkins replied on February 5, 1965: "Although it has been three and a half months since you wrote me that nice note, I am glad to report that I am now ready to have that 'drink to the perdition of our enemies' ").

25. Betty Hickman to Walter Jenkins, October 29, 1964, San Antonio folder, box 70, PPWJ; Edmund G. Brown to Walter Jenkins, October 27, 1964, box 43, PPWJ; Connie Kazen to Marjorie Jenkins, October 26, 1964, Misc. Texas Cities folder, box 70, PPWJ; Sister M. Elizabeth Anne to Marjorie Jenkins, October 16, 1964, box 41, PPWJ; Jack Bush to Marjorie Jenkins, October 16, 1964, box 42, PPWJ.

26. Adele Reinhartz, "Sexuality, Stoning, and Supersessionism in Biblical Epic Films of the Post-World War II Era," in *The Oxford Handbook of Feminist Approaches to the Hebrew Bible*, ed. Susanne Scholz (Oxford University Press, 2021), 313–25.

27. Catherine Ballinger to Walter Jenkins, n.d., New York folder, box 51, PPWJ; Thomas Fletcher to Walter Jenkins, October 27, 1964, Connecticut folder, box 39, PPWJ.

28. Mrs. D. H. Whitehill to Marjorie, Walter and Family, October 26, 1964, box 154, PPWJ; Josie Loggie and Bill Loggie to Walter Jenkins, October 15, 1964, box 154, PPWJ; Mrs. Grover Johnson to Walter Jenkins, n.d., box 154, PPWJ; Mrs. M. F. Woodlief to Marjorie Jenkins, n.d., Virginia folder, box 51, PPWJ; Mrs. D. J. Poarch to Marjorie Jenkins, n.d., Kansas folder, box 39, PPWJ.

29. Thomas Fletcher to Walter Jenkins, October 27, 1964, Connecticut folder, box 39, PPWJ; Pearl Parriott to Marjorie Jenkins, October 24, 1964, Iowa folder, box 39, PPWJ; Richard F. Martin to Walter Jenkins, October 29, 1964, California folder, box 51, PPWJ; George McCullough to Walter Jenkins, October 16, 1964, New York folder, box 51, PPWJ.

30. Minnie Lee Wire to Marjorie Jenkins, October 18, 1964, Virginia folder, box 70, PPWJ; Gloria Marx to Marjorie Jenkins, October 23, 1964, South Carolina folder, box 51, PPWJ.

31. Jerry Voorhis to Walter Jenkins, October 19, 1964, box 224, PPWJ; Mrs. Brenda Smith to Walter Jenkins, n.d., Foreign folder, box 39, PPWJ. On Voorhis, see John A. Farrell, *Richard Nixon: The Life* (Vintage, 2017), 28–41.

32. Oscar Arnold, SM, to Walter Jenkins, October 29, 1964, DC folder, box 39, PPWJ; Earl E. Markey to Walter Jenkins and Marjorie Jenkins, October 28, 1964, New York folder, box 51, PPWJ.

33. "An understanding friend" to Walter Jenkins, October 19, 1964, Virginia folder, box 51, PPWJ. One woman wrote that it was "some one very close." J. M. L. to Lady Bird Johnson, October 27, 1964, in "Jenkins, Mr. & Mrs. Walter (only)" folder 2 of 2, box 1022, White House Social Files, LBJL.

34. Unsigned letter to Marjorie Jenkins, October 24, 1964, DC folder, box 39, PPWJ. Of the twenty-one letters, two came from the greater Washington area; three each from New York, New Jersey, and California; two from Ohio; one each from Arizona, Kentucky, Tennessee, Pennsylvania, Connecticut, Maryland, and Michigan; and one from Canada.

35. "Because lesbian oral history projects privilege the stories of those women who eventually divorced and began new lives, such stories dominate this book." Lauren Jae Gutterman, *Her Neighbor's Wife: A History of Lesbian Desire Within Marriage* (University of Pennsylvania Press, 2019), 5.

36. "A stranger, who wishes you well" to Walter Jenkins, October 21, 1964, Pennsylvania folder, box 51, PPWJ; unsigned letter to Walter Jenkins, October 25, 1964, Ohio folder, box 51, PPWJ; R. F. M. to Walter Jenkins, October 29, 1964, California folder, box 51, PPWJ.

37. J. B. D. to Walter Jenkins, October 26, 1964, Tennessee folder, box 51, PPWJ; C. C. T. to Walter Jenkins, November 3, 1964, Arizona folder, box 70, PPWJ; "Don" to Walter Jenkins, October 24, 1964, Foreign folder, box 39, PPWJ; W. D. to Walter Jenkins, October 21, 1964, New York folder, box 51, PPWJ.

38. Gutterman, *Her Neighbor's Wife*, 16; Alison Lefkovitz, "'The Peculiar Anomaly': Same-Sex Infidelity in Postwar Divorce Courts," *Law and History Review* 33, no. 3 (August 2015), 665–701, here 669.

39. W. J. H. to Walter Jenkins, n.d., New Jersey folder, box 51, PPWJ (he wrote again on February 5, 1965: "I have a new job now, and it's not always easy but one has to brave the storm"); J. B. D. to Walter Jenkins, October 26, 1964, Tennessee folder, box 51, PPWJ.

40. Sumner Welles, the undersecretary of state who resigned without publicity in 1943 and was outed by *Confidential* magazine in 1956, was married three times; Lester C. Hunt Jr., the senator's son arrested in 1953, later married. Chris Parkes, "The Trouble with Sumner Welles: Sexuality, Race, and the Limits of Mythmaking in Queer History," *Journal of American Studies* 57 (2023), 371–92; Rodger McDaniel, *Dying for Joe McCarthy's Sins: The Suicide of Wyoming Senator Lester Hunt* (Cody, Wyoming: WordsWorth, 2013). See also *Pride* (2021 documentary miniseries), episode 1 ("1950s: People Had Parties"), directed by Tom Kalin.

41. "A friend" to Walter Jenkins, October 28, 1964, New York folder, box 51, PPWJ. The writer enclosed the *Staten Island Advance* editorial "Sickness Not Issue" (October 27, 1964), which likened homosexuality to alcoholism, drug addiction, and other "ugly facts of life," calling it "probably the most understanding and non-vicious article written about you." The editorial portrayed Jenkins's "sickness" as ubiquitous and nonpartisan—discoverable "anywhere" by those who snoop—and arising from medical, social, and moral, not political, causes.

42. M. B. to Marjorie Jenkins, October 17, 1964, New Jersey folder, box 51, PPWJ; M. B. to Walter Jenkins, n.d., Kentucky folder, box 39, PPWJ.

43. F. A. F. to Walter Jenkins, November 12, 1964, box 41, PPWJ; H. B. to Walter Jenkins, October 18, 1964, Texas folder, box 51, PPWJ.

44. Mrs. M. H. R. to Marjorie Jenkins, November 8, 1964, Pennsylvania folder, box 51, PPWJ.

45. W. D. to Walter Jenkins, October 22, 1964, New York folder, box 51, PPWJ; J. C. P. to Walter Jenkins, October 23, 1964, California folder, box 71, PPWJ; "An understanding friend" to Walter Jenkins, n.d. (October 19, 1964), Virginia folder, box 51, PPWJ; William R. Parker and Elaine St. Johns, *Prayer Can Change Your Life: Experiments and Techniques in Prayer Therapy* (Prentice-Hall, 1957), 66–67. Philip Zaleski and Carol Zaleski call the book "the first well-publicized study, cited to this day in many books lauding prayer's curative powers," despite its "many drawbacks and defects." *Prayer: A History* (Houghton Mifflin, 2005), 341.

46. "A friend indeed" to Marjorie Jenkins, October 24, 1964, Connecticut folder, box 39, PPWJ.

47. Unsigned letter to Marjorie Jenkins, October 19, 1964, Ohio folder, box 51, PPWJ.

48. Charles Jackson to Walter Jenkins, n.d., New Jersey folder, box 51, PPWJ. Jackson wrote, "P.S. If I have intruded, please believe that it was well-meant. We all need love." Jenkins's polite reply, dated December 31, said, "Of course I know your work well and believe you are one of the most talented writers we have in the country." *The Fall of Valor* (Rinehart, 1946) drew mixed reviews and sold and disappointing sales compared to his first book.

49. Tucker Ashworth to Walter Jenkins, n.d., and reply dated January 30, 1965, New York folder, box 51, PPWJ,.

50. RWWJ, 80 (Popple), 75 (a Commerce Department employee who had worked for Jenkins on the Senate staff from 1957 to 1961), 31 (Burris).

51. Celello, *Making Marriage Work*, 10, 75. Experts, Celello notes, increasingly "warned white middle-class wives that their husbands were in grave danger of premature illness and death from working too hard in the cutthroat corporate world" (81).

52. Stephanie Coontz, *Marriage, a History: How Love Conquered Marriage* (Penguin, 2005), 247.

53. Mrs. Arthur E. Goldschmidt to Walter Jenkins, October 18, 1964, box 70, PPWJ; J. M. L. to Lady Bird Johnson, October 27, 1964, in "Jenkins, Mr. & Mrs. Walter (only)" folder 2 of 2, box 1022, White House Social Files, LBJL.

54. Walter Jenkins to Mrs. Ross Corlett, April 9, 1965, copy, box 70, PPWJ.

55. Lady Bird Johnson, *A White House Diary* (Holt, Rinehart, and Winston, 1970), 204; Lady Bird Johnson, audio diary and annotated transcript, November 17, 1964, LBJL. President Johnson told Abe Fortas, a week after the election, that in their recent phone call Walter had mentioned "about three thousand letters he'd received." Telephone conversation no. 6335, sound recording, LBJ and ABE FORTAS, November 11, 1964, 10:30 p.m., LBJL.

CHAPTER 7

1. Beverly Gage, *G-Man: J. Edgar Hoover and the Making of the American Century* (Viking, 2022), 450 ("perhaps"), 578, 600.

2. Telephone conversation no. 5891, sound recording, LBJ and NICHOLAS KATZENBACH, October 15, 1964, 7:26 a.m., LBJL; telephone conversation no. 5892, sound recording, LBJ and NICHOLAS KATZENBACH, October 15, 1964, 7:26 a.m., LBJL; telephone conversation no. 5893, sound recording, LBJ and NICHOLAS KATZENBACH, October 15, 1964, 7:26 a.m., LBJL; telephone conversation no. 5894, sound recording, LBJ and NICHOLAS KATZENBACH, October 15, 1964, 7:26 a.m., LBJ; telephone conversation no. 5933, sound recording, LBJ and CARTHA "DEKE" DELOACH, October 20, 1964, 9:08 p.m., LBJL. The request Hoover countermanded was that "we interview Jenkins regarding possible equivocations in an affidavit furnished by Jenkins in the Baker" case. W. V. Cleveland to Mr. Evans, October 16, 1964, in FBI file 161-HQ-2848.

3. RWWJ, 27–52, quotation at 52; Ed Witzenburger to Walter and Marjorie Jenkins, October 16, 1964, Wyoming folder, box 70, PPWJ; Doc and Betty Watson to Marjorie Jenkins, n.d., box 43, PPWJ; Helen Grace Gould to Marjorie and Walter Jenkins, October 17, 1964, box 120, PPWJ; Norman Heine Powell to Walter Jenkins, November 11, 1964, box 231, PPWJ.

4. Morton Mintz and Alfred E. Lewis, "Jenkins Case Was Handled Routine Way," *Washington Post*, October 16, 1964; "'Y' Closes Its Public Rest Room," *Washington Post*, October 18, 1964; RWWJ, 53. When the Kennedy administration took office in 1961 and Johnson asked that Jenkins be issued a White House pass, the Secret Service learned only that there had been an arrest for "Investigation (Suspicious Person)."

5. RWWJ, 84 ("any and all"), 18 ("would rather die"); "NSC Meetings Attended by Mr. Jenkins," Walter Jenkins folder, box 10, National Security File—Intelligence File, Presidential Papers, LBJL.

6. RWWJ, 59–61, 69–70, and exhibit D-1.

7. RWWJ, 64. Other men with morals arrests were a high school classmate and someone who had "roomed in the same building" at the University of Texas (58, 65–66). See Margot Canaday, *Queer Career: Sexuality and Work in Modern America* (Princeton University Press, 2023), 122.

8. "The Charge: Washington Police Reporters Failed," *Bulletin of the American Society of Newspaper Editors* 481 (December 1, 1964).

9. C. D. DeLoach, memo to Mr. Mohr, October 15, 1964, in FBI file 161-HQ-2848; W. V. Cleveland to Mr. Evans, October 15, 1964, in FBI file 161-HQ-2848; RWWJ, 21; Cleveland to Evans, October 16, 1964, in FBI file 161-HQ-2848.

10. Telephone conversation no. 5971, sound recording, LBJ and CARTHA "DEKE" DELOACH, October 27, 1964, 1:45 p.m., LBJL; report attached to J. Edgar Hoover to Bill D. Moyers, October 29, 1964, in FBI file 161-HQ-2848.

11. RWWJ, exhibit D-1 and 72. James Kirchick has shown that a nongay friend betrayed Waldron during an earlier Civil Service Commissison investigation concerning his potential appointment to Johnson's Space Council (*Secret City: The Hidden History of Gay Washington* [Henry Holt, 2022], 307–12). On October 18, DeLoach called Bill Moyers to say that Waldron had admitted to homosexual acts but had interrupted an interview with FBI agents in San Antonio "explaining that he had to attend a social function at the LBJ Ranch." Moyers then blocked Waldron's appearance (DeLoach to Mr. Mohr, October 19,

1964, in FBI file 161-HQ-2854). Kirchick interprets this as evidence that Moyers maliciously purged homosexuals from the White House and implies he helped destroy Waldron's career, out of rivalry for Johnson's favor (336–37). The record suggests otherwise: by then, given the FBI's findings, Waldron's resignation was inevitable; Moyers neither precipitated it nor caused the devastation Waldron felt at his friend's betrayal. Keeping him from the LBJ Ranch event not only protected the campaign (just over two weeks before Election Day) but reduced the risk of Waldron's being outed publicly should the press learn he was under a cloud. (Recall that no one was sure how reporters had learned of Jenkins's arrests, but Republicans seemed to have played a role.) The real question was when and how—not whether—Waldron would leave the federal payroll and whether it would draw damaging publicity; in the end he, unlike Jenkins, resigned quietly with no publicity.

12. RWWJ, 45, 32.

13. J. Edgar Hoover to Tolson, Belmont, Evans, Rosen, Sullivan, DeLoach, October 22, 1964, in FBI file 161-HQ-2848.

14. FBI, "For Immediate Release, October 22, 1964," in FBI file 161-HQ-2848; C. D. DeLoach to Mr. Mohr, October 23, 1964, in FBI file 161-HQ-2848 (which says the report initially "came over the wire service ticket at 8:51PM"); M. A. Jones to DeLoach, October 23, 1964, in FBI file 161-HQ-2848.

15. J. Edgar Hoover, memo to Tolson et al., October 23, 1964, 10:34 a.m., in FBI file 161-HQ-2848; M. A. Jones to DeLoach, October 23, 1964, in FBI file 161-HQ-2848; telephone conversation no. 5948, sound recording, LBJ and J. EDGAR HOOVER, October 23, 1964, 6:00 p.m., LBJL.

16. Untitled statement by Jenkins, n.d., Jenkins Investigation folder, box 29A, Office Files of Mildred Stegall, LBJL.

17. Telephone conversation no. 6368, sound recording, LBJ and CARTHA "DEKE" DELOACH, November 16, 1964, 4:40 p.m., LBJL.

18. Eric Cervini, *The Deviant's War: The Homosexual vs. the United States of America* (Farrar, Straus and Giroux, 2020), 44, 141, 227.

19. "Johnson on Jenkins, Baker . . . New GOP Charges," *New York Herald-Tribune*, October 25, 1964; telephone conversation no. 5969, sound recording, LBJ and KERMIT GORDON, October 27, 1964, 1:32 p.m., LBJL; telephone conversation no. 5974, sound recording, LBJ and MCGEORGE BUNDY, October 27, 1964, 1:59 p.m., LBJL; telephone conversation no. 5975, sound recording, LBJ and ROBERT MCNAMARA, October 27, 1964, 2:39 p.m., LBJL; telephone conversation no. 5977, sound recording, LBJ and WALTER HELLER, October 27, 1964, 2:45 p.m., LBJL; telephone conversation no. 5979, sound recording, LBJ and RICHARD GOODWIN, October 27, 1964, 2:59 p.m., LBJL.

20. President's Daily Diary, October 28, 1964, LBJL; "Johnson Tells of Morals Case in Eisenhower Administration," *St. Louis Post-Dispatch*, October 29, 1964.

21. Quoted from a verbatim transcript that KSON (San Diego country-music station) reporter Dan McKinnon sent to the White House at George Reedy's request: Dan McKinnon to Willie Day Taylor, October 30, 1964, copy in Ex FG 11-8-1/Jenkins, Walter folder, box 86, Presidential Papers, LBJL. Johnson quickly added a reference to Sherman Adams and alluded to Truman and Roosevelt also facing similar problems. But he could

not retract the sentence referring—unmistakably, to those in the know—to Arthur H. Vandenberg Jr. "Looks like I might not have said just quite what I intended to say," he told Nicholas Katzenbach, and asked him to obtain the facts about Vandenberg. Telephone conversation no. 5980, sound recording, LBJ and NICHOLAS KATZENBACH, October 28, 1964, 11:43 p.m., LBJL.

22. "LBJ Says Ike Had Own Jenkins Case," *Newark Evening News*, October 29, 1964; "Johnson Says Eisenhower Had His 'Jenkins Case'" (AP), *Fresno Bee*, October 29, 1964; Robert Barkdoll, "Had No 'Jenkins Case,' Eisenhower Declares," *Los Angeles Times*, October 30, 1964; "Rep. Miller Says LBJ Disregards Truth" (AP), *Salisbury [MD] Times*, October 31, 1964; "Nixon: LBJ 'Smeared Thousands' Under Ike" (AP), *San Francisco Examiner*, October 31, 1964; telephone conversation no. 5981, sound recording, LBJ and CLARK CLIFFORD, October 29, 1964, 7:27 a.m., LBJL. In a televised news conference, Richard Nixon charged that Johnson had smeared "the thousands of people in the Eisenhower administration." At least one paper ran AP stories on both Johnson's claim and Eisenhower's denial. "LBJ Says Ike Faced Jenkins-Type Problem" (AP) and "Ike Cannot Recall It" (AP), in *Daily Advance* [Lynchburg, VA], October 29, 1964. On the private life of Eisenhower's national security advisor, a gay man, see Peter Shinkle, *Ike's Mystery Man: The Secret Lives of Robert Cutler* (Steerforth Press, 2018).

23. Dom Bonafede, "Jenkins Home, 'Coming Along Fine,'" *New York Herald-Tribune*, November 11, 1964; telephone conversation no. 6335, sound recording, LBJ and ABE FORTAS, November 11, 1964, 10:30 p.m., LBJL. In 1963, Jenkins had advised Bobby Baker to settle Ralph Hill's lawsuit. Baker deeply regretted his failure to take Jenkins's advice, which led to Baker's resignation and disgrace (Baker with Larry L. King, *Wheeling and Dealing: Confessions of a Capitol Hill Operator* [W. W. Norton, 1978], 175–76).

24. Lady Bird Johnson, audio diary and annotated transcript, November 17, 1964, LBJL.

25. Lyndon B. Johnson OH, August 19, 1969, by Harry Middleton, LBJL.

26. Walter Jenkins to Hobart Taylor Jr., December 16, 1964, box 306, PPWJ; Walter Jenkins to Lacey C. Sharp, February 23, 1965, box 41, PPWJ; Walter Jenkins to Mrs. D. Whitehill, November 22, 1965, box 154; Walter Jenkins to Hon. Philip A. Kazen, December 29, 1964, box 154, PPWJ; Walter Jenkins to David W. Cunningham, March 29, 1965, box 180, PPWJ; Walter Jenkins telegram to Oliver A. Quayle III, January 27, 1965 (annotated in Jenkins's handwriting "Had for cocktails in NY 2/10/1965"), copy, box 70, PPWJ; Walter Jenkins to Eddie Weisl Jr., February 12, 1965, box 70, PPWJ.

27. Charlie Jenkins to Walter Jenkins, January 28, 1965, and Walter Jenkins to Charles H. Jenkins, February 5, 1965, copy, box 157, PPWJ; Rowland Evans and Robert Novak, *Lyndon B. Johnson: The Exercise of Power* (New American Library, 1966), 480; income tax returns, box 105, PPWJ.

28. Mary Lasker to Walter Jenkins, December 23, 1964, box 70, PPWJ ("I know"); Mary Lasker to Lyndon B. Johnson, December 23, 1964, copy, Lyndon Baines Johnson folder, box 276, Mary Lasker Papers, Columbia University Library, New York (suggestion; if Johnson kept the original of Lasker's letter, I have not found it); George R. Brown to Walter and Marjorie Jenkins, December 7, 1964, box 180, PPWJ; Paul Starr, *The Social*

Transformation of American Medicine (Basic Books, 1982), 342–46; Shirley Haley, *Angel in Mink: The Story of Mary Lasker's Crusade for Medical Research and the National Institutes of Health* (ACT for NIH Foundation, 2022), 197–205. Lasker later became a key funder of the First Lady's Washington beautification program, and in 1966 she subsidized "press hospitality" during Lady Bird's 1966 trip to Big Bend National Park. Jan Jarboe Russell, *Lady Bird: A Biography of Mrs. Johnson* (Simon & Schuster, 1999), 277–78; Winzola McLendon and Scottie Smith, *Don't Quote Me: Washington Newswomen and the Power Society* (E. P. Dutton, 1970), 117.

29. Bill Weaver to Walter Jenkins, January 11, 1965, and Walter Jenkins to Bill Weaver, January 16, 1965, copy, box 41, PPWJ; telephone conversation no. 6335, sound recording, LBJ and ABE FORTAS, November 11, 1964, 10:30 p.m., LBJL.

30. Luther Holcomb OH II, July 8, 1969, by T. H. Baker, LBJL; Betty Beale, "Inaugural Doings Not Only Festivities," *Wilmington [DE] Evening Journal*, January 23, 1965, 19.

31. "Walter Jenkins' Twin Sons Will Live in Texas" (AP), *Sioux City Journal*, January 28, 1965; "Walter Jenkins Not Moving" (AP), *Lexington Herald-Leader*, January 28, 1965; Robert S. Allen and Paul Scott, "Jenkins May Yet Escape Testifying in Baker Case," *Camden Courier-Post*, January 20, 1965; "Walter Jenkins To Move Here?" *Austin American-Statesman*, January 26, 1965; "Political Intelligence" column, *Texas Observer*, March 19, 1965, 16.

32. Robert S. Allen and Paul Scott's column appeared under headlines such as "Abandoned Car Adds to Jenkins Mystery" (*Capital Times* [Madison, WI], January 30, 1965), "Mystery of Abandoned LBJ Car Involves Walter Jenkins" (*Casper Morning Star*, January 29, 1965), "Jenkins in Car Puzzle" (*Lubbock Avalanche-Journal*, February 1, 1965), "Abandoned Car Mystery Intrigues Washington" (*Lexington Herald-Leader*, January 29, 1965), "New Mystery Surrounds Jenkins" (*Sioux City Journal*, January 29, 1965); interview with Beth Jenkins Bromberg and Walt Jenkins Jr., Bee Cave, Texas, June 4, 2016.

33. Marjorie Jenkins letter to whom it may concern, January 16, 1965, Balbina Suarez folder, box 41, PPWJ; "Baker Probers Notify Jenkins He Is to Testify on Jan. 25," *Washington Evening Star*, January 15, 1965; Paul Hope, "Private Jenkins Quiz Slated for Thursday," *Washington Evening Star*, January 29, 1965; John Barron, "Psychiatrist Tells Probers Quiz Could Harm Jenkins," *Washington Evening Star*, February 5, 1965.

34. "Senators Let Jenkins Avoid Probe Subpoena," *Washington Evening Star*, February 9, 1965; Paul Hope, "Baker Probers Draft Questions for Jenkins," *Washington Evening Star*, February 11, 1965; John Barron, "Jenkins Absent from Hearing on Baker Case," *Washington Evening Star*, February 4, 1965; Gerry van der Heuvel, "Hint Jenkins Won't Heed Call," *New York Daily News*, February 4, 1965; US Congress, Senate, Committee on Rules and Administration, *Hearings re: S. Res. 212 S. Res. 367*, 88th Cong., part 10, testimony of Walter W. Jenkins (in the Form of Interrogatories and Answers Thereto), February 24, 1965, 981; Laurence Stern, "Jenkins Admits Part in Reynolds TV Deal," *Washington Post*, February 24, 1965; Carl T. Curtis OH I, March 10, 1978, by Michael L. Gillette, LBJL, 21.

35. Walter Jenkins to Beverly Aldridge, February 1, 1965, box 41, PPWJ (apartment and twins' school); Walter Jenkins to Irving Ferman, February 8, 1965, box 41, PPWJ ("pretty well"); Walter Jenkins to Willard A. Hawkins, February 24, 1965, box 215, PPWJ

("reasonably good"); income tax returns, box 105, PPWJ; telephone interview with Sandy Silver, August 22, 2016; telephone interview with George Bristol, June 11, 2022.

36. Walter Jenkins to Mrs. Ross Corlett, April 9, 1965, box 70, PPWJ (move-in date); Walter Jenkins to Roberta Forbes, April 9, 1965, box 41, PPWJ ("we have"); Walter Jenkins to Mr. and Mrs. W. R. Jenkins, April 19, 1965, Misc. Texas Cities folder, box 70, PPWJ ("I bought"); Walter Jenkins to Mr. and Mrs. Reginald C. Martin, May 14,1965, Misc. Texas Cities folder, box 70, PPWJ ("One of").

37. Doris Hancock to Walter Jenkins, April 2, 1965, in Beth Jenkins Bromberg Personal Papers, Bee Cave, Texas ("I am directed"); Claude C. Wild to Walter Jenkins, August 16, 1965, box 120, PPWJ (subsequent invitation).

38. John W. Finney, "Johnson, for Fun, Has a Hideaway Ranch," *New York Times*, July 7, 1964; Marjorie Jenkins to Lady Bird Johnson, n.d. (filed July 17, 1965), in "Jenkins, Mr. & Mrs. Walter (only)" folder 2 of 2, box 1022, White House Social Files, LBJL; Julia Sweig, *Lady Bird Johnson: Hiding in Plain Sight* (Random House, 2021), 172 (incorrectly describing this as a dinner hosted by both Johnsons); interview with Beth Jenkins Bromberg and Walt Jenkins Jr., Bee Cave, Texas, June 4, 2016.

39. Walter Jenkins to J. Cordell Moore, August 30, 1965, box 303, PPWJ; Walter Jenkins to Perry R. Bass, October 4, 1965, box 157, PPWJ; Perry R. Bass to Walter Jenkins, October 21, 1965, box 157, PPWJ; Walter Jenkins to J. C. Kellam, July 19, 1965, in David Cunningham folder, box 180, PPWJ.

40. Interview with George Bristol, Fort Worth, TX, October 3, 2022; telephone interview with George Bristol, June 11, 2022 (quote).

41. Telephone interview with George Bristol, June 11, 2022 ("frankly," "I forget"); interview with George Bristol, Fort Worth, TX, October 3, 2022 ("always").

42. President's Daily Diary for November 26, 1964, December 20, 1964, December 23, 1964, and June 27, 1965, LBJL.

43. Kirchick, *Secret City*, 340, 647–48; Bob Waldron to Marge and Walter Jenkins, February 22, 1965 (mistakenly dated 1964), and Bob Waldron to Marge Jenkins, n.d. (Walter's reply dated December 5, 1966), box 306, PPWJ; Robert E. Waldron OH II, February 1, 1976, by Michael L. Gillette, LBJL.

44. Thomas R. Eisenmann, "The U.S. Cable Television Industry, 1948–1995: Managerial Capitalism in Eclipse," *Business History Review* 74, no. 1 (Spring 2000), 1–40, here 6–7; "Sooners Have Quarterbacks Galore, Too," *Austin Statesman*, October 6, 1955; "Okies Want Another Bud," *Austin American*, January 13, 1964; "Miss Spurrier and Jay O'Neal Are Married in Mexico City," *Ada Weekly News*, July 13, 1961; interview with George Bristol, Fort Worth, TX, October 3, 2022.

45. Isabelle Shelton, "L.B.J.'s Beagle Starts Flap at Fort," *Record* (Hackensack, NJ), May 17, 1965; interview with George Bristol, Fort Worth, TX, October 2, 2022; telephone interview with George Bristol, June 11, 2022; S. I. Newhouse Jr. to Mrs. Lyndon B. Johnson, sent "c/o Mr. Walter Jenkins," July 21, 1967, box 231, PPWJ.

46. Interview with Beth Jenkins Bromberg and Walt Jenkins Jr., Bee Cave, Texas, June 4, 2016; Helen Thomas to Walter and Marjorie Jenkins, February 17, 1966, box 306, PPWJ; interview with George Bristol, Fort Worth, TX, October 3, 2022; Lady Bird Johnson

to Walter Jenkins, January 14, 1967, copy in "Jenkins, Mr. & Mrs. Walter (only)" folder 2 of 2, box 1022, White House Social Files, LBJL.

47. Walter Jenkins to Robert C. Hill, December 12, 1966, folder 32, box 100, Robert C. Hill Papers, Hoover Institution Library and Archives, Stanford, CA.

48. Income tax returns, box 105, PPWJ; "Cromwell Investment Club of Austin, Texas, Partnership Agreement" (June 1967), Cromwell Investment Club folder, box 107, PPWJ; interview with George Bristol, Fort Worth, TX, October 3, 2022.

49. Telephone conversation no. 5877, sound recording, LBJ and ABE FORTAS, October 14, 1964, 3:56 p.m., LBJL.

50. Paul M. Popple to Melvin Sisk, October 27, 1964, Chronological—October 1964 folder, box 6, Office Files of Paul M. Popple, LBJL; Paul M. Popple to Dr. Frank Stanton, October 20, 1964, Chronological—October 1964 folder, box 6, Office Files of Paul M. Popple, LBJL (quote); Rowland Evans and Robert Novak, "Inside Report . . . : Trouble in the White House," *Washington Post*, November 4, 1964.

51. Emmette S. Redford and Richard McCulley, *White House Operations: The Johnson Presidency* (University of Texas Press, 1986), 57, 138 (see also 62, 183). Redford and McCulley argue that the high staff turnover for which Johnson became known was in fact confined to the press operation; elsewhere, "very substantial stability" prevailed (31). The media followed Johnson in describing Moyers as Jenkins's successor, as when Charles Roberts wrote in 1965, "Since the fall of Walter Jenkins, who was clearly LBJ's No. 1 aide after Dallas, Moyers has taken over more of Jenkins' duties than any other staffer" (*LBJ's Inner Circle* [Delacorte Press, 1965], 53). In his 2017 book on the presidency, Jeremi Suri contends that Johnson was the last president to have a successful first year in office (xxi). He argues that Johnson's presidency soon lost focus: "His calendars show longer and longer days, ceaseless meetings and phone calls, and debilitating routines. . . . The pressure was too intense to think beyond the immediate matter" (222). Suri further maintains that the Kennedy and Johnson administrations "mark a turning point when the power of the modern executive grew almost unmanageable" (224). Jeremi Suri, *The Impossible Presidency: The Rise and Fall of America's Highest Office* (Basic Books, 2017), xxi.

52. Julian E. Zelizer, *Taxing America: Wilbur D. Mills, Congress, and the State, 1945–1975* (Cambridge University Press, 2000), 18; George Reedy OH I, December 20, 1968, by T. H. Baker, LBJL; interview with Bill Moyers, New York City, August 8, 2017.

53. Heller quoted in *The Johnson Presidency: Twenty Intimate Perspectives of Lyndon B. Johnson*, ed. Kenneth W. Thompson (University Press of America, 1986), 194–95. The overall size of the federal budget had been a major concern early in Johnson's presidency. Under the plan, up to a quarter of the money would have been reserved for the poorest states, with the remainder allocated by population. See Edwin L. Dale Jr., "President Favors Giving the States Share of Revenue," *New York Times*, October 28, 1964; Robert L. Heilbroner, "The Share-the-Tax-Revenue Plan," *New York Times*, December 27, 1964.

54. James Rowe to Walter Jenkins, March 12, 1965, box 305, PPWJ.

55. Harry C. McPherson OH IV, March 24, 1969, by T. H. Baker, LBJL, 2.

56. George Reedy OH I, December 20, 1968, by T. H. Baker, LBJL, 5.

57. Interview with Bill Moyers, New York City, January 18, 2018.

58. Exceptions to his vanishing from the news included the 1965 hearings over Fortas's nomination to the Supreme Court, when Jenkins's case was raised; far-right smears falsely tying him to a Job Corps facility; and a 1966 American Nazi Party picket outside his Austin home. Telephone conversation no. 8413, sound recording, LBJ and NICHOLAS KATZENBACH, July 29, 1965, 9:20 p.m., LBJL; Meta Dinklage to John J. Williams, September 17, 1965, and Sargent Shriver to John J. Williams, October 6, 1965, both in folder 112, box 32, John J. Williams Papers, University of Delaware Library Special Collections, Newark, DE; F. J. Baumgardner to W. C. Sullivan, February 14, 1966, in FBI file 161-2848; "Nazis Picket Residence of Jenkins" (AP), *Fort Worth Star-Telegram*, February 14, 1966.

59. Ruth Montgomery, "Brushoff from White House Angers Democratic Politicos," *Philadelphia Inquirer*, November 22, 1966, in Willie Day Taylor folder, box 119, PPWJ; Ruth Montgomery, "Many Demos Disturbed by Lack of Links With White House," *San Antonio Light*, November 20, 1966, in J. J. Pickle folder, box 42, PPWJ.

60. NSC Action 2497, in National Security Council Record of Actions, August 4, 1964, in "Records of Actions, National Security Council Meetings, August 4, 1964" folder, box 1, Meeting Notes File, Presidential Papers, LBJL.

61. Bromley Smith to Lyndon B. Johnson, August 21, 1967, copy in Walter Jenkins folder, "J" box 67, White House Central Files, Name File, LBJL. "Our records indicate that Jack Valenti was not at this meeting," Smith noted. For the context, see E. W. Kenworthy, "Congress Warned to Reassert Role," *New York Times*, August 17, 1967; E. W. Kenworthy, "President Observes Congress Can Void Its Vote on Tonkin," *New York Times*, August 19, 1967; E. W. Kenworthy, "Katzenbach Sees Tonkin Vote Peril," *New York Times*, August 22, 1967; Thomas W. Ottenad, "Move Growing in Senate to Change Tonkin Resolution," *St. Louis Post-Dispatch*, August 27, 1967; Robert David Johnson, *Congress and the Cold War* (Cambridge University Press, 2006), 138–41.

62. Mildred Stegall to Lyndon B. Johnson, August 25, 1967; "Notes Taken at Leadership Meeting on August 4, 1964"; and untitled memo, August 27, 1967, all in "August 4 Leadership" folder, box 1, Meeting Notes File, Presidential Papers, LBJL.

63. George Reedy OH I, December 20, 1968, by T. H. Baker, LBJL; Vicky Cammon McHugh Murphy and Simon McHugh OH II, by Michael L. Gillette, June 8, 1975, LBJL; Clark M. Clifford OH II, July 2, 1969, by Paige E. Mulhollan, LBJL.

64. Joe Califano to Larry Temple, December 9, 1968, in EX FG 11-8-1/Holborn, box 86, Presidential Papers, LBJL.

65. George Reedy OH I, December 20, 1968, by T. H. Baker, LBJL; Hobart Taylor Jr. OH I, January 6, 1969, by Stephen Goodell, LBJL.

66. Mary Margaret Wiley Valenti OH I, July 24, 1969, by Joe B. Frantz, LBJL; Sally O'Brien MacDonald and Sarah McClendon OH I, February 16, 1972, by Joe B. Frantz, LBJL.

67. Vicky Cammon McHugh Murphy and Simon McHugh OH II, June 8, 1975, by Michael L. Gillette, LBJL; Al Weisel Jr., "LBJ's Gay Sex Scandal," *Out* 73 (December 1999), 131.

68. Walter Jenkins to Mildred Stegall, July 8, 1971, box 209, PPWJ.

69. Interview with Beth Jenkins Bromberg and Walt Jenkins Jr., Bee Cave, Texas, June 4, 2016.

70. Interview with Beth Jenkins Bromberg and Walt Jenkins Jr., Bee Cave, Texas, June 4, 2016; Walter Jenkins to Mrs. Jack Kern (Sandy Kern), May 11, 1976, Cromwell Investment Club folder, box 107, PPWJ; interview with Beth Jenkins Bromberg, Dallas, Texas, June 28, 2017.

71. Interview with Beth Jenkins Bromberg, Dallas, Texas, June 28, 2017; Dorothy Alford to Hotel Maria Isabel, August 6, 1973, Mexico—Gene Archer folder, box 295, PPWJ.

72. Walter Jenkins to Mr. and Mrs. Charles H. Jenkins, October 27, 1972, box 157, PPWJ.

73. Lady Bird Johnson to Walter Jenkins, January 29, 1973, in LBJ—General folder, box 83, PPWJ; Wayne Jackson and Holly Hudlow, "Thousands Pay Final Respects at LBJ Library," *Austin American*, January 24, 1973; Walter Jenkins to Lady Bird Johnson, February 6, 1973, in LBJ—General folder, box 83, PPWJ; Michael L. Gillette, telephone conversation with author, January 6, 2021.

74. Bill Moyers, "LBJ and the FBI," *Newsweek*, March 10, 1975; Lillian Faderman, *The Gay Revolution: The Story of the Struggle* (Simon and Schuster, 2015), 262–64; Regina Kunzel, *In the Shadow of Diagnosis: Psychiatric Power and Queer Life* (University of Chicago Press, 2024), 133–35; Canaday, *Queer Career*, 119–22.

75. The 1980 interview by Emmette S. Redford and Richard McCulley was later added to the oral history collection.

76. John Macy to Walter Jenkins, December 21, 1976, box 302, PPWJ.

77. James W. Mangan, "Witness Tells How LBJ 'Stole' Senate Election," *Austin American-Statesman*, July 31, 1977; the same article ran in the same day's *Fort Worth Star-Telegram*, also on the front page ("Man Admits Fixing LBJ's '48 Election").

78. Bob Bain, "Campaign Aides Defend Johnson," *Fort Worth Star-Telegram*, August 2, 1977 (morning ed.); Jon Ford, "LBJ Aides Deny He Plotted to Rig Disputed Election," *Austin American-Statesman*, August 2, 1977; Merle Miller, *Lyndon: An Oral Biography* (G. P. Putnam's Sons, 1980), 166.

79. "For the Defense" (standalone photo), *Fort Worth Star-Telegram*, August 2, 1977 (morning ed.); Bob Bain, "Campaign Aides Defend Johnson"; "Friends Rally to Defend Johnson in Ballot Box Issue" (UPI), *Port Arthur Daily News*, August 7, 1977; "Friends, Aides Deny Story" (AP), *Amarillo Globe-Times*, August 2, 1977.

CHAPTER 8

1. Telephone conversation no. 5884, sound recording, LBJ and CARTHA "DEKE" DELOACH, October 14, 1964, 9:00 p.m., LBJL. Later he complained to J. Edgar Hoover about his inability to detect homosexuals: "I swear, I can't recognize them." Telephone conversation no. 5989, sound recording, LBJ and J. EDGAR HOOVER, October 31, 1964, 10:35 a.m., LBJL.

2. Sidey to Parker, October 15, 1964, Johnson, Lyndon (16 of 22) folder, box 31k, THWP; Theodore H. White, "The Making of the President 1964" (book excerpt), *Chicago Tribune*, October 26, 1965.

3. John, telephone interview by Whitney Strub and Timothy Stewart-Winter for the Queer Newark Oral History Project, March 29, 2017, http://queer.newark.rutgers.edu/sites/default/files/transcript/2017-03-29%20John%20interview%202%20final%20to%20post.pdf.

4. "Silver Lining," *Citizens News* 4, no. 1 [n.d. but between October 14 and October 31, 1964], 6; "Opinion and Analysis," *Citizens News* 4, no. 2 [n.d.], 2.

5. Undated typed notes (ca. early 1990s) in folder 1, box 41, Dick Leitsch Papers, New York Public Library.

6. Margot Canaday, *The Straight State: Sexuality and Citizenship in Twentieth-Century America* (Princeton University Press, 2009), 216–21; David K. Johnson, *The Lavender Scare: The Cold War Persecution of Gays and Lesbians in the Federal Government* (University of Chicago Press, 2004), 197; Marc Stein, *Rethinking the Gay and Lesbian Movement*, 2nd ed. (Routledge, 2022), 72.

7. Jean White, "Homophile Groups Argue Civil Liberties," *Washington Post*, October 11, 1964. The *Evening Star* covered the conference as well: "Civil Liberties Union Hits Homosexual Ban," *Evening Star*, October 11, 1964.

8. Pender M. McCarter, letter to the editor, *Out*, February 2000, 8; John, telephone interview by Whitney Strub and Timothy Stewart-Winter for the Queer Newark Oral History Project, March 29, 2017, http://queer.newark.rutgers.edu/sites/default/files/transcript/2017-03-29%20John%20interview%202%20final%20to%20post.pdf; United States Congress, "BAUMAN, Robert Edmund," accessed August 26, 2025, https://bioguide.congress.gov/search/bio/B000244; Robert E. Bauman, *The Gentleman from Maryland: The Conscience of a Gay Conservative* (Arbor House, 1986), 177–90; "Programme" for a birthday party, San Francisco, November 10, 1964, "Flyers and Other Ephemera: San Francisco, 1958–1979," Ephemera Collection, GLBT Historical Society, San Francisco, California.

9. Mr. T. (Arlington, VA), letter to the editor, *ONE*, March 1965, 29–30; Mr. S. (New York City), letter to the editor, *ONE*, September 1965, 32.

10. "Silver Lining."

11. Undated typed notes (ca. early 1990s), folder 1, box 41, Dick Leitsch Papers, New York Public Library; Don Slater, "Editorial," *ONE* 12, no. 11 (November 1964), 4–5, at 5; Franklin E. Kameny to *Washington Daily News*, October 25, 1964, folder 11, box 128, Kameny Papers.

12. Franklin E. Kameny to Jean White, January 17, 1965, folder 1, box 134, Kameny Papers.

13. Jean M. White, "Those Others: A Report on Homosexuality," *Washington Post*, January 31, 1965; Edward Alwood, *Straight News: Gays, Lesbians, and the News Media* (Columbia University Press, 1996), 57.

14. White, "Scientists Disagree on Basic Nature of Homosexuality," *Washington Post*, February 1, 1965. White's lede drew on Freud's 1935 letter to a gay son's mother, expressing doubt over whether therapy could make him heterosexual. Pomeroy was a coauthor of Kinsey's *Sexual Behavior in the Human Male* (1948) and *Sexual Behavior in the Human Female* (1953). By this point Hooker had published "A Preliminary Analysis

of Group Behavior of Homosexuals," *Journal of Psychology* 42 (1956), 217–25, and "The Adjustment of the Male Overt Homosexual," *Journal of Projective Techniques* 21 (1957), 18–31, with additional articles underway.

15. Jean M. White, "49 States and the District Punish Overt Homosexual Acts as Crimes," *Washington Post*, February 3, 1965; "Homosexuals' Militancy Reflected In Attacks on Ouster From U.S. Jobs," *Washington Post*, February 4, 1965. The preceding articles were "Those Others: A Report on Homosexuality," January 31, 1965; "Scientists Disagree on Basic Nature of Homosexuality, Chance of Cure," February 1, 1965; and "Homosexuals are in All Kinds of Jobs, Find Place in Many Levels of Society," February 2, 1965. White's first article appeared on the front of the Sunday Outlook section; the other four each ran on page A1.

16. John M. Goshko, "'Morality' Talk Slows Sex Hearing," *Washington Post*, August 9, 1963; John M. Goshko, "House Group Continues Homosexuality Hearing," *Washington Post*, August 10, 1963; "2 Groups Object to Ban on Mattachine Soliciting," *Washington Post*, September 9, 1963; Paul A. Schuette, "Dowdy Bill Attacked by 9 in House," *Washington Post*, March 21, 1964; Elise Carper, "House Action Put Off On Fund Soliciting Bill," *Washington Post*, July 28, 1964; "ACLU Asks Solicitation Bill's Defeat," *Washington Post*, August 10, 1964; National Capital Area Civil Liberties Union, statement on Jenkins Case, December 1964, folder 3, box 53, Dick Leitsch Papers, New York Public Library; "Enticement," *Washington Post*, December 29, 1964.

17. Eric Cervini, *The Deviant's War: The Homosexual vs. the United States of America* (Farrar, Straus and Giroux, 2020), 303–4.

18. *Scott v. Macy*, 349 F.2d 182 (DC Cir. 1965); "Job Denial By U.S. Ruled Improper," *Washington Evening Star*, June 17, 1965; Margot Canaday, *Queer Career: Sexuality and Work in Modern America* (Princeton University Press, 2023), 116.

19. Alwood, *Straight News*, 52, 57; undated typed notes (ca. early 1990s), folder 1, box 41, Dick Leitsch Papers, New York Public Library.

20. Brothers answered that although prison might not make a gay person straight, she argued—citing psychiatrists—that an arrest could "be of valuable aid to the therapist in motivating the individual to thinking about his difficulty." "Arrest, Not Prison, Will Curb Deviation," *Kenosha News*, November 15, 1967. Into the early 1970s she continued to tell readers that change was possible; by the decade's end, however, she rebuked a letter writer for firing an employee because of his homosexuality and condemned California's antigay Briggs initiative, adding that she felt "very strongly that a homosexual teacher doesn't harm children." Andrew E. Stoner, *Dear Abby, I'm Gay: Newspaper Advice Columnists and Homosexuality in America* (McFarland & Company, 2021), Kindle, loc. 1899.

21. Cervini, *Deviant's War*, 173–74; chapter vice president Dick Leitsch, handwritten note, n.d., folder 1, box 41, Dick Leitsch Papers, NYPL. Leitsch wrote to correct Toby Marotta's statement that Frank Kameny "had to dissuade Wicker and his cohorts from picketing the FBI" over Jenkins's arrest in *The Politics of Homosexuality* (Houghton Mifflin, 1981), 28. According to Leitsch, "Frank didn't do the 'dissuading.' Julian Hodges did."

22. Cervini, *Deviant's War*, 199–201; "Mattachine Pickets White House," *Citizens News* 4, no. 13 [n.d. but summer 1965], 16; "Homosexuals Stage Protest in Capital," *New York Times*, May 30, 1965; "Pickets Demand Fair Treatment for Homosexuals" (AP),

Washington Evening Star, May 30, 1965; Marc Stein, "LGBT Direct Action Bibliography, Chronology, and Inventory, 1965–1975" (updated October 2024), https://outhistory.org/exhibits/show/direct/inventory; "Comment and Warning," *Drum* 4, no. 10 (December 1964), 2; Leo Richards, "Magazines, 1964," *Drum* 5, no. 3 (May 1965), 24.

23. Joseph Young, "Preretirement Counseling Plan for U.S. Employes Asked in Bill," *Washington Evening Star*, June 25, 1965; Cervini, *Deviant's War*, 206–7; L. MacA., "Highlights from ECHO Conference Speeches," *Tangents* 1, no. 2 (November 1965), 10 (quote); Stein, "LGBT Direct Action Bibliography, Chronology, and Inventory, 1965–1975."

24. "The Homosexual in the Great Society," *The Ladder* 10, no. 4 (January 1966), 8–12.

25. Johnson, *Lavender Scare*, 199; Cervini, *Deviant's War*, 214. At the very same time, Macy himself was assuming one of Jenkins's former duties: vetting personnel for presidential appointments across the executive branch. Jenkins's personal papers show that during these months he regularly sent Macy recommendations on behalf of friends and acquaintances. Macy's memoir makes no mention of the antigay policies he vigorously defended and suggests that he never regarded the issue as substantive or important. He left the commission in 1969 and died in 1986. John W. Macy, *Public Service: The Human Side of Government* (Harper & Row, 1971); William G. Blair, "John W. Macy Jr., 69, Ex-Leader of Civil Service Commission, Dies," *New York Times*, December 25, 1986.

26. Nan Alamilla Boyd, *Wide-Open Town: A History of Queer San Francisco to 1965* (University of California Press, 2003), 233–35; "A Brief of Injustices: An Indictment of Our Society in Its Treatment of the Homosexual" (Council on Religion and the Homosexual, June 1965), folder 3, box 42, Kameny Papers; *The Challenge of Homosexual Law Reform* (Council on Religion and the Homosexual, 1968), 21. The Jefferson quotation, from an 1816 letter, appears on the memorial's Southeast Portico and begins, "I am not an advocate for frequent changes in laws and constitutions, but laws and institutions must go hand in hand with the progress of the human mind" (https://www.nps.gov/thje/learn/photosmultimedia/quotations.htm).

27. Jon J. Gallo et al., "The Consenting Adult Homosexual and the Law: An Empirical Study of Enforcement and Administration in Los Angeles County," *UCLA Law Review* 13, no. 3 (March 1966): 643–832; *Terry v. Ohio*, 392 U.S. 1 (1968); *Katz v. United States*, 389 U.S. 347 (1967).

28. *Katz v. United States*, 389 U.S. 347 (1967), Justice Harlan, concurring; David Alan Sklansky, "'One Train May Hide Another': *Katz*, Stonewall, and the Secret Subtext of Criminal Procedure," *UC Davis Law Review* 41, no. 3 (2008), 912; Joyce Murdoch and Deb Price, *Courting Justice: Gay Men and Lesbians v. the Supreme Court* (Basic, 2001), 108.

29. *Norton v. Macy*, 417 F.2d 1161 (DC Cir. 1969). In the earlier case, the court observed: "In the view of the community, the stain is a deep one; indeed, it has become a badge of infamy"—all the more so "in time of cold war and hot emotions." *Wieman v. Updegraff*, 344 U.S. 183, 190–91 (1952).

30. Fletcher Knebel, *Vanished* (Doubleday, 1968), 166 (quotes), 250.

31. *Vanished* (dir. Buzz Kulik, NBC television, 1971); William C. Woods, "'Vanished': Soap Opera," *Washington Post*, March 11, 1971.

32. "The 'Disease' Fights Back," *Gay Flames*, October 24, 1970, 1.

33. "Carswell Arrested, Enters a Hospital" (AP), *Washington Post*, June 27, 1976; Martin Dyckman, "Carswell Indicted on 2 Charges," *Washington Post*, July 1, 1976; Tom Sherwood and Joann Stevens, "Hill Police Arrest Congressman on Sodomy Charge," *Washington Post*, February 5, 1981; Judy Wieder, "All the Way Out: George Michael," *Advocate*, January 19, 1998, 24–41; Carl Hulse, "Guilty Plea Stands, But Craig Won't Quit Senate," *New York Times*, October 5, 2007; Randy Shilts, "Is 'Outing' Gays Ethical?" *New York Times*, April 12, 1990; Eleanor Randolph, "The Media, At Odds Over 'Outing' of Gays," *Washington Post*, July 13, 1990; George Chauncey, *Why Marriage? The History Shaping Today's Debate Over Gay Equality* (Basic, 2004), 51–52; PSRA/Newsweek survey cited in Karlyn Bowman and Adam Foster, *Attitudes About Homosexuality and Gay Marriage* (updated June 3, 2008), available at https://www.aei.org/wp-content/uploads/2011/10/20080603-Homosexuality.pdf?x85095.

34. "Gay Revolution Comes Out," in Marc Stein, *The Stonewall Riots: A Documentary History* (NYU Press, 2019), 188.

35. Jonathan Alter, "Gays in Washington," *Newsweek*, September 25, 1989, 19–20; Brian McNaught, "Disturbed Peace," *Washington Blade*, September 1978, 13.

EPILOGUE

1. Alan W. Ross to Steve Endean, August 26, 1979, folder 47, box 5, Human Rights Campaign Records, Human Sexuality Collection, Cornell University, Ithaca, New York; Barry M. Dank, "Coming Out in the Gay World," *Psychiatry* 34, no. 2 (May 1971), 180–97, at 185. Dank's interview with the latter man was likely conducted between 1969 and 1971; see Dank, "The Development of a Homosexual Identity: Antecedents and Consequences" (PhD diss., University of Wisconsin, 1973).

2. Testimony by Dr. Ralph Blair before City Council's General Welfare Committee on Bill No. 475, City Hall, December 17, 1971, folder 9, box 83, Barbara Gittings and Kay Tobin Lahusen Papers, New York Public Library.

3. Richard E. Neustadt, *Presidential Power and the Modern Presidents: The Politics of Leadership from Roosevelt to Reagan* (Free Press, 1990), 346n60; Brian Miller, "A Scholarly Taxi to the Toilets," *The Advocate*, April 15, 1982, 39–40; Eric Cervini, *The Deviant's War: The Homosexual vs. the United States of America* (Farrar, Straus and Giroux, 2020), 305. In 1982 Humphreys began, but never completed, a book that colleagues later described as "a rambling character assassination of conservative leaders caught in the act of sexual deviance." John F. Galliher, Wayne H. Brekhus, and David P. Keys, *Laud Humphreys: Prophet of Homosexuality and Sociology* (University of Wisconsin Press, 2004), 88.

4. John Mitzel, "Highlights from My Imaginary Interview with the Trick in the Stall with Walter Jenkins Way Back When," in Mitzel, *Some Short Stories About Nasty People I Don't Like* (Manifest Destiny, 1977), 29–34.

5. Prompted by the John F. Kennedy Assassination Records Collection Act of 1992, the LBJ Library began processing the White House telephone recordings in 1993. Rather than release only the 684 assassination-related calls, the Library opened the full corpus—about 800 hours of mostly telephone conversations of which Jenkins's secretary Mildred Stegall had been the guardian. Mary K. Knill, "The Lyndon B. Johnson Library in the

Information Age," *Government Information Quarterly* 12, no. 1 (1995), 57–70, esp. 66–67. For an early discussion of the October 15 call between the Johnsons, see James Warren, "On the Brink of Scandal, LBJ Showed How to Act Very Fast," *Chicago Tribune*, March 28, 1999.

6. Robert Schenkkan, *All the Way* (Grove Press, 2014), 116. Schenkkan places Jenkins on the Dallas-to-Washington flight on November 22, 1963, and has J. Edgar Hoover, rather than Abe Fortas, tell Johnson of the arrest. He also stages a pair of behind-the-scenes counsel moments, with Jenkins offering useful suggestions while, across the stage, Ralph Abernathy gives Martin Luther King Jr. the same advice. Steven Elliott Jackson's *The Seat Next to the King* (Toronto Fringe Best New Play, 2017; J. Gordon Shillingford, 2018) pushes the parallel between Jenkins and an advisor to King further by imagining Jenkins and Bayard Rustin meeting in a Washington tearoom in September 1964, kissing, and spending the night in a motel; Jackson has Rustin lecture Jenkins on homosexuality and racism, with explicit urinal dialogue highlighting Jenkins's discomfort with Rustin's Blackness (26, 30). *All the Way* was later adapted by HBO, with Bryan Cranston playing Johnson, as he had in the Broadway production. Rob Reiner's *LBJ* (2016), starring Woody Harrelson, likewise makes Jenkins a central figure but ends before the scandal and depicts him as a swaggering, bullying mini-LBJ—for example, trying to dissuade Johnson from accepting the vice presidential nod at the 1960 convention and ordering Ted Sorensen around after the assassination. Jenkins was present at both moments, but this portrayal is improbable.

7. Vance Muse, "LBJ's Greatest Loss," *George* (May 1999), 104; Al Weisel Jr., "LBJ's Gay Sex Scandal," *Out* 73 (December 1999), 130. Weisel, a New York–based freelance journalist, drew on the FBI's report, obtained via the Freedom of Information Act. He interviewed Carpenter, Stegall, Joseph Califano, and former attorney general Ramsey Clark, who said of Jenkins, "There was a sense he was too gentle to be a political figure" (79). Without naming Heine, Weisel reported that Jenkins had paid collateral for a fellow Johnson aide arrested in a tearoom. He also quoted Andy Choka as later saying he had had sex with men only due to "age and lack of funds," implying he otherwise would have hired female sex workers (81). I have been unable to locate the source for the Choka quotation; Weisel died in 2010.

8. Interview with Luci Baines Johnson, Austin, Texas, April 5, 2018.

INDEX